Watering

A good-quality **hose** is a sound investment. The extra expense is worthwhile if the hose kinks less and lasts longer. Look for a hose that has no visible veining and features a long brass nozzle and brass screw-ends. Even if you have a sprinkler system, you'll need a garden hose for supplying water to freshly planted trees and shrubs.

Soaker hoses have thousands of tiny pores that allow water to slowly seep from them. They can be buried under soil or mulch.

Drip irrigation kits are a water-smart way to maximize your water use. They apply the water at the base of the plants, keeping your water bill to a minimum.

A **watering wand** attaches to the end of your hose. Its long handle makes it easy to water hard-to-reach corners of beds as well as containers and hanging baskets. The wand head showers plants like raindrops instead of blasting them with a hard stream of water.

Timers are great for regulated watering. Use timers to turn on garden hoses, soaker hoses, or drip systems. Automatic irrigation systems with underground piping can also be controlled by specialized timers. Because watering early in the day is better than later, rely on timers to get the watering done while you're still asleep. They're also useful for keeping your landscape healthy while you're out of town.

A **watering can** always comes in handy. Choose one with a large head to disperse water gently. A rounded handle makes the can easier to grip when it's full.

Good Stuff

Hose-end sprayers, also known as siphon injectors, turn your hoses into sprayers. Granules or liquids are mixed with the water from the hose. Water pressure spreads the mixture. Hose-end sprayers are handy for applying liquid fertilizer.

Garde... from cuts, dirt, and abrasion. Choose well-fitting gloves that allow you to pick up small items. The mud-type gloves shown here are excellent and machine wash well. Buy several pairs so you always have one clean.

Leather gloves are necessary for heavy-duty landscaping projects and hauling stone or concrete. They protect your hands against thorns, sharp branches, and tools. Look for gloves that tighten at the wrist to keep out dirt.

A **garden hat** protects your face from the sun. Open-weave material breathes to keep you from overheating. Use a sun hat and sunscreen when you're working outdoors.

A **wheelbarrow** is the landscaping workhorse, saving time and your back when you're transplanting trees and shrubs, or moving soil amendments, gravel, and tools. The more you spend on a new wheelbarrow, the longer you can expect it to last. Always store your wheelbarrow hanging up so it isn't resting on its tire. Keep a spare replacement tire handy.

Pump sprayers are simple to operate and to maintain. A pump handle forces air into the plastic basin, forcing the liquid mixture out a tube with an adjustable nozzle. It's very difficult to clean a sprayer thoroughly. Mixing herbicides and fertilizers can wreak havoc in your landscape. Keep several on hand and label them for different chemicals.

A **tarp** is useful for many tasks. Spend the extra money for quality. A sturdy version will last longer and prove more practical than the inexpensive variety. Use it to protect trees and shrubs on the ride home from the store, to slide heavy plants into place, and to stockpile soil removed from planting holes.

Kneeling is part of gardening and a good pair of **knee pads** makes the job a lot less painful.

Flower Gardening 1-2-3™

Meredith Book Development Team
Project Editor: John P. Holms
Art Director: John Eric Seid
Writer: Veronica Lorson Fowler
Illustrator: Mavis Augustine Torke
Contributing Writers: Laura C. Martin, Monica Brandies, Erin Hynes, Sally Wasowski
Photographer: Doug Hetherington
Designer: Bill Nelson
Contributing Designer: Tim Abramowitz
Copy Chief: Terri Fredrickson
Copy and Production Editor: Victoria Forlini
Editorial Operations Manager: Karen Schirm
Managers, Book Production: Pam Kvitne, Marjorie J. Schenkelberg
Contributing Copy Editor: Lorraine Ferrell
Contributing Proofreaders: Mary Duerson, Beth Ann Edwards, Fran Gardner, Beth Lastine, Barbara Stokes
Indexer: Donald Glassman
Electronic Production Coordinator: Paula Forest
Editorial Assistant: Renee E. McAtee

Meredith® Books
Editor in Chief: James D. Blume
Design Director: Matt Strelecki
Managing Editor: Gregory H. Kayko
Executive Editor, Gardening and Home Improvement: Benjamin W. Allen

Director, Sales, Special Markets: Rita McMullen
Director, Sales, Premiums: Michael A. Peterson
Director, Sales, Retail: Tom Wierzbicki
Director, Book Marketing: Brad Elmitt
Director, Operations: George A. Susral
Director, Production: Douglas M. Johnston

Vice President and General Manager: Douglas J. Guendel

Meredith Publishing Group
President, Publishing Group: Stephen M. Lacy
President-Publishing Director: Bob Mate

Meredith Corporation
Chairman and Chief Executive Officer: William T. Kerr

Chairman of the Executive Committee: E. T. Meredith III

The Home Depot®
Senior Vice President, Marketing and Communications: Dick Sullivan
Marketing Manager: Nathan Ehrlich

Contact us by any of these methods:
1 Leave a voice message at **(800) 678-2093**
2 Write to **Meredith Books, Home Depot Books, 1716 Locust Street, Des Moines, IA 50309-3023**
3 Send e-mail to **hi123@mdp.com**. Visit The Home Depot website at **homedepot.com**

Flower GARDENING 1-2-3

Design ▪ Plan
Select ▪ Plant ▪ Care
STEP-BY-STEP

Meredith BOOKS

Flower Gardening 1-2-3
Table of Contents

Marigolds
Tagetes,
page 212

Chapter 4 — Maintenance — 98

Chapter 5 — Specialized Flower Gardening — 140

Chapter 6 — Flower Encyclopedia — 156

Tickseed
Coreopsis,
page 176

Flower Gardening 1-2-3
How To Use This Book

Flower Gardening 1-2-3 is from the gardening experts at the Home Depot. Inside you'll find almost everything you need to get you started on the flower garden of your dreams.

First, you will learn about the importance of climate and ways to cope with climate needs. Then you will go through steps for designing, preparing, planting, and maintaining your flower garden. There are also ideas for specialized kinds of flower gardens. Finally, the Flower Encyclopedia provides precise information on the most popular flowers.

There's nothing better than a quiet place to sit in a beautiful garden.

Flower Encyclopedia

The encyclopedia entry for each plant includes light and soil needs, mature size, special features, and care and selection information. It also includes zones in which the plant thrives (see page 12). Zone information should be used as a rough guide. Local conditions are the real test for what grows.

Gaillardia spp.   *annual or perennial*
blanket flower

Light Needs:

Full sun

Mature Height: *10"–3'*
Mature Width: *10"–2'*

Zones: *2–11*

Features:

Good for seaside gardens

Heat- and drought-tolerant

Long-blooming

Blooms mid- to late summer.

Needs: Fertile to average, sandy, well-drained soil; tolerates seashore conditions. Allow to dry between waterings; heat- and drought-tolerant.

Plant in spring; perennial type can also be planted in fall. Fertilize lightly, if at all; trim spent blooms and plant will likely bloom until early autumn or even frost.

This plant is prone to powdery mildew and leaf hoppers. It is also prone to crown rot in wet conditions.

Choices: Flowers are usually bicolored in autumn colors—reds, golds, yellow, burgundy, and cream.

Gaillardia pulchella is the annual blanket flower and can be grown in Zones 2–11; *Gaillardia × grandiflora* is the perennial type and can be grown in Zones 2–10.

Annual or Perennial? It Depends on Where You Live

Annuals are plants that grow and bloom in a single growing season. (Remember the "A" for "a year.") Perennials come back year after year. In this book a certain plant, such as salvia, may be referred to as an annual or a perennial.

That's because it may or may not come back each year, depending on your region, zone, climate and growing conditions, and type of plant. To get more information, check the Flower Encyclopedia starting on page 156.

Step-by-Step Projects

Clear step-by-step directions make garden projects easy.

STUFF YOU'LL NEED

✔ Bare-root rose
✔ Large bucket
✔ Pruning shears
✔ Spade
✔ Compost
✔ Watering can or hose

What to Expect
New growth in the form of red shoots should start a week or two after planting.

Every project includes a list of tools and materials you'll need to get the job done right.

Plant lists get you started with specific plants. Both common names and botanical names are provided, as well as zones and the page number the plant appears in the flower encyclopedia.

Must-Have Annuals

Looking for plants so easy to grow even a child can do it? Then go for these annuals. They are some of the most maintenance-free, the ones every gardener who professes a brown thumb should try:

Name	Zones	Page
Ageratum, flossflower	2–11	160
Ageratum houstonianum		
Celosia, cockscomb	2–11	170
Celosia		
Cosmos	2–11	176
Cosmos spp.		
Dusty miller	2–11	171
Centaurea cineraria		
Geranium	2–11	203
Pelargonium spp.		
Impatien	2–11	190
Impatiens spp.		
Marigold	2–11	212
Tagetes spp.		
Petunia	2–11	205
Petunia spp.		
Salvia	2–11	209
Salvia		
Sweet alyssum	2–11	196
Lobularia maritima		
Vinca, periwinkle	2–8	170
Catharanthus roseus		
Wax begonia	2–11	166
Begonia × *semperflorens-cultorum*		
Zinnia	2–11	215
Zinnia spp.		

DesignTip

Calling in the Pros
Stumped for ideas? Talk to your garden center staff. Experienced staff may come up with quick designs based on your photographs, drawings, and measurements of your yard's layout. They'll save you time and money!

You'll find lots of design tips to help you skillfully lay out your flower beds and borders.

TRIP SAVER

Picture This
Keep photos of your garden and key measurements in your wallet or purse. Then you'll always have them with you when shopping to refer to or to show garden center staff for suggestions. It will save time and money.

Save trips to the garden center with these clever tips for using what you have or using materials more resourcefully.

Learn to work more effectively.

Work Smarter!

Observe Those Microclimates
In coastal regions, microclimates (see page 11) can change significantly even from neighborhood to neighborhood. Take note of what does well in your area and compare to other areas even a few blocks away, or a few miles away.

Homer's Hindsight

Leave It Up
I got carried away and deadheaded some plants I wish I would have left alone. Thinking I was doing a good cleanup job in the fall, I cut back my ornamental grasses, sedum, and other plants. Turns out, these flower and seed heads dry right on the stalk and look great. So all winter long I had to enjoy my neighbor's perennials instead of my own.

Homer shares his experience to help you avoid common gardening mistakes.

Save money with tips on buying plants and supplies.

BUYER'S GUIDE

Rose Talk
Confused about all the terms rose fanciers use to describe a rose? Terms such as shrub rose, low-maintenance rose, and landscape rose are used interchangeably.

Learn more with tidbits of extra information.

CLOSER LOOK

What Is a Bulb?
Some flowers we commonly think of as bulbs really aren't bulbs at all. True bulbs look a little like an onion with many layers. Lilies, hyacinths, amaryllis, and daffodils, for example, are true bulbs. Others are actually corms, tubers, or rhizomes (see page 136 for planting information). Don't let the terminology throw you, though. They're not treated any differently. Just follow the label directions.

TOOL TIP

Masonry Bits
A simple masonry bit can turn ceramic, clay, or pottery containers without holes into pots with good drainage. Simply drill a hole or two with the bit. (Wear safety glasses.) Some containers may crack even with a masonry bit so drill a test hole in a pot that's already cracked or damaged.

Having the right tool and knowing how to use it makes all the difference.

Here's an Idea:

Line Raised Beds
Raised beds (page 68) filled with purchased topsoil and compost create the perfect planting bed. However, when a raised bed is placed on sand, the soil tends to wash out. Line the bottom of the raised bed with porous landscape fabric to hold in the soil.

Smart ideas that make gardening simpler or easier are scattered throughout.

Golden Rules of Flower Gardening

1 **Invest in your soil.** Spend time and money first on improving your soil. Loose, rich, well-drained soil reduces watering, makes weeding easier, fights diseases, and helps flowers grow bigger and better in a way no chemicals can. The no-fail way is to work in plenty of compost—it's almost impossible to add too much—and to keep adding it year after year. See page 62 for more details on enriching your soil.

2 **Put the right plant in the right place.** Choose plants that are well-suited to your climate—they will require minimal attention, watering, sprays, altered pHs, staking, or digging up each year. See page 10 for other ways to work with nature rather than against it.

3 **Look at your garden every day.** Spend a little time in the morning before work or steal a few moments each evening. You'll enjoy your garden, get ideas, and spot problems while they're small and can be remedied easily.

4 **Learn and plan.** Read and research plants and gardening techniques. Look through mail-order catalogs and gardening magazines. Browse the Web. You'll get ideas that will help you garden better and more efficiently. See page 32 for more planning ideas—it's a great way to spend the winter!

5 **Have patience.** Gardening is a gradual process. It takes time —often years—to master techniques and time for gardens to reach their potential. Learning to appreciate nature's pace is actually one of gardening's great lessons.

6 **Read the instructions.** Whether it's a plant label or a package, read the instructions and follow them exactly. You'll save time and money.

7 **Have fun!** Working in your garden provides great relief from the trials and stresses of everyday life. Great gardens evolve with a combination of creativity and persistence! Fulfillment, enjoyment and personal satisfaction are what flower gardening is all about.

The Name of the Game

What's so important about those funny Latin names?

Most plants have at least two names—a common name and a botanical or Latin name. The common name is the one most people use when they want to talk about a plant. The Latin or botanical name is assigned to each plant by botanists for accurate identification.

Common names are easy to remember and often charming (Johnny-jump-up, love-lies-bleeding, lady's mantle) but common names can vary widely by region. And two or three different plants might share the same common name, as in the case of African daisy (which refers to both *Arctotis* and *Dimorphoteca*). **Botanical names** can be hard to remember and be tongue-twisters, but each plant has only one botanical name.

That's why, in the Flower Encyclopedia starting on page 156, plants are listed by their botanical names. It's the surest way to help you find the right plant for your garden. If you are searching for a plant by common name, check the index of plants in the back of the book. Also refer to the general index to search for specific information on gardening techniques and processes.

The Language of Flower Gardening

Gardening has its own language. It can seem confusing; but if you master basic terms, your gardening experience will be much easier.

Annual: Grows, blooms, and dies or is significantly weakened at the end of a single growing season. Some plants are annuals in one part of the country but may grow for many years in a warmer region (page 44).

Perennial: Comes back year after year. Foliage usually dies back at the end of the growing season, but plants return in spring (page 46).

Biennial: Takes two years to flower, spending the first year growing foliage and the second year flowering. Plants then die (page 46).

Deciduous: Loses all leaves in the fall.

Evergreen: Keeps most leaves or needles throughout the year.

Full sun: A full day or close to a full day of direct sun (page 74).

Part shade: Also called part sun. About a half day of sun or a full day of dappled or filtered shade (page 74).

Full shade: Also called deep shade. Little or no direct sunlight. (page 74).

Deadheading: Trimming spent blooms off plants to tidy them and to encourage further flowering (page 118).

Mulch: Any material placed over or around a plant to protect it (page 104).

Fertilizer: Any material, organic or chemical, given to a plant to promote growth (page 106).

Reseeder: Also called a self-sower or self-seeder. A plant that scatters its seed by itself and successfully establishes new plants by that method (page 126).

Homer's Hindsight

I Should Have Called First!

I was so excited to start planting that I cut a power line while digging my new flower bed. It was an expensive lesson. Don't begin digging until you know what's buried beneath your shovel. Electrical, telephone, gas, cable, and water service can be hidden where you want a hole. Check with your utility company or county office first.

If You Want to Hire a Pro

Expert Qualifications

Hiring a pro often can save you time and money by preventing costly mistakes in building structures and choosing plants. No matter whom you hire, always ask for references, visit their sites in progress, and see completed jobs before you negotiate a contract. Show the person yardscapes you like. Set a budget and stick to it and never pay the entire fee upfront.

Associates at home and garden centers often offer informal design advice as part of their service. Can be expert gardeners.

Garden designers might not be licensed, but they are often very qualified and can offer advice on planning and preparing your landscape. They will charge fees for design services.

Landscape architects are professionals licensed to prepare plans and guide planting, grading, and landscape construction. Expect a licensed architect to charge a higher fee.

Landscape contractors will often provide free design services as long as they're hired to do the work as well.

Chapter 1

Regional Flower Gardening

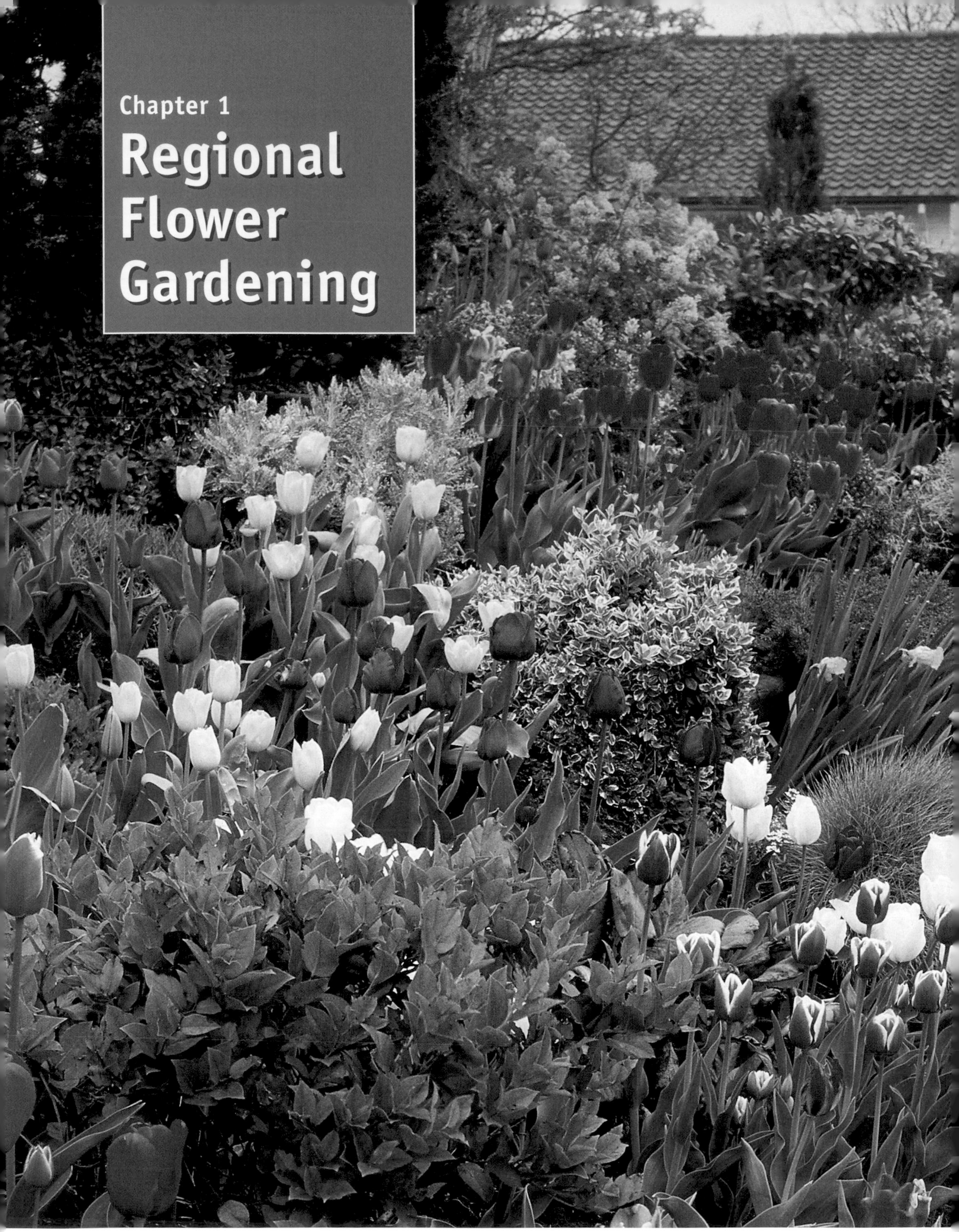

Growing beautiful, healthy flowers is really about knowing what's happening in the microclimate you call your own backyard. What works for a gardener in Los Angeles is different than for a gardener in Boston. Every garden has its own set of requirements and needs.

In this chapter you'll learn what's common as well as what's different about the soils, climates, and conditions that characterize major gardening regions. You will find information on planting and maintenance, plant lists tailored for specific needs, and tips and techniques that will make your gardening more successful.

One of the golden rules of gardening is to take advantage of all the good advice you can get, but also to remember that the best judge of your garden's microclimate is you. This chapter will help you make the right choices for your own little corner of the world.

This annual, Lisianthus (Eustoma; page 182), grows well in a variety of climates if it has plenty of moisture and rich, well-drained soil.

Gardening Smart Wherever You Live

Understanding the climate in your area is key to successful gardening.

Take notice of how much rain you get and when, the average low and high temperatures, the type of winds, and the nature of winters, springs, summers, and autumns in your area. As much as possible, read up on your climate and browse the Web. Also ask your local garden center and local experienced gardeners. With this information you can orchestrate a garden that's beautiful and healthy. Here's how:

In the lush, cool climate of the Pacific Northwest, many plants thrive but must be resistant to slugs, mildews, and steady rain.

BUYER'S GUIDE

Go Native!

Plants that are native to your region thrive naturally in your climate. Ask for regional native plants at your garden center.

Name	Zones	Page
Boltonia *Boltonia asteroides*	4–9	167
Butterfly weed *Asclepias tuberosa*	4–10	164
Coreopsis *Coreopsis* spp.	3–9	176
Gaura *Gaura lindheimeri*	5–9	184
Goldenrod *Solidago* hybrids	5–9	211
Joe-Pye weed *Eupatorium* spp.	3–9	182
Pasque flower *Pulsatilla vulgaris*	4–8	208
Pink turtlehead *Chelone lyonii*	3–8	173
Purple coneflower *Echinacea purpurea*	3–9	180
Summersweet *Clethra alnifolia*	4–9	228
Trumpet vine *Campsis radicans*	4–9	237
Woodland phlox *Phlox divaricata*	3–9	205

■ *Invest in a Rain Gauge*

Keep track of rainfall. Most plants do well with one inch of water a week, so a rain gauge is critical for figuring out how much watering you'll need to do. It also helps you see patterns so you can decide which plants are best for your garden, when you'll need to do the most watering, and how you can plan ahead with soil amending and watering strategies.

■ *Check the Weather Page*

Look in the newspaper or browse the Web for regional weather information.

Look at record rainfalls and droughts, cold snaps and heat waves, winds, snows, and spells of foul or fair weather. Then you'll know what to expect and be prepared. Use this informa-tion to guide plant buying and planting. If you know that temperatures in your area regularly dip below -20°F (-30°C), you won't be tempted to buy a flowering shrub that's hardy only to -10°F (-24°C).

■ *Compare Other World Climates*

If you live in Southern California, you'll find that your climate is fairly similar to many regions of the Mediterranean. Parts of the upper Midwest have climates similar to Siberia. The botanical names of potential flowers for your garden may give you some ideas. For example, if it has the word *sibirica* in it and you live in Minnesota, you know you're probably making a good choice.

■ *Look at Plants in Untended Places*

Take notice of flowers thriving in local untended lots, in alleys and cemeteries, along railroad tracks, or around abandoned houses. They'll do well for you in your more cultivated garden too.

■ Learn About Microclimates

If you live in the Great Plains and drying winds are a problem, put plants near fences or windbreaks. In the South and the arid West, plant trees that give cooling shade to plants that otherwise would take full sun. Plant moisture-lovers on the north and east sides of the house and heat-lovers on the south and west sides of the house. Avoid planting early spring-blooming plants on the south side of a building or against a dark or masonry building, where passive solar heat can trick them too early into thinking it's spring. Low spots gather frost, so avoid spring-blooming plants that might be damaged by a late cold snap. The area under an eave gets less water while the spot at the end of a gutter gets more.

■ Choose Star Plants

Once you find a plant that performs well, look for others that share similar characteristics. Silver- and hairy-leaved plants, for example, tend to resist drought. Hostas with thick, dense leaves fend off slugs better than hostas with thin leaves. In wet climates, roses with single petals that shed water easily may thrive in your garden better than roses with many tightly packed petals.

In the arid Southwest, beautiful gardens are easy to achieve as long as you seek out plants that thrive in heat with little water.

Zone and Frost Date Maps

No matter where you live, it's important to know approximately what "zone" you live in. The U.S. Department of Agriculture has divided the country into zones to help gardeners decide which plants do best where. More specific information on zones is often available on the internet. Plant labels will also offer the zonal range. For instance the label may tell you that a specific plant does best "in Zones 4 to 11." The lower the number, the colder the region.

Knowing your zone will save you frustration later. You'll avoid planting flowers that die out in harsh winters. You can also use zone designations to keep from planting flowers that would shrivel in a too-warm climate.

On these pages, you'll also see two frost date maps. Throughout the book, reference is made to planting times and plant maintenance in relationship to the time in spring when you're unlikely to get any more frost and the time in fall when you're likely to get the first frost.

U.S.D.A. Hardiness Zone Map

Range of Average Annual Minimum Temperatures for Each Zone

Zone 1: Below -50° F (below -45.6° C)
Zone 2: -50 to -40° F (-45.5 to -40° C)
Zone 3: -40 to -30° F (-39.9 to -34.5° C)
Zone 4: -30 to -20° F (-34.4 to -28.9° C)
Zone 5: -20 to -10° F (-28.8 to -23.4° C)
Zone 6: -10 to 0° F (-23.3 to -17.8° C)
Zone 7: 0 to 10° F (-17.7 to -12.3° C)
Zone 8: 10 to 20° F (-12.2 to -6.7° C)
Zone 9: 20 to 30° F (-6.6 to -1.2° C)
Zone 10: 30 to 40° F (-1.1 to 4.4° C)
Zone 11: Above 40° F (above 4.5° C)

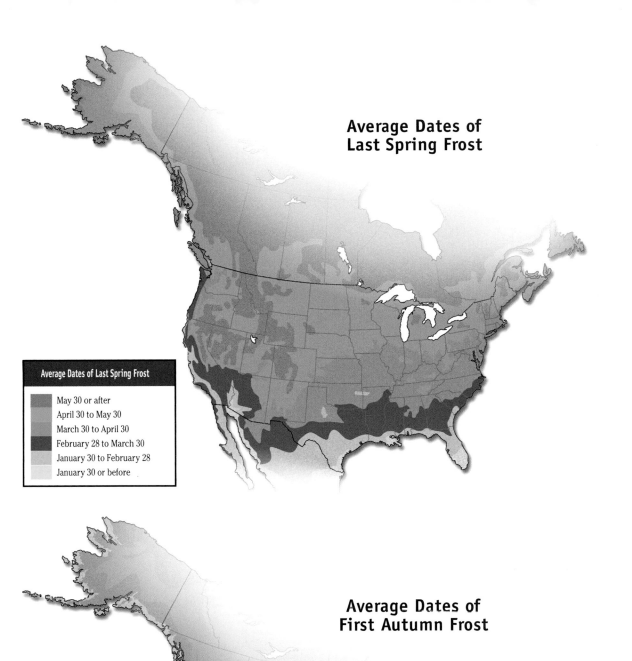

Average Dates of Last Spring Frost

Average Dates of Last Spring Frost

- May 30 or after
- April 30 to May 30
- March 30 to April 30
- February 28 to March 30
- January 30 to February 28
- January 30 or before

Average Dates of First Autumn Frost

Average Dates of First Autumn Frost

- June 30 to July 30
- July 30 to August 30
- August 30 to September 30
- September 30 to October 30
- October 30 to November 30
- November 30 to December 30

Cold-Climate Gardening

Flower Gardening in the Northeast and the Midwest

Whether you live in Minnesota or Maine, surviving winters is the challenge. Other parts of the Midwest and the Northeast face other challenges—everything from dry weather in Kansas to coastal conditions in Massachusetts—but all share frigid winters.

While the cold prevents you from planting some flowers, it also allows others to thrive. The following tips will help you make the most of your climate.

■ *Extending the Season*
• **Plant cool-season annuals.** Unlike heat-loving, warm-season annuals, these flowers like it on the cool side. They will often bloom even with a bit of snow around them. They include stock, snapdragons, pansies, lobelia, violas, calendula, and godetia. Plant in spring four to six weeks before your region's last frost date (see page 13). Cool-season annuals bloom until temperatures regularly hit the 80s, then stop blooming. In cold climates, if cut back, they'll often start blooming again in early autumn.

• **Cover up.** Cold frames (page 15) are great for starting flowers such as cosmos or marigolds from seed, six to eight weeks earlier than they are usually planted directly in the soil. And superspun fabric is ideal for throwing over favorite flowers in autumn when frost threatens to fell them. It lets in sunlight and rain, but protects from frost. Cloches made from milk jugs with the bottoms cut out are good for protecting small, individual plants.

• **Add winter interest.** Plant sedums, berries, ornamental grasses, and shrubs with bright barks that look great even with snow and ice on them.

■ *Preventing Winter Losses*
Another challenge of cold-climate gardening is preventing perennials (and some shrubs) from dying out in the winter. Here's how to minimize winter loss or damage:

• **Choose hardy plants.** Know your U.S.D.A. Zone (see page 12). Read plant labels carefully and skeptically. If you want to be sure to keep a plant, make sure you're at least one zone warmer than the coldest zone the plant will take. If you're in Zone 5, for example, plant only those plants that are listed as hardy to Zone 4.

• **Prepare the soil to provide good drainage.** Plants hate wet feet during the winter. If the soil is crumbly, rich, and well drained, plants are less likely to die out during harsh weather.

• **Mulch intelligently.** Perennials and small shrubs need light mulch to protect them during the winter. Cover with bits of pine boughs or rake chopped autumn leaves right onto the beds. (Chop leaves first by running over them with a mower.) Leaving perennial foliage on plants over the winter also helps. Don't cover the plants with anything too heavy because they could rot or suffocate. Remove mulch in early spring once the plants show signs of new growth.

• **Fight frost heave.** Freeze and thaw cycles throughout winter can heave plants right out of the ground. On nice days in late winter or very early spring, go out into the flower bed and gently tamp down the soil around heaved plants with your foot.

Since cold-region gardens spend so much time under a blanket of snow, it's smart to design them with winter in mind. Here, a low evergreen hedge and a stylish container look great even in the middle of winter.

Building a Cold Frame

• **Take advantage of your site.** Plants on the south side of a building, fence, hedge, or other protection are less likely to be damaged by north winds. Protected sites with southern exposures may cause early bloomers to come on too soon and then be nipped by a late frost. Plant early bloomers on the north or east side. (See Learn About Microclimates on page 11.)

Cold frames are miniature greenhouses. They absorb the sun's heat and concentrate it during cold weather, allowing you to start seedlings, force bulbs (see page 151), and help plants adjust to cooler temperatures in early spring. Cold frames are simple to make. All you need are a few lengths of pressure-treated lumber and an old storm window or a piece of translucent fiberglass for a top.

1 **Build the frame.** The cold frame should be at least 10 inches high. Using the cover you've chosen as a guide for measurements, cut cedar or pressure-treated lumber to the proper lengths and widths. Nail or screw the pieces together.

2 **Sink the cold frame into the ground.** Slope it to the south to collect maximum sunlight. Remove the grass inside the frame and replace with properly balanced and amended soil before you plant.

3 **Position the top.** Set the window or fiberglass on top of the frame. Weight it down with bricks or stones if needed. Remove accumulations of snow or debris as needed.

Must-Have Plants for Cold-Weather Gardens

Note: Some flowers will perform as annuals or perennials depending on your zone and local growing conditions in your garden. For more information on the plants below, check the Flower Encyclopedia beginning on page 156 and consult with associates at your local garden center.

Name	Zones	Page	Name	Zones	Page
Amethyst sea holly *Eryngium amethystinum*	2–9	181	Obedient plant *Physostegia virginiana*	2–9	207
Blanket flower *Gaillardia × grandiflora*	2–11	184	Peony *Paeonia* spp.	2–8	202
Blue lungwort *Pulmonaria angustifolia*	2–8	208	Potentilla *Potentilla fruticosa*	2–7	233
Canadian roses	2–8	88	Rugosa roses	2–9	91
Cardinal flower *Lobelia cardinalis*	2–9	196	Siberian squill *Scilla sibirica*	2–8	224
Creeping phlox *Phlox stolonifera*	2–8	206	Snow-in-summer *Cerastium tomentosum*	2–9	172
Fringed bleeding heart *Dicentra eximia*	2–9	179	Viburnum *Various species, check label*	2–9	235
Moss phlox *Phlox subulata*	2–9	206			

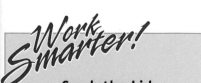

Work Smarter!

Crack the Lid

Crack the lid of the cold frame at least 1 inch on warm, sunny days to keep plants from overheating.

Warm-Climate Gardening

Flower Gardening in the South

Southern gardeners should choose plants that can tolerate the dual hazards of heat and humidity.

Because most regions of the South have extended periods of frost-free days, bugs and pests are also a great challenge. In these tough conditions, here's how you get picture-perfect plants:

■ *Take a Soil Test*

Many Southern soils are very acidic, that is, they have a low pH. Test your soil with a pH kit. Then choose plants that do well in that pH range and/or amend the soil. (See page 62.)

• **Good drainage is essential.** Many southern soils have a high clay composition, which absorbs poorly in wet weather and bakes into a brick in dry weather. Adding organic matter will improve both the drainage and composition of the soils.

■ *Pay Attention to Light*

The South is blessed with many great species of trees. If you have great trees in your landscape, take advantage of them by planting shade-loving flowers underneath.

• **Trees protect flowers.** Plant additional trees to give partial-shade plants a break from the grueling southern sun.

• **Learn from nature.** Southern woodlands are home to some of the world's most beautiful plants. Create a gorgeous, shady southern garden.

Formal gardens with lots of brickwork have a long, rich tradition in the South.

■ *Provide for Good Air Circulation*

Because humidity creates a perfect environment for fungal and other diseases, leave ample space around susceptible plants.

■ *Water Wisely*

• **Irrigate deeply.** During periods of low rainfall, irrigate deeply and less frequently, rather than shallow and often.

• **Water at ground level.** Avoid wetting leaves, which encourages fungal diseases. (See page 100 for more watering tips.)

■ *Choose Plants Carefully*

Choose plants that are suited to your own local growing conditions. Consider both cold hardiness and tolerance for heat and humidity (see page 12 for a hardiness map).

• **Use native plants.** Choose plants that are well acclimated to conditions in the South.

• **Plants for all seasons.** With a careful selection you can have flowers almost all year long, even in winter. For best results, seek out cool-season annuals (see page 45) and perennials that thrive in the cooler temperatures of late autumn, winter, and very early spring.

Design Tip

Give Plants Room

Make sure you've allotted enough space to allow the plant plenty of room at maturity. Use flour or landscaping spray paint to mark the mature size before you dig the hole. Plant annual color or use containers to fill in the gaps while your first choices are reaching maturity.

Must-Have Plants for Southern Gardens

Note: Some flowers will perform as annuals or perennials depending on your zone and specific growing conditions. For more information on the plants below, check the Flower Encyclopedia beginning on page 156 and consult with associates at your local garden center.

Name	Zones	Page
Annuals/Perennials		
Black-eyed Susan *Rudbeckia*	3–10	209
Blue lilyturf *Liriope muscari*	6–9	195
Garden phlox *Phlox* spp.	5–7	206
Goldenrod *Solidago* hybrids	3–9	211
Goldenstar *Chrysogonum virginianum*	5–9	173
Hosta *Hosta* spp.	3–9	190
Lantana *Lantana camara*	2–11	192
Lenten rose *Helleborus* spp.	3–9	188
Pentas *Pentas lanceolata*	3–11	204
Purple coneflower *Echinacea purpurea*	3–9	180
Salvia *Saliva* spp.	2–11	209

Name	Zones	Page
Society garlic *Tulbaghia*	8–11	225
Sweet william *Dianthus* spp.	2–11	178
Verbena *Verbena* spp.	2–11	214
Viola *Viola* spp.	2–11	215
Windflower *Anemone*	4–9	217
Woodland phlox *Phlox divaricata*	3–9	205
Yarrow *Achillea* spp.	3–9	159
Shrubs and Roses		
Azalea *Rhododendron* spp.	3–9	233
Butterfly bush *Buddleia* spp.	5–10	227
Camellia *Camellia* spp.	6–11	228
China roses *Rosa*	6–10	89
Daphne *Daphne* spp.	4–9	229

■ *Group Plants According To Their Needs*

Group sun-loving plants together in one spot and shade-loving plants in another area. The same holds true for thirsty plants and drought-tolerant plants, which every Southern garden should include to save on irrigation costs and to conserve water.

■ *Visit Regional Gardens*

There are beautiful public gardens throughout the South and many will have similar climate and soil conditions to your garden. Visit them, take notes, talk to gardeners who work there, and get ideas for creating your own paradise right at home. Visit these sites during difficult growing times, such as high summer, to get a sense of the problems you will face.

Both marigolds (Tagetes spp., page 212) and red salvia (Salvia splendens, page 209) do beautifully in the heat and humidity of the South.

Flower Gardening on the Coasts

It's important to understand beach microclimates. Take note of what plants thrive in relationship to their distance from the water, salt tolerance, temperature highs and lows, light levels, soil and rock composition, and wind patterns. Even once you understand the effects of the elements, remember that they can vary radically throughout the season and even throughout the day. But you can create a microclimate in your garden to nurture some of your favorite flowers. Here are some tips for dealing with the toughest challenges:

■ *Choose the Right Plants*
• **Seek out salt-tolerant plants.** A handful of plants cope with salty conditions (soil or spray) better than most. They aren't salt-proof, but they will thrive in moderately salty conditions. Keep in mind that salt spray travels a tremendous distance, blowing several miles inland in some areas.
• **Environmental realities.** Beaches and the land near them are environmentally fragile areas and should be gardened with great care. Some garden plants can be invasive, crowding out important local plants. The role of some plants, such as American beach grass and sea oats, is so critical that some states prohibit their destruction. If in doubt, consult with a local nursery or call your state or county department of natural resources for more information.
• **Let the name guide you.** Many plants well suited to coastal

Even a low wall, such as this one, can protect flowers from salt spray and relentless coastal winds.

conditions have "sea" or "beach" in their names.
• **Fewer petals.** Choose roses and flowers with just a few petals. The fog and dew common to most coastal areas makes thickly petaled flowers rot and fall before they open.

■ *Cope with Wind*
• **Choose low growers.** Low-growing plants hug the ground and, unlike vertical plants, do not require staking.
• **Choose strong rooters.** Strong, deep roots anchor plants in sandy soil and strong winds, and help them find moisture far into the soil. Flowering shrubs usually do better than annuals, which have more shallow root stems.

• **Watch wind patterns.** Winter winds can rapidly dry out many plants. Plant in protected areas alongside the house, garage, or other buildings.
• **Build windbreaks wisely.** A solid fence or wall can create strong turbulence on the leeward side. A dense hedge, on the other hand, is ideal for slowing down the wind. You might also consider a combination of an open-work fence and a hedge for fast yet effective wind protection.

■ *Improve Sandy Soil*
Add plenty of compost, sphagnum peat moss, soil conditioner, and soil amendments. This improves soil's ability to retain water.

Must-Have Plants for Coastal Gardens

Note: Some flowers will perform as annuals or perennials depending on your zone and local growing conditions in your garden. For more information on the plants below, check the Flower Encyclopedia beginning on page 156 and consult with associates at your local garden center.

Name	Zones	Page
Annuals/Perennials		
Black-eyed Susan	3–10	209
Rudbeckia spp.		
Catmint	4–9	201
Nepeta spp.		
Coreopsis	3–9	176
Coreopsis spp.		
Dusty miller	2–11	171
Centaurea cineraria		
Dwarf morning glory	2–11	175
Convolvulus tricolor		
Gaillardia	2–11	184
Gaillardia spp.		
Gazania	2–11	185
Gazania rigens		
Geranium	2–11	203
Pelargonium spp.		
Lavender	5–10	192
Lavandula spp.		
Lavender cotton	6–9	210
Santolina chamaecyparissus		
Moss rose	2–11	207
Portulaca		
Periwinkle	4–7	241
Vinca minor		
Russian sage	5–7	204
Perovskia atriplicifolia		

Name	Zones	Page
Sea lavender	2–11	194
Limonium spp.		
Vinca, periwinkle	2–11	170
Catharanthus roseus		
Yarrow	3–9	159
Achillea spp.		
Roses (Rosa)		
'Betty Prior' (floribunda)		90
'Carefree Wonder' (other shrub)		91
'Fruhlingsgold' (other shrub)		91
Meidiland roses (other shrub)		91
'Robusta' (rugosa)		91
Rugosa roses		91
Rosa wichuraiana (climbing)		93
Shrubs		
Butterfly bush	5–10	227
Buddleia spp.		
Cinquefoil	2–7	233
Potentilla fruticosa		
Potentilla	2–7	233
Potentilla fruticosa		
Purple smokebush	5–8	229
Cotinus coggygria		
Spirea, bridalwreath	3–9	234
Spiraea spp.		

• **Add water absorbers.** Try the new polymer crystals that absorb and hold water in the soil. Use as directed on the package. They don't work well in large beds but are excellent in small plantings or in pots. These crystals will last for several seasons.

• **Plant in pots.** Plant roses and prized perennials in large (5-gallon plus) pots with drainage holes that you sink directly into the sandy soil. Fill with a mixture of compost, potting soil, and a soilless potting mix. This gives flowering plants the rich soil they prefer, and the soil won't wash away. You can also recycle plastic containers, such as the bottoms of old garbage cans, to create these buried gardens in the sand.

• **Build raised beds.** Create raised beds of wood, stone, or other materials (see page 68). Fill with a mixture of high-quality black topsoil and compost.

Look for plants that are salt-tolerant and not bothered by high winds.

Work Smarter!

Observe Those Microclimates

In coastal regions, microclimates (see page 11) can change significantly even from neighborhood to neighborhood. Take note of what does well in your area and compare to other areas even a few blocks away, or a few miles away.

Here's an Idea:

Line Raised Beds

Raised beds (page 68) filled with purchased topsoil and compost create the perfect planting bed. However, when a raised bed is placed on sand, the soil tends to wash out. Line the bottom of the raised bed with porous landscape fabric to hold in the soil.

Flower Gardening in the Arid West and Southwest

Flowers can bloom all year if you select native and drought-tolerant species and plant them under the dappled shade of lacy-leaved desert trees.

■ Conserving Water

Average rainfall ranges from 4 to 16 inches per year, but some years only half the average may fall, and the next year it might be double. In El Paso, rain is most likely to occur in late summer; in Southern California, rain comes in the winter; and in Phoenix, the rainy season is divided between summer and winter. Talk to neighbors and your garden center staff about specific rainfall patterns. Make the most of limited rainfall by doing the following:

• **Minimize your lawn.** Wrap your flower garden around a covered patio or a small lawn of buffalograss and blue gramagrass.

• **Install drip irrigation.** Water when the sun is down to limit evaporation.

• **Create swales and berms.** Low spots and high spots capture water from roofs, driveways, and patios.

• **Position plants on the south edge** of a slight hollow to trap water and shade their roots.

• **Make walls.** Enclose gardens with masonry walls to hold in water, cast shade, and lessen evaporation.

• **Mulch.** Mulch with gravel or decomposed granite to prevent weeds and conserve moisture.

■ Choose Drought-Tolerant Plants

Plants native to desert areas are drought-tolerant and becoming easier to find.

• **Yuccas, agaves, cacti, and other succulent evergreens** will create focal points when flowers aren't blooming.

• **Short native flowering shrubs** will provide bright spots of color.

• **Plant bunch grasses,** such as Mexican feather grass, deergrass, bamboo muhly, or pink muhly for soft accents.

• **Plant reseeders.** Tie everything together with reseeding desert flowers such as California poppy, desert marigold, butter daisy, fragrant evening primrose, globe mallow, and calylophus.

California poppies (Eschscholzia californica, page 181) will reseed freely in most parts of the West and the Southwest.

Flowers for Southwest Gardens*

Name

Flowering Succulent Evergreens

Agave
  Agave
Aloe
  Aloe
Claretcup cactus
  Echinocereus triglochidiatus
Mojave yucca
  Yucca schidigera
Red yucca
  Hesperaloe parviflora

Short Flowering Shrubs

Autumn sage
  Salvia greggii
Chuparosa
  Justicia californica
Damianita
  Chrysactinia mexicana
Desert milkweed
  Asclepias subulata
Feather dalea
  Dalea formosa
Mountain marigold
  Tagetes lemmonii
Pink fairyduster
  Calliandra eriophylla
Scarlet bouvardia
  Bouvardia ternifoli

Availability varies. Check with your local garden center.

Name

Drought-Tolerant Bunch Grasses

Mexican feather grass
  Stipa tenuissima
Muhly grasses
  Muhlenbergia

Long-Lived Flowers

Coral bells
  Heuchera sanguinea
Douglas iris
  Iris douglasiana
Penstemon
  Penstemon spp.
Zauschneria
  Epilobium canum

Short-Lived Flowers

Butter daisy
  Melampodium paludosum
California poppy
  Eschscholzia californica
Calylophus
  Calylophus hartwegii
Chocolate flower
  Berlandiera lyrata
Desert marigold
  Baileya multiradiata
Fragrant evening primrose
  Oenothera caespitosa
Globe mallow
  Sphaeralcea

Flower Gardening in Texas

Texas is a state of climatic extremes: East Texas is hot, wet, and muggy; West Texas is hot and dry; northern Texas offers constant wind, gruelingly hot summers, and frigid winters. Soil types range from clay to thin dust on top of rocks.

A casually designed garden filled with drought-tolerant flowers is the perfect foil for this rustic Texas home.

■ *Coping with Extremes*

• **Grow native and naturalized plants.** Pamper them with a little extra water and fertilizer. Consider time-tested heirlooms such as crinum and four-o-clocks. Look at ditches and abandoned farmsteads for thriving remnants of long-abandoned gardens.

• **Take advantage of the seasons.** In central and southern Texas, winter, spring, and autumn are the best times to garden. In the Panhandle it's autumn and spring. Plant annuals such as pansies, sweet pea, and snapdragon in autumn for winter and spring color.

• **Include ornamental grasses.** Consider those with attractive flowers such as gulf muhly or Mexican feather grass.

• **Look for microclimates—** those little niches in the garden protected from extremes of sun, wind, and weather. Buy specimens of inexpensive plants and test them in different areas.

■ *Whack Away*

Digging is hard work in the clay-laden and rocky soils so often found in Texas. Instead of using a spade, try a pick mattock, which has a pointed blade at one end and a flat blade at the other. Swing it as you would an ax—carefully and remember to be fully focused on the task at hand.

Must-Have Flowers for Texas Gardens

Name	Zones	Page
Annuals/perennials		
Annual red sage *Salvia coccinea*	2–11	209
Blanket flower *Gaillardia pulchella*	2–11	184
Butter daisy *Melampodium paludosum*	2–11	198
Flowering tobacco *Nicotiana alata*	2–11	201
Four-o-clock *Mirabilis jalapa*	2–11	199
Mexican heather *Cuphea hyssopifolia*	2–11	177
Texas bluebonnet *Lupinus texensis*	2–11	197
Shrubs		
Butterfly bush *Buddleia* spp.	5–10	227
Purple beautyberry *Callicarpa americana*	5–8	227
Roses		
China roses		89
'Cécile Brunner' (polyantha)		91

Name
Indian paintbrush *Castilleja indivisa*
Paper-white narcissus *Narcissus papyraceus*
Showy evening primrose *Oenothera speciosa*
Texas lantana *Lantana horrida*
Turk's-cap *Malvaviscus arboreus var. drummondii*
Wild ageratum *Eupatorium coelestinum*
Zexmenia *Wedelia hispida*
Grasses
Gulf muhly *Muhlenbergia capillaris*
Lindheimer muhly *Muhlenbergia lindheimeri*
Mexican feather grass *Stipa tenuissima*
Shrubs
Cenizo *Leucophyllum candidum*
Texas mountain laurel *Sophora secundiflora*
Roses
'Archduke Charles' (China)
Musk roses
Noisette roses
'Penelope' hybrid (musk)
'Rêve d'Or' (noisette)

Other Options*

Name
Annuals/perennials
Autumn sage *Salvia greggii*
Chile pequin *Capsicum annuum*
Crinum *Crinum bulbispermum*

*Availability varies. Check with your local garden center.

Flower Gardening in California

California climates are as diverse as the people who live there. California has four of the five major climate zones found in the world—Mediterranean, semi-arid, desert, and alpine. Tropical is the only one not making the list.

On the same day, the northern part of the state may be in the low 60s°F (16°C) and cloudy, while deserts surrounding Bakersfield in Southern California may be above 100°F (38°C). Along California's northwest coast, annual rainfall averages 110 inches, while Bakersfield receives just 10. The northwest coast has a climate much like that of southern Ireland, while the southwest corner resembles the northern Sahara desert.

Even in the same city in California, climates from one yard to another can vary depending on elevation and distance from the ocean. What grows in your garden depends not only on your region but also on your neighborhood. A California gardener needs to be a master of the microclimate (see page 11). The best information will come from your neighbors and garden center staff who understand your garden's unique climate.

Know your garden's specific needs for soil and rainfall. If you get frost, know the last frost in spring and the first frost in fall. Track weather patterns in your local paper. Watch for articles that address your area's needs.

■ Arid California

• **Buy drought-tolerant plants.** Your local garden center will highlight plants that use minimal water.

• **Group plants according to water needs.** Create a small "oasis" of plants with higher water needs near the house to make watering easier.

• **Improve the soil.** Low rainfall can make the soil more alkaline. In general, don't add lime to the soil, because it raises the pH further. Instead, work in organic matter, primarily compost, leaves, and grass trimmings.

• **Think salt.** Coastal gardens are vulnerable to salty ocean spray. Low rainfall also contributes to high salt concentration in the soil— a problem for many plants even if they're quite far inland. If salt is a problem, talk to your garden center staff about choosing salt-tolerant plants and soil amendments for your garden.

• **Install an irrigation system.** Water is not only a natural resource, it's also expensive. An irrigation system will pay for itself.

• **Create shade.** Many plants will do better in hot, dry regions if they have light shade. Acacia, palo verde, and desert willow cast the dappled light shade plants like best. Position a tree so it gives afternoon shade.

• **Mulch!** Whether you do it with gravel or wood chips, it keeps soil cooler and moister—and it minimizes weeds.

Must-Have Flowers for Arid California

Note: Some flowers will perform as annuals or perennials depending on your zone and local growing conditions in your garden. For more information on the plants below, check the Flower Encyclopedia beginning on page 156 and consult with associates at your local garden center.

Name	Zones	Page	Name	Zones	Page
Agapanthus *Agapanthus*	2–11	217	Oleander *Nerium oleander*	5–7	232
Bougainvillea *Bougainvillea*	9–11	237	Ranunculus *Ranunculus asiaticus*	8–10	224
California poppy *Eschscholzia californica*	2–11	181	Santolina *Santolina chamaecyparissus*	6–9	210
Fuchsia *Fuchsia* spp.	2–11	183	Wisteria *Wisteria* spp.	5–9	241
Gazania *Gazania rigens*	2–11	185			

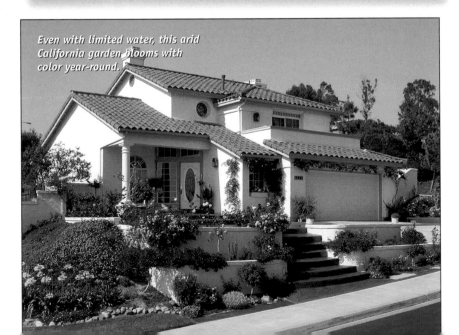

Even with limited water, this arid California garden blooms with color year-round.

Mountainous California

• Know when spring is due.
Spring in the mountains is notoriously fickle, with balmy weather one day and snow the next. Keep track of your last spring frost dates or talk to people who know.

• Make the most of a short growing season. Look for perennials that thrive in cooler temperatures and familiarize yourself with cool-season annuals (see page 45). Many spring-blooming bulbs (see page 49) also do well in the cool temperatures and excellent drainage found in some mountain areas.

• Garden at an angle.
Gardening on a slope involves (see page 144 for information on rock gardening) disturbing the least amount of soil when planting or weeding to prevent erosion. Build low, informal terraces to retain water and slow erosion. Plant moisture-lovers at the lower part of a slope and drought- tolerant plants at the top.

• Outsmart the critters. Great mountain views often include a glimpse of deer, rabbits, woodchucks, raccoons, and other wildlife that love your garden too. Buy plants that wildlife are less likely to eat (see page 133) and consider a deer fence.

• Realize your light is brighter. Gardens at 3,000 feet and higher receive 20 percent more light then those at sea level. If a plant likes part or full shade at sea level, you will want to give it a little more shade in higher altitudes.

Must-Have Flowers for Mountainous California

Note: Some flowers will perform as annuals or perennials depending on your zone and local growing conditions in your garden. For more information on the plants below, check the Flower Encyclopedia beginning on page 156 and consult with associates at your local garden center.

Name	Zones	Page
Blanket flower *Gaillardia × grandiflora*	2–11	184
California poppy *Eschscholzia californica*	2–11	181
Cinquefoil *Potentilla fruticosa*	2–7	233
Cosmos *Cosmos* spp.	2–11	176
Gazania *Gazania rigens*	2–11	185
Larkspur *Consolida ambigua*	2–11	175
Lupine *Lupinus* hybrids	4–9	197

Name	Zones	Page
Oriental poppies *Papaver orientale*	2–7	203
Pansy *Viola* spp.	2–11	215
Poppies, annual types *Papaver* spp.	2–11	203
Santolina *Santolina chamaecyparissus*	6–9	210
Shasta daisy *Leucanthemum × superbum*	4–9	193
Snapdragon *Antirrhinum majus*	2–11	162

Cool, Moist California

• Plant in fall. Get a head start on early spring by planting perennials and shrubs in fall.

• Choose roses well. Thickly petaled roses tend to ball up and rot in steady rain and mist. Choose single or double roses, which have fewer petals. As a rule, pink roses are more resistant to the region's fungal diseases. Rugosa roses also tend to perform well.

• Take advantage of the cool, moist winter by planting cool-season annuals that will provide winter color (see page 45).

• Clean up dead foliage (especially irises and roses) in fall to prevent blight, molds, and mildews.

• Slug it out. Deter slugs, a major problem in cool, moist climates, by hand-picking and by creating wood ash or copper strip barriers around favorite plants. Use slug bait as needed.

• Dig summer-blooming bulbs. Wet soil will rot many summer-blooming bulbs. Dig and store them (see page 136).

Must-Have Cool, Moist, California Annuals

Name	Zones	Page
Annuals / Perennials		
California poppy *Eschscholzia californica*	2–11	181
Clematis *Clematis* spp.	4–9	238
Coral bells *Heuchera*	3–8	189
Edging lobelia *Lobelia erinus*	2–11	195
Foxglove *Digitalis purpurea*	4–9	179
Hosta *Hosta* spp.	3–9	190
Nasturtium *Tropaeolum majus*	2–11	214

Name	Zones	Page
Pansy *Viola* spp.	2–11	215
Snapdragon *Antirrhinum majus*	2–11	162
Shrubs		
Camellia *Camellia* spp.	6–11	228
Hydrangea *Hydrangea* spp.	4–9	231
Rhododendron, azalea *Rhododendron* spp.	3–9	233

Flower Gardening in Florida and the Gulf Coast

Gardening successfully in Florida means gardening in a way very different from the rest of the country. Seasons are upside down, nearly the opposite of much national gardening advice. That means you'll need to become expert at adapting information and at observing what works best in your own Florida garden.

■ *A Long Growing Season*

- **Enjoy color year-round.** Blooms are spread over an amazingly long period of the year. However, the disadvantage is that color seldom comes in the same intensity as it does in cooler climates. Not everything blooms at the same time.
- **Timing is vital.** While there is seldom quite the same pressure as in other parts of the country to plant, prune, and maintain in a narrow window of time, it's still important to do the right task at the right time.
- **Plants perform differently** here from the rest of the country. Many plants, such as petunias and nasturtiums, grow well from fall until spring but die out in the heat of summer. Some, such as impatiens and peppers, are annuals elsewhere but may be perennials here. Still others that are perennial in most of the country, such as delphinium, thyme, and yarrow, are best treated as annuals in Florida because the summer heat often kills them. Peonies and lilacs may not grow at all. However, for every plant that doesn't grow here, 10 more exotics well-suited to the region will thrive beautifully.

Despite heat, humidity, and lots of bugs, gardening in Florida can be a lush treat, especially if you understand how different it is from the rest of the country.

Beat the Frost

In central and Southern Florida, group together annual flowers that are frost sensitive. That way you can throw a sheet or burlap over the whole group when the temperature dips and save the plants without any problem, avoiding costly replacements.

■ *The Highs and the Lows*

• **Heat is hot.** An increased interest in gardening in desert and subtropical regions has led plant merchants to include information about heat tolerance on plant labels.

• **Plants grow more slowly in the winter.** With its short days and different sun and shade patterns, winter dramatically slows the growth of plants. Reduce watering and feeding accordingly.

• **Don't be bitten by frost.** Keep a list of your cold-sensitive plants and be ready to cover them, move them, or take cuttings to renew them whenever frost is predicted. Good maintenance and abundant compost in the soil can give you a few extra degrees of protection.

■ *Water and Soil Smarts*

• **Water, water everywhere.** Where there are heavy summer rains as well as heat, make another list of plants that are likely to melt down in the high humidity. You'll soon learn what is worth trying to save and what is best restarted in the fall. Plants that don't like too much water, such as lavender,

can be grown in pots, where the excellent drainage can save them. Containers also have the advantage of being movable so you can place them in a shadier spot for the summer or under the eaves during rainy spells.

• **Lend a helping hand.** After a summer of heavy rainfall, desert conditions often abound for the rest of the year. Irrigation is essential for the thirstier plants.

• **Know your soil.** Some areas have soil so sandy that it provides anchorage only—no nutrients. In other places, the soil is solid as rock. In either case, add as much compost and other organic matter as you can to enrich the soil (see page 63).

Must-Have Flowers for Florida and the Gulf Coast

Name	Zones	Page
Annuals/Perennials		
Alyssum † *Lobularia maritima*	2–11	196
Butter daisy* *Melampodium paludosum*	2–11	198
Globe amaranth* *Gomphrena globosa*	2–11	186
Impatiens* *Impatiens* spp.	2–11	190
Lantana NCS *Lantana camara*	2–11	192
Periwinkle, vinca* *Catharanthus roseus*	2–11	170
Moss rose* *Portulaca*	2–11	207
Nasturtium* *Tropaeolum majus*	2–11	214
Pentas NCS *Pentas lanceolata*	3–11	204
Petunia* † *Petunia* spp.	2–11	205
Salvias NCS *Salvia* spp.	2–11	209, 210
Snapdragon † *Antirrhinum majus*	2–11	162
Violas and pansies † *Viola* spp.	2–11	215
Wax begonia* *Begonia × semperflorens-cultorum*	2–11	166
White gaura NC *Gaura lindheimeri*	5–9	184
Wishbone flower* *Torenia fournieri*	4–11	213
Zinnia* *Zinnia* spp.	2–11	215

Name	Zones	Page
Flowering shrubs/Vines		
Azaleas NC *Rhododendron* spp.	3–9	233
Bougainvillea CS *Bougainvillea*	9–11	237
Camellia NC *Camellia* spp.	6–11	228
Hibiscus CS *Hibiscus* spp.	5–11	231
Jasmine NCS *Jasminum*	6–9	239
Plumbago CS *Ceratostigma plumbaginoides*	5–9	172

Other Options**

Perennials

Aloe
Aloe CS

Australian violet
Viola hedera NCS

Begonias CS
Begonias spp.

Firebush NCS
Hamelia patens

Moonflower CS
Ipomoea alba

Rain lily NCS
Zephyranthes

Flowering shrubs

Crepe myrtle NCS
Lagerstroemia indica

Ixora
Ixora coccinea CS

Thryallis
Galphimia glauca CS

* Protect from frost.
† Does best during cooler months
N: Does well in north Florida;
    withstands frost
C: Does well in central Florida
S: Does well in south Florida

**Availability varies. Check with your local garden center.

Bougainvillea (page 237) is an ideal flowering vine for Florida gardens.

Flower Gardening in the Mountain West

With the possibility of snow at highest elevations in any season, flower gardening in the mountains can be a risky business. But a look at nature's own high-altitude gardens demonstrates that it is possible to grow flowers in glorious profusion in the mountains.

■ Take Note of Key Elements

• **Heat.** During the growing season, take advantage of any heat that comes your way. Use south-facing exposures or place tender plants near large rocks, boulders, or stone walls that absorb the heat during the day and release it slowly at night.

• **Light.** Full sun areas at elevations of 3,000 feet and higher receive 20 percent more light than full sun areas at sea level. Although some plants thrive in this excessive light, others need some shade protection.

• **Water.** If you garden on a slope, terrace your plants to slow rainwater runoff. Use groundcovers such as creeping juniper to further prevent eroding soils. Use mulch to conserve as much soil moisture as possible. Irrigate plants during dry months by watering deeply and seldom rather than shallow and often, encouraging the plants to develop deep roots.

• **Soil.** Most mountainous soils are rocky and shallow, so the addition of organic matter to the soil is a necessity. Add compost, well-rotted manure, leaf litter, or other organic materials to enhance the nutrient value and the composition of the soil. Use readily available loose stone to your advantage, building raised beds and filling them with topsoil.

■ Be Ready to Spring In Spring

As soon as you can begin to work the soil, start digging and enriching the soil so that you can garden in earnest as soon as warm weather arrives.

TRIP SAVER

Ready, Set, Plant!

Gardeners at high altitudes should take advantage of every sunny summer day by having plants ready to put in the ground as soon as it looks as if warm temperatures are here to stay. Starting plants from seed indoors can extend the growing and blooming season by several weeks. If you can, grow enough seedlings for several successive plantings. The first time you plant, set out a portion of your seedlings, keeping some back just in case the first ones are nipped by a late frost.

Must-Have Flowers for the Mountain West

Common Name	Zones	Page
Annuals/Perennials		
Bee balm	4–8	200
Monarda didyma		
Bellflower	3–8	170
Campanula spp.		
Blanket flower	2–11	184
Gaillardia spp.		
Bleeding heart	2–9	179
Dicentra spp.		
Catmint	4–9	201
Nepeta spp.		
Columbine	3–10	162
Aquilegia spp.		
Coreopsis	3–9	176
Coreopsis spp.		
Cosmos	2–11	176
Cosmos spp.		
Delphinium	2–7	178
Delphinium elatum		
Gazania	2–11	185
Gazania rigens		
Larkspur	2–11	175
Consolida ambigua		
Lobelia	2–11	195–196
Lobelia spp.		
Love-in-a-mist	2–11	202
Nigella damascena		
Lupine	4–9	197
Lupinus hybrids		
Marigold	2–11	212
Tagetes spp.		
Morning glory	2–11	239
Ipomoea spp.		

Common Name	Zones	Page
Oriental poppy	2–7	203
Papaver orientale		
Pansy	2–11	215
Viola spp.		
Petunia	2–11	205
Petunia spp.		
Pot marigold	2–11	169
Calendula		
Rugosa roses	2–9	91
Shasta daisy	4–9	193
Leucanthemum × superbum		
Snapdragons	2–11	162
Antirrhinum majus		
Violet	2–11	215
Viola spp.		
Yarrow	3–9	159
Achillea spp.		
Zinnia	2–11	215
Zinnia spp.		
Shrubs		
Cinquefoil	2–7	233
Potentilla fruticosa		
Lilac	2–8	235
Syringa spp.		
Spirea	3–9	234
Spiraea spp.		

■ *Use Cold, Bright Days*

Sunny days in winter are ideal for gardening chores, including pruning trees and shrubs. (If you prune spring-blooming shrubs in winter you risk trimming off buds with the branches. Wait until right after they bloom to prune these shrubs.) Also be on the lookout for frost-heaved perennials and small shrubs. If you see exposed roots, pat soil around the base of the plant to protect the roots.

■ *Choose Plants Wisely*

Because mountainous areas have fewer frost-free days than most other gardening regions, it's important to choose flowers that produce blooms quickly. If you live at an extremely high elevation, include flowers such as violas, pansies, lobelia, and calendula. These are tolerant of cooler temperatures. (See page 45 for a list of cool-season annuals that thrive in cooler temperatures.)

Many native plants thrive in mountainous regions, creating a colorful plant palette for a wildflower garden.

Flower Gardening in the Pacific Northwest

In the rainy winters and dry, moderate summers of the Pacific Northwest, a tremendous variety of plants will thrive beautifully.

Imported and unusual species of rhododendrons, azaleas, dogwoods, and brilliantly blooming rock garden and alpine plants thrive in the Pacific Northwest.

Here's how to maximize your gardening in the Pacific Northwest:

■ A Long Growing Season

Spring starts as early as February in the Pacific Northwest, with hardy primroses and minor bulbs breaking forth beneath the protection of tall evergreens. Plant in fall to ensure colorful and early spring blooms.

• **Underplant.** Midspring explodes with blooms from rhododendrons and azaleas. Underplant them with shade-tolerant, blooming groundcovers such as ajuga, lamium, and lungwort.

• **Cut back.** For summer bloom, extend perennials' flowering season by cutting back faded flowers in spring. Phlox, hollyhocks, and foxgloves, for example, will all bloom a second time if you cut them back. This second bloom can be encouraged further with an extra application of fertilizer at the same time you cut them back.

• **Use the seasons.** Fall is like a second spring in the Northwest, with annuals such as begonias and impatiens continuing to bloom until the first hard frost in mid autumn. Plant cold-tolerant pansies, snapdragons, dusty miller, and stock.

• **Dig and divide.** Digging and dividing crowded perennials can be done in early spring, late spring, or fall. Soil is moist at these times, so cuttings of easily

Periods of cool, misty weather make the Pacific Northwest a nearly perfect gardening climate.

propagated plants root readily if just pushed into the soil.

■ *The Cold Facts*

Along the coast where a heavy freeze is rare, winter rains cause more damage than cold weather. Canna, dahlia, and gladiola bulbs rot before they freeze. Dig and store them in a dry spot indoors (see page 136). Sun-loving perennials such as lavender, Russian sage, and artemesias also can drown in the wet. Raised beds (see page 68) and quick-draining soil amended with sand, gravel, or other grit are insurance against losing plants in wet winters.

• **Clean up in the fall.** Blights, molds, and mildews (see page 130-131) thrive in the cool, damp winter season. Fall cleanup of dead foliage (especially that of peonies, irises, and roses) prevents fungi from making it through the winter and reviving in spring.

• **Install nonslip pathways.** In winter, patios and paths of gravel or cedar chip are much preferred to those of brick and tile or soggy grass, which grow slippery with moss and rain.

■ *Shade Specifics*

• **Provide filtered shade.** Evergreen trees provide the filtered shade that's ideal for rhododendrons, camellias, azaleas, and small-leaved Japanese maples.

• **Go shade-tolerant.** Shade-tolerant perennials such as astilbe, corydalis, hostas, and coral bells bloom well beneath the skirts of understory trees and shrubs such as vine maple and dogwood.

• **Go native.** The Pacific Northwest has many native shade lovers. Try small bulbs such as scilla and snowdrop as well as wildflowers such as trilliums, violets, skunk cabbage, piggyback plant, hardy cyclamen, and primroses.

• **Slug the slugs.** Shady gardens need vigilant watch against slugs. Pick slugs out one-by-one, use environmentally safe slug bait, or set up barriers of wood ashes or copper strips around slug magnets like hostas.

Must-Have Flowers for the Pacific Northwest

Name	Zones	Page
Annuals/Perennials		
Astilbe *Astilbe* spp.	3–8	165
Basket-of-gold *Aurinia saxatilis*	3–7	166
Candytuft, annual type *Iberis umbellata*	3–10	190
Coral bells *Heuchera*	3–8	189
Cosmos *Cosmos* spp.	2–11	176
Creeping phlox *Phlox stolonifera*	2–8	206
Edging lobelia *Lobelia erinus*	2–11	195
Foxglove *Digitalis purpurea*	4–9	179
Fuchsia (hardy types) *Fuchsia* spp.	8–11	183
Hardy geranium *Geranium* spp.	4–8	185
Hosta *Hosta* spp.	3–9	190
Impatiens *Impatiens* spp.	2–11	190
Lady's mantle *Alchemilla* spp.	3–8	161
Nasturtium *Tropaeolum majus*	2–11	214
Tuberous begonia *Begonia* × *tuberhybrida*	2–11	218
Wax begonia *Begonia* × *semperflorens-cultorum*	2–11	166
Shrubs		
Azalea *Rhododendron* spp.	3–9	233
Camellia *Camellia* spp.	6–11	228
Hydrangea *Hydrangea* spp.	4–9	231
Rhododendron *Rhododendron* spp.	3–9	233
Viburnum *Viburnum* spp.	2–9	235
Vines and Groundcovers		
Clematis *Clematis* spp.	4–9	238
Honeysuckle *Lonicera* spp.	3–9	239
Sweet woodruff *Galium odoratum*	4–8	184
Wisteria *Wisteria* spp.	5–9	241

Roses

In general, pink roses are more resistant to the region's fungal diseases, and yellow and red roses do not fade in the afternoon sun as they do elsewhere. Roses with fewer petals do better than those with many petals since they don't ball up and rot as easily after days of rain. Any of the rugosa roses also do well. Other top rose performers include:

Name	Page
'Bonica' (other shrub)	91
'Flower Carpet' (other shrub)	91
'Peace' (hybrid tea)	92
'Queen Elizabeth ' (grandiflora)	90
'The Fairy' (polyantha)	91

Other Options*

Annuals/Perennials

English Primrose
Primula vulgaris
Lungwort
Pulmonaria spp
Poor man's orchid
Schizanthus pinnatus
Saxifrage
Saxifraga stolonifera
Spotted dead nettle
Lamium maculatum

Shrubs

Japanese pieris
Pieris japonica
Leucothoe
Leucothoe

Vines and Groundcovers

Ajuga
Ajuga reptans
Scarlet runner bean
Phaseolus coccineus

Availability varies. Check with your local garden center.

Chapter 2
Design Basics

I f you can decorate a room or organize a closet, you can design a flower garden. The same principles of color, texture, scale, organization, and practicality apply.

In this chapter, you'll learn how to start planning a flower garden by paying special attention to your own personal style, the basic structure of the garden, color combinations, and bloom season. You'll also learn how to use plants according to their growth habit (annual, perennial, vine, and more) and how to incorporate fragrance, function (outdoor living, entry area) and garden accessories into your designs.

So pull out your paper, sharpen your pencil, and start planning!

When planning for cool-season color in late fall or early spring, consider the bold color of many pinks (Dianthus, page 178).

Planning Your Flower Garden

■ *Where to Begin?*

Whether you have a yard that's bare except for the sod the builder left or you have a landscape that seems like an overgrown jungle, the starting point is the same—gathering ideas.

It's best to live in your house one full year before plunging into any major landscape projects. This allows you to get an idea of soil, sun and shade exposure, local climate, and pests. During that time, go on garden tours, visit local public gardens, and browse through magazines and books. Put all your favorite photos and lists of your favorite plants into one folder or notebook.

After you've gathered ideas, sketch out your plans on graph paper. Some gardeners prefer to work with the real thing. Lay out a garden hose where you want the edges of your flower beds and borders. Take photos of the site and sketch in new beds and borders with grease pencil, or lay a piece of tracing paper over the photo and draw your ideas on that with a regular pencil.

Start slowly, plant a small area or two at a time. Gorgeous gardens don't happen in a year or two. They're usually the product of 10, 15, or even 20 years of committed gardening.

Black-eyed Susans (Rudbeckia, page 209) are so easy to grow they should be included in nearly every garden plan.

STUFF YOU'LL NEED

✔ Measuring tape
✔ Wooden stakes
✔ ¼" grid tracing paper
✔ Straightedge
✔ Compass
✔ Pencils

Design Tip

Designing on the Spot

Use powdered lime, gypsum, flour, landscape spray paint, or a garden hose to mark future beds and borders. Look at them for a day or two to make sure you like their shape and position.

② **Using grid paper, position the fixed points on your plan.** It is useful to prepare an underlay of just the portions of your garden design that will not change, like mature trees, structural elements, and walkways. Then design your garden on a tracing paper overlay. That way, you have to redraw only the things that are changeable as you experiment with garden designs.

Making a Garden Plan

① **Measure the distances between fixed elements in your garden landscape.** Your garden design will be limited by the fixed points in your landscape that you can't change. Measure accurately and locate these benchmarks on your garden plan.

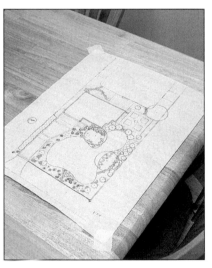

③ **Fill in with plantings and accessories.** Take into consideration the mature heights and widths of your plantings, the color of the blooms, seasonal progression of blooms, and soil type, as well as the light and water requirements of plant groups. You might try several garden layouts before you find one you like.

What Do I Want in My Garden?

Ask yourself some basic questions:

• **How much time do I want to spend gardening?** Figure an average of about a half hour a week during the growing season to maintain a 5×20-foot bed.

• **What's my budget?** Flowers, tools, and supplies can add up quickly. Make a budget and stick to it.

• **What are my growing conditions?** How much sun and shade do I get in various parts of my yard? What's my soil like? How wet or dry is my climate at various times of the year? What are record temperature lows and highs?

• **What look do I want?** Formal, country, English cottage garden, native, manicured, eclectic?

• **What is my home's architectural style?** How do I create a garden that works with my house?

• **What's my region's style?** What sort of gardens look at home in my part of the country? Drought-tolerant native plants? Lush tropical plants? Prairie natives? Mountain wildflowers?

• **What's my lifestyle?** How do I want to use my garden? As a retreat? As a place for entertaining? Will children play there? Will pets have access?

• **What are my favorite colors?** Will the flowers look good with the existing structures, such as houses, fences, and garages?

• **What animals do I want to attract or deter?** Birds, butterflies, and hummingbirds (page 146) are welcome guests while deer and rabbits (page 132) are not.

• **Do I want flowers for cutting?** If so, be sure to plant plenty of flowers that are good for cutting (page 152) from spring to frost.

• **How important is fragrance?** Incorporate plenty of scented plants (page 54).

• **Should my garden look good all growing season?** Am I home all year long and do I want something blooming all the time? Or am I aiming for a peak bloom in spring, summer, or fall?

No-Fail Flowers

Note: Some flowers will perform as annuals or perennials depending on your zone and local growing conditions. For more information on the plants below, check the Flower Encyclopedia beginning on page 156 and consult with associates at your local garden center.

Name	Zones	Page
Annuals/Perennials		
Black-eyed Susan *Rudbeckia*	3–10	209
Catmint *Nepeta* spp.	4–9	201
Coreopsis *Coreopsis* spp.	3–9	176
Daffodil *Narcissus* spp.	3–11	223
Daylily *Hemerocallis* spp.	3–10	189
Geranium *Pelargonium* spp.	2–11	203
Hosta* *Hosta*	3–9	190
Impatiens *Impatiens* spp.	2–11	190
Marigold *Tagetes* spp.	?–11	212
Moss rose *Portulaca*	2–11	207
Vinca *Catharanthus roseus*	2–11	170
Petunia *Petunia* spp.	2–11	205
Sedum *Sedum* 'Autumn Joy'	3–11	211
Siberian iris* *Iris sibirica*	3–10	191
Sweet william *Dianthus* spp.	2–11	178
Wax begonia *Begonia × semperflorens-cultorum*	2–11	166

* Does well in all regions except the desert Southwest.

Design Tip

Calling in the Pros

Stumped for ideas? Talk to your garden center staff. Experienced staff may come up with quick designs based on your photographs, drawings, and measurements of your yard's layout. They'll save you time and money!

Easy, care-free geraniums (Pelargonium, page 203) are practically no-fail flowers.

Your Garden's Style

The best advice on garden style is to have one. The most successful gardens are unified; everything makes sense in relation to everything else. It's tempting to choose garden structures, accessories, and plants based on what appeals at the moment, but in the long run clear and unified choices are far more satisfying.

Garden styles are as individual as the gardeners themselves, yet they still reflect both personal taste and the environment they exist in. The choices are limited only by your imagination: an Asian-inspired tropical garden; a garden featuring a collection of birdhouses, a wildflower garden outside a New England saltbox, a landscape showcasing a daylily collection, a formal brick-and-boxwood beauty surrounding a traditional pillared Southern home, a garden surrounded by woods that welcomes wildlife, or a garden of roses enclosed by a picket fence surrounding a bungalow.

Here's what to consider when you're planning a garden:

■ *Your Home's Architecture*
Your house is part of your garden too. When designing your garden, take cues from the architecture and the building materials of your home.

A brick home looks great with brick paths. A simple wood ranch calls for simple wood structures in the yard. A '30s clapboard bungalow is the perfect foil for a charming picket fence.

■ *What's Already There*
Work with existing features.

This rustic home is complemented perfectly by equally rustic window boxes.

A wooded lot calls for a woodland garden. A tiny urban yard, hemmed in by tall buildings, would be a natural for a courtyard garden.

Landscapes and structures you'll look at along with your own garden must also be taken into account. Be sure to look at the big picture while you're planning so you won't be surprised after it's too late.

■ *Formal vs. Informal*
Formal gardens tend to have straight and geometric lines, such as a garden divided into four or six or eight squares or rectangles. They can also be circular or a perfect oval, perhaps with straight or curving paths running off the circle or oval.

Many formal gardens include a central axis, a long straight path that runs through the center of the planting beds, giving an illusion of depth.

Formal gardens don't have to be stuffy. True, very traditional formal gardens tend to have tightly clipped hedges, uniformly planted flowers, and strict themes, such as a rose garden. But even a wildflower garden could be formal if the paths cut through it are in a geometric pattern.

Informal gardens are more free in form. Beds and borders are usually abstract, flowing shapes. Their layouts are unpredictable, and paths may make many turns. If you look at the garden from a bird's-eye viewpoint, the garden would not be symmetrical in the way formal gardens so often are.

■ *Hardscape Materials*
What you use for your paths, fences, patios, porches, decks, and other "hardscape" in the garden affects the garden's style as well.

Paths, for example, can be

Design Tip

Paper Gardens

As you're deciding which style is best for your garden, do what interior designers recommend to their clients: Tear out photos of gardens you love from magazines, newspapers, and fliers. File them in a folder. After a while, you'll have a large collection of photos. Go through them and check what the photos have in common. An abundance of yellow flowers? A formal layout? An English cottage look? Use this information to guide you to a unified garden style all your own.

■ *Personality*

Let your personality shine through in your garden. After all, personal expression is a big part of why you're spending all this time and money.

Use your favorite colors. If you love purple, use lots of it. If you're a bird-watcher, fill your garden with birdhouses and wildlife-friendly flowers. If you like a soft, country look, incorporate ornamental grasses and lively, richly colored flowers.

TRIP SAVER

Picture This

Keep photos of your garden and key measurements in your wallet or purse. Then you'll always have them with you when shopping to refer to or to show garden center staff for suggestions. It will save time and money.

constructed of several different materials. Wood chips set a casual tone, while brick is formal. Pea gravel edged with brick is somewhere in between.

Unify the hardscape. A white wooden arbor works with a white wooden bench. Brick paths may look out of place with a flagstone patio.

■ *Region and Neighborhood*

Your garden doesn't need to be a copy of all the other landscapes in your neighborhood, but it should fit in.

A grand, lush, water-thirsty garden with a large lawn and high-maintenance annuals is out of place in a modest neighborhood in the desert Southwest. Use some of the same type of fencing or the same trees you see in the neighborhood. This is especially important in the public spaces such as your front yard where your garden will be on display to passersby.

An old fireplace front becomes a whimsical, freestanding garden accent.

Garden Structure

Like all real beauties, extraordinary gardens have great bone structure. Hardscape elements pull the whole garden together and keep it looking good all year-round. Whatever you want to call it, your garden's structure consists of the following:

• **Decks, patios, and porches** serve as transitions from the outdoors to the indoors. They serve a practical function as a hard surface on which to put outdoor furniture, grills, pots, and other accessories. They reduce dirt and mud tracked into a home and frame the view from your windows, creating an outdoor room.

• **Paths** direct traffic in your garden. People—and even some pets—are amazingly obedient about following paths. Paths can be as simple as wood chips or turf, or as elaborate as flagstone or brick. Just make sure they're wide enough. Two feet is right for a small access path through a wide perennial bed, a path only you would use to work the beds. Three feet is comfortable for visitors to use to stroll through. And paths need to be 4 feet or wider if you'd like two people to be able to walk side by side.

• **Arbors, trellises, and pergolas** add height and interest to the garden. Arbors should be used at the entrance of paths or other entries (never just put one in the middle of a lawn). Trellises and pergolas are ideal supports for vines and can be designed as shelters for dining or sitting areas as well. Use them creatively either against your house or in a far corner of the garden as a destination to draw people through the garden.

• **Hedges, fences, and walls** offer privacy as well as a backdrop. Hedges can be one green plant or a combination of several with varying foliage colors and different flowers. Fences and walls can be of varying materials and heights (always check local laws on materials, heights, and setbacks). However, if a fence or wall is to be more than 4 or 5 feet tall, consider using lattice or another open design to lighten it up.

Hedges and fences have another wonderful benefit: They block winds, creating a gentle microclimate in your garden.

• **Retaining walls** hold soil in place and add structure to a slope or a raised bed. Although every situation is different, it's more attractive (and safer) to have a series of low retaining walls rather than one very tall one. On a steep 8-foot slope, it would be better to have three low retaining walls, each just a few feet high, rather than one 8-foot-tall wall.

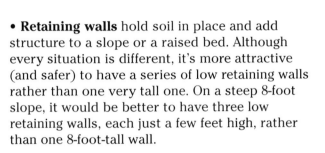

• **Edging** gives beds and borders crisp definition, making them look well kept even if you've been a little lax with the hoe and pruning shears. Choose an edging compatible with other materials in your garden. Landscape timbers work well if other natural wood is nearby. Brick edging is especially nice if there are brick paths or the house is built of brick.

Combining Plants

Combining plants effectively is the key to a good design.

■ Color

Mix pastels with pastels and brights with brights. If you're a beginner, work with a reliable, easy color scheme such as pink, blue, and white.

• **Colors change with the seasons.** Pinks and blues are easier to find in spring flowers. Maroons, russets, and oranges are easier to find in autumn flowers. Summer gives a wide range with nearly every color imaginable.

• **Most color schemes can benefit from the addition of a little white.** White adds punch and freshness, making the colors near it stand out, especially at night.

• **Color makes a space feel bigger or smaller.** Blues and dark reds blend into the background, creating the effect of being farther away. Yellows, clear reds, oranges, whites, and bright pinks seem closer.

• **Color sets mood.** A garden with lots of red is vibrant and exciting. A garden with blues feels soothing and almost misty. A white garden is serene. A garden with pink and blue together is sweet and romantic.

• **Coordinate.** Consider the color of your home, fences, and nearby buildings when choosing a color scheme. Orange flowers against a red house can be jolting, and white flowers in front of a white house can get lost.

■ Foliage

A flower's foliage is just as important as its bloom. A pretty flower with good-looking foliage is a treasure. Some, such as Oriental poppies, have spectacular flowers; however, the foliage shrivels shortly after bloom, presenting the gardener with cleanup problems. Others, such as astilbe and peonies, have pretty, glossy foliage throughout the growing season. Some, such as hostas, lamb's-ears, and dusty miller, have such wonderful foliage that they are planted primarily for their leaves. Many plants have variegated forms, sporting striking leaf markings.

Green is also a color. In the garden it ranges from the palest gray-green to deep burgundy-green to almost yellow spring-green. Mix in a variety of foliage colors.

A Well-Designed

A spiky plant or two adds contrasting shape to the border, which is dominated by sprawling, "fluffy" plants. Ornamental grasses have also been included for a strong vertical element and yet another contrasting shape.

A touch of white flowers freshens the look and adds welcome contrast.

Plants are placed fairly close together for a lush look.

Yellow torch lily

White roses

Lady's mantle

Lavender

This border has a subtle color scheme: Purple flowers are used with touches of yellow flowers and plants with gold foliage.

■ Texture and Shape

When combining plants in your flower garden, go for a contrast in leaf shape, size, texture, and color. For example, put a silvery, hairy-leaved plant next to a glossy, large-leaved plant. Tuck in a feathery plant as well as one with strappy, grasslike leaves.

Experiment with plant combinations by plucking a leaf from each plant and holding them together in your hand. If you like the combination, it will probably look good in your flower bed too.

■ Height

Arranging plants by height is easy. Put the tall ones (4 to 6 feet) in the back; the mid-sized ones (2 to 4 feet) in the middle; and the shorter ones (2 feet and under) in the front.

• **How will your flower bed be viewed?** If your flower bed will be viewed from all sides, put tall sizes in the center, shorties along the edges, and middle sizes in the middle.

• **How do you know how tall a plant will get?** Checking the plant in the Flower Encyclopedia (page 156) or simply reading the label is best, but be aware that plant heights can vary according to climate, rainfall, soil, nitrogen levels, and your microclimate.

■ Seasonality

Colors, heights, textures, and shapes change with the seasons.

In spring bulbs may fill your garden with color, but then fade away. For fall, plant ornamental grasses and other perennials that have good color or stand during winter. Make note of a plant's characteristics from earliest spring through late fall and winter and plant accordingly.

■ Growing Conditions

As important as visual elements are, all will be for naught if the plants you've combined don't also have similar growing needs.

Group plants with similar water requirements together as well as those with similar light and soil requirements.

Perennial Border

Butterfly bush

Yucca

Lower, neater perennials are used as edging plants.

A purple-leaved plant breaks up what would otherwise be a dull mass of green.

This border has an attractive background—a wooded area. Other good backgrounds include tall fences or the side of a building.

Tall, more unruly perennials are placed in back where they lend height while other plants disguise their leggy habit.

Mid-height plants are placed in the middle.

Foliage is as important to this border as flowers. It contains plants with a variety of leaf colors, including purple and yellow.

Design Tip

Mix It Up

There's a garden saying "Put a roundy by a frilly by a spiky." And it works. A composition using those shapes will look good for months, long before and after the flowers have peaked.

Color All Year Long

Careful planning makes it possible to have a garden that blooms from early spring through winter. Try these ideas.

■ Choose Long-Blooming Perennials

Some perennials bloom for just a few days, while others bloom for months. Plant as many of the long-bloomers as possible (see page 47). A good long-blooming perennial will bloom for two or even three months.

■ Deadhead to Extend Bloom Time

Deadheading (page 119) keeps your garden tidy and encourages plants to bloom longer.

Some plants respond better to deadheading than others. And some, like coreopsis, have so many sprawling blooms that it's best to cut or shear them all back at once, taking a little of the plant's foliage with them, to clean up the plant and encourage new flushes of bloom.

Cut back plants with long, bare stalks, such as irises and daylilies, to the base—long stalk and all.

A Year of Bloom from Perennials and Roses

early spring   midspring   early summer

Daffodils
Narcissus
page 223

Tulip
Tulipa
page 225

Columbine
Aquilegia spp.
page 162

Siberian iris
Iris sibirica
page 191

Peony
Paeonia
page 202

Shrub rose
Rosa
pages 88-91

■ Seek Early Through Late-Season Bloomers

Some tulips will bloom while snow is on the ground, others are midseason cultivars, and still others will bloom with the earliest roses. Each type may bloom only two or three weeks, but planted together, they will extend tulip time to more than two months.

■ Seek Repeat Bloomers

Some plants will bloom in flushes with a first, heavy flowering. If you're diligent in deadheading or cutting the plant back slightly (page 118), they'll often respond with a second, third, or even continual series of blooms. Hardy geraniums are a good example of this, as are many roses.

Here's an Idea:

Plan for Winter Interest

No matter what your climate, you can have a beautiful garden, even in winter. In warm climates, seek out evergreen flowers or flowers that bloom in winter. In colder climates, tall sedums, ornamental grasses, berries, shrubs, and trees with colorful barks create visual interest even in deepest snow. Visit local public gardens and neighborhood gardens, and chat with garden center staff even in winter to learn more about these useful off-season plants.

midsummer   late summer   autumn

| Asiatic or Oriental lily *Lilium* spp. page 222 | Garden phlox *Phlox paniculata* page 206 | Daylily *Hemerocallis* spp. page 189 | Aster *Aster* page 165 | Perennial mum *Chrysanthemum* spp. page 173 | Sedum *Sedum* 'Autumn Joy' page 211 |

Flowers by Color

The flowers in these lists are organized by color. If a plant is listed more than once, it is available in more than one color. Check with your garden center for other color options available in your region.

Autumn crocus (Colchicum autumnale, page 219)

White

Name	Zones	Page
Agapanthus *Agapanthus*	2–11	217
Asiatic and Oriental lilies *Lilium* spp.	3–9	222
Astilbe *Astilbe* spp.	3–8	165
Autumn crocus *Colchicum autumnale*	5–7	219
Azure Monkshood *Aconitum carmichaelii*	3–7	159
Baby's breath *Gypsophila paniculata*	3–9	186
Balloon flower *Platycodon grandiflorus*	3–8	207
Bellflower *Campanula* spp.	3–8	170
Bleeding heart *Dicentra* spp.	2–9	179
Candytuft *Iberis* spp.	3–10	190
Columbine *Aquilegia* spp.	3–10	162
Cupflower *Nierembergia*	3–11	201
Dahlia *Dahlia*	2–11	220
Delphinium *Delphinium elatum*	2–7	178
English daisy *Bellis perennis*	4–10	167
Flowering tobacco *Nicoliana* spp.	2–11	201
Lily-of-the-valley *Convallaria majalis*	3–7	175
Peony *Paeonia* spp.	2–8	202
Petunia *Petunia* spp.	2–11	205
Phlox, moss or creeping *Phlox subulata* or *stolonifera*	2–9	206
Snow-in-summer *Cerastium tomentosum*	2–9	172

Name	Zones	Page
Trillium *Trillium* spp.	4–8	224
Tulip *Tulipa* spp.	3–11	225
Windflower *Anemone* spp.	4–9	217

Delphinium (Delphinium elatum, page 178)

Blue and Purple

Name	Zones	Page
Agapanthus *Agapanthus*	2–11	217
Ageratum *Ageratum houstonianum*	2–11	160
Amethyst flower *Browallia*	2–11	168
Aster *Aster* spp.	4–8	165
Bachelor's button *Centaurea cyanus*	3–10	171
Balloon flower *Platycodon grandiflorus*	3–8	207
Bellflower *Campanula* spp.	3–8	170
Blue daisy *Felicia amelloides*	7–11	183
Blue false indigo *Baptisia australis*	3–9	166
Blue flax *Linum perenne*	4–9	195
Blue lilyturf *Liriope muscari*	6–9	195
China aster *Callistephus chinensis*	2–11	169
Chinese forget-me-not *Cynoglossum amabile*	2–9	177
Cranesbill *Geranium* spp.	4–8	185
Delphinium *Delphinium elatum*	2–7	178
Edging lobelia *Lobelia erinus*	2–11	195
Forget-me-not *Myosotis sylvatica*	4–9	200
Globe thistle *Echinops* spp.	3–8	180
Grape hyacinth *Muscari* spp.	3–8	223
Hyacinth *Hyacinthus orientalis*	3–11	222
Iris *Iris* spp.	3–10	191
Larkspur *Consolida ambigua*	2–11	175
Lavender *Lavandula* spp.	5–10	192
Lilac *Syringa* spp.	2–8	235
Lungwort *Pulmonaria* spp.	2–8	208

Name	Zones	Page
Lupine *Lupinus* hybrids	4–9	197
Penstemon *Penstemon* spp.	3–9	204
Perennial cornflower *Centaurea montana*	3–8	171
Russian sage *Perovskia atriplicifolia*	5–7	204
Salvia (both annual and perennial) *Salvia* spp.	2–11	209, 210
Scabiosa *Scabiosa caucasica*	3–7	210
Squill *Scilla* spp.	2–8	224
Statice *Limonium* spp.	2–11	194
Swan River daisy *Brachycome iberidifolia*	2–11	167
Sweet alyssum *Lobularia maritima*	2–11	196
Sweet william *Dianthus* spp.	2–11	178
Texas bluebonnet *Lupinus texensis*	2–11	197
Veronica *Veronica* spp.	3–8	214
Violet *Viola* spp.	2–11	215
Virginia bluebells *Mertensia virginica*	3–8	199

Coreopsis, (Coreopsis, page 176)

Yellow and Gold

Name	Zones	Page
Annual sunflower *Helianthus annuus*	2–11	187
Asiatic and Oriental lily *Lilium* spp.	3–9	222
Basket-of-gold *Aurinia saxatilis*	3–7	166
Black-eyed Susan *Rudbeckia* spp.	3–10	209
Blanket flower *Gaillardia* spp.	2–11	184
Butterfly weed *Asclepias tuberosa*	4–10	164
California poppy *Eschscholzia californica*	2–11	181
Canna *Canna hybrids*	2–11	218
Celosia *Celosia* spp.	2–11	170
Columbine *Aquilegia* spp.	3–10	162
Coreopsis *Coreopsis* spp.	3–9	176

Name	Zones	Page
Cosmos *Cosmos* spp.	2–11	176
Daffodil *Narcissus* spp.	3–11	223
Dahlia *Dahlia*	2–11	220
Daylily *Hemerocallis* spp.	3–10	189
Evening primrose *Oenothera* spp.	3–8	202
False sunflower *Helianthus* spp.	4–9	187
Foxglove *Digitalis purpurea*	4–9	179
Goldenrod *Solidago* hybrids	3–9	211
Lilies, especially Asiatic *Lilium* spp.	3–9	222
Marigold *Tagetes*	2–11	212
Mexican sunflower *Tithonia rotundifolia*	2–11	213
Perennial mum *Chrysanthemum* spp.	4–9	173
Perennial sunflower *Helianthus* spp.	4–9	187
Pot marigold *Calendula*	2–11	169
Statice *Limonium* spp.	2–11	194
Strawflower *Helichrysum bracteatum*	2–11	187
Violet *Viola* spp.	2–11	215
Yarrow *Achillea* spp.	3–9	159
Zinnia *Zinnia* spp.	2–11	215

Dahlias
(*Dahlia*,
page 220)

Pink

Name	Zones	Page
Asiatic and Oriental lily *Lilium* spp.	3–9	222
Aster *Aster* spp.	4–8	165
Astilbe *Astilbe* spp.	3–8	165
Bleeding heart *Dicentra* spp.	2–9	179
Boltonia *Boltonia asteroides*	4–9	167
Canna *Canna* hybrids	2–11	218
Celosia *Celosia* spp.	2–11	170
Columbine *Aquilegia* spp.	3–10	162
Coreopsis *Coreopsis* spp.	3–9	176

Name	Zones	Page
Cosmos *Cosmos* spp.	2–11	176
Creeping phlox *Phlox stolonifera*	2–8	206
Dahlia *Dahlia*	2–11	220
Foxglove *Digitalis purpurea*	4–9	179
Garden phlox *Phlox* spp.	5–7	206
Moss rose *Portulaca*	2–11	207
Obedient plant *Physostegia virginiana*	2–9	207
Peony *Paeonia* spp.	2–8	202
Perennial mum *Chrysanthemum* spp.	4–9	173
Purple coneflower *Echinacea purpurea*	3–9	180
Rose *Rosa* spp.	2–11	86-93
Spider flower *Cleome hassleriana*	2–11	174
Sweet pea *Lathyrus odoratus*	2–11	192
Sweet william *Dianthus* spp.	2–11	178
Wax begonia *Begonia × semperflorens-cultorum*	2–11	166
Yarrow *Achillea* spp.	3–9	159

Crocosmia
(*Crocosmia x crocosmiiflora*,
page 219)

Orange

Name	Zones	Page
Blanket flower *Gaillardia* spp.	2–11	184
Butterfly weed *Asclepias tuberosa*	4–10	164
California poppy *Eschscholzia californica*	2–11	181
Canna *Canna* hybrids	2–11	218
Dahlia *Dahlia*	2–11	220
Daylily *Hemerocallis* spp.	3–10	189
Fritillary *Fritillaria* spp.	3–7	221
Gazania *Gazania rigens*	2–11	185
Geranium *Pelargonium* spp.	2–11	203
Gerber daisy *Gerbera*	3–10	185
Lilies, especially Asiatic *Lilium* spp.	3–9	222

Name	Zones	Page
Marigold *Tagetes* spp.	2–11	212
Mexican sunflower *Tithonia rotundifolia*	2–11	213
Moss rose *Portulaca*	2–11	207
Nasturtium *Tropaeolum majus*	2–11	214
Oriental poppy *Papaver orientale*	2–7	203
Zinnia *Zinnia* spp.	2–11	215

Tulips
(*Tulipa*,
page 225)

Red

Name	Zones	Page
Annual phlox *Phlox drummondii*	2–11	205
Annual red salvia *Salvia splendens* and *coccinea*	2–11	209
Aster *Aster* spp.	4–8	165
Astilbe *Astilbe* spp.	3–8	165
Bee balm *Monarda didyma*	4–8	200
California poppy *Eschscholzia californica*	2–11	181
Cardinal flower *Lobelia* spp.	2–9	196
Coral bells *Heuchera*	3–8	189
Geranium *Pelargonium* spp.	2–11	203
Impatiens *Impatiens* spp.	2–11	190
Love-lies-bleeding *Amaranthus caudatus*	2–11	161
Lupine *Lupinus* hybrids	4–9	197
Nasturtium *Tropaeolum majus*	2–11	214
Perennial mum *Chrysanthemum* spp.	4–9	173
Primrose *Primula* spp.	3–10	208
Rose *Rosa* spp.	3–11	86-95
Snapdragon *Antirrhinum majus*	2–11	162
Stock *Matthiola incana*	3–11	198
Tulip *Tulipa* spp.	3–11	225
Verbena *Verbena* spp.	2–11	214
Wax begonia *Begonia × semperflorens-cultorum*	2–11	166
Yarrow *Achillea* spp.	3–9	159
Zinnia *Zinnia* spp.	2–11	215

Designing with Annuals

It's no coincidence that annuals are given to children for their first gardens. Annuals are inexpensive, grow quickly, and provide an explosion of color. Since you plant annuals each year, experiment with different color schemes and designs. (See pages 66 and 76 and Chapter 4 for information on planting and maintenance.)

■ Choosing Annuals

It's easy to grow annuals from seed, but many gardeners prefer to buy them as established seedlings. Consider the following:

• **Is it the right plant for the right place?** Read the label to check light, soil, and height information. Look for awards or prizes the plant has won—a good sign that it's reliable with great growing characteristics.

• **Is it healthy?** What you see is

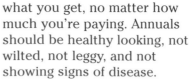

CLOSER LOOK

What Is an Annual?

An annual is a plant that grows for just one year. However, an annual in one part of the country might live as a perennial for several years in a warmer region.

Some labels and books make further distinctions such as hardy annuals, half-hardy annuals, half-hardy perennials, or tender perennials. Those labels just mean that the plant is borderline.

To further blur matters, some flowers have both annual and perennial varieties. For example, some salvias are annuals in nearly all parts of the country, while others are perennials everywhere.

If you're confused, look at the Flower Encyclopedia (page 156), check the label, or ask garden center staff.

what you get, no matter how much you're paying. Annuals should be healthy looking, not wilted, not leggy, and not showing signs of disease.

• **What is its growth habit?** A tumbling, vinelike annual is great for a window box, but a disaster in the back of the border where it will get lost. A tall leggy plant, like a sunflower, is regal for a few weeks when planted behind shorter plants, but can be unattractive growing by itself.

■ Using Annuals

Follow these tips for great annual plantings:

• **Give them company.** Plant in large groups. Twenty marigolds

Must-Have Annuals

Looking for plants so easy to grow even a child can do it? Then go for these annuals. They are some of the most maintenance-free, the ones every gardener who professes a brown thumb should try:

Name	Zones	Page
Ageratum, flossflower *Ageratum houstonianum*	2–11	160
Celosia, cockscomb *Celosia*	2–11	170
Cosmos *Cosmos* spp.	2–11	176
Dusty miller *Centaurea cineraria*	2–11	171
Geranium *Pelargonium* spp.	2–11	203
Impatien *Impatiens* spp.	2–11	190
Marigold *Tagetes* spp.	2–11	212
Petunia *Petunia* spp.	2–11	205
Salvia *Salvia*	2–11	209
Sweet alyssum *Lobularia maritima*	2–11	196
Vinca, periwinkle *Catharanthus roseus*	2–8	170
Wax begonia *Begonia × semperflorens-cultorum*	2–11	166
Zinnia *Zinnia* spp.	2–11	215

The brilliant red and yellow annual poppies in this flower bed are cool-season annuals that add gorgeous color in early summer. By mid-summer, they'll begin to fade and brown and should then be pulled up.

in a group have a bigger, more attractive impact than three in a group. Most annuals grow in groups in nature and like it that way in the garden, too.

• **Leave pockets for annuals.** Perennial borders are lovely but, unless perfectly planned, can be too green certain times of the year. Leaving an open space for annuals lets you enhance the color.

• **Alternate warm-season and cool-season annuals.** Get more color longer in prime spots, such as window boxes or planters, by planting cool-season annuals in winter or spring. Then, when the cool-season flowers fade in late spring, replace with warm-season annuals.

• **Fertilize regularly.** Since they're growing so much in one year, annuals need abundant food. Work in a slow-release fertilizer or compost at planting time. If possible, supplement with a liquid fertilizer four or five times during the growing season.

• **Use reseeders.** Some annuals reseed each spring (page 126). Although they may not grow exactly like the parents, it's fun (and inexpensive) to let them grow. Thin and transplant as desired.

These marigolds (Tagetes spp., page 212) are warm-season annuals that thrive once temperatures soar.

These annual lobelia (Lobelia erinus, page 195), which are cool-season annuals, do well as long as temperatures don't exceed the 80s.

Warm-Season Annuals versus Cool-Season Annuals

Understanding warm-season and cool-season annuals puts you on your way to having a garden that looks good throughout the growing season.

Cool-season annuals do well during cool weather, be that spring, fall, or even winter in warm climates. They take a little frost—and often snow—but tend to brown and shrivel when temperatures regularly hit 80 to 85°F (26 to 29°C).

Warm-season annuals love it hot. Planted in spring, they'll sulk if the weather is cold; but when very warm weather hits, they take off and thrive for weeks or months until frost.

Name	Zones	Page
Cool-season Annuals		
California poppy *Eschscholzia californica*	2–11	181
Edging lobelia *Lobelia erinus*	2–11	195
Godetia *Clarkia amoena*	2–11	174
Larkspur *Consolida ambigua*	2–11	175
Pansy *Viola* spp.	2–11	215
Pinks, annual type *Dianthus chinensis*	3–11	178
Pot marigold *Calendula*	2–11	169
Snapdragon *Antirrhinum majus*	2–11	162
Sweet alyssum *Lobularia maritima*	2–11	196
Sweet pea *Lathyrus odoratus*	2–11	192
Violet *Viola* spp.	2–11	215

Name	Zones	Page
Warm-season Annuals		
Ageratum, flossflower *Ageratum houstonianum*	2–11	160
Amethyst flower *Browallia*	2–11	168
Annual salvia *Salvia*	2–11	209
Celosia *Celosia* spp.	2–11	170
Cosmos *Cosmos* spp.	2–11	176
Flowering tobacco *Nicotiana* spp.	2–11	201
Globe amaranth *Gomphrena globosa*	2–11	186
Impatiens *Impatiens*	2–11	190
Marigold *Tagetes* spp.	2–11	212
Petunia *Petunia* spp.	2–11	205
Spider flower *Cleome hassleriana*	2–11	174
Zinnia *Zinnia* spp.	2–11	215

Designing with Perennials

Perennials are a flower gardener's friend, coming back year after year, saving expense, planting time, and maintenance. (See pages 66 and 76 and Chapter 4 for information on selection and maintenance.)

■ *Choosing Perennials*

• **Look for good value in comparison to size.** Mail-order perennials, for example, can be very small or bare-root and may take years to get to good blooming size. The large, more expensive 1-gallon perennials will bloom sooner, but often cost far more. Smaller perennials, those in 3- or 4-inch pots, are often the best value.

• **Check the roots.** Don't be afraid to knock the plant out of its pot a little in the store. You want a plant that has a well-developed root system, not a small, weak cutting that's hardly established itself.

• **Buy healthy plants, preferably not in bloom.** Don't purchase plants that look diseased or wilted. They may spread the problem. Also, it's best to buy when flowers are not in bloom. Although they're gorgeous, it will take longer for them to establish, because they have to put their energy into flowering as well as root development.

• **Consider foliage.** Perennials are short bloomers. Most of the time you'll be looking at the foliage. Choose plants with foliage that looks fresh all season (hostas, ever-blooming bleeding heart, Siberian irises) and are a contrast in color and texture to the other foliage in the garden.

Many of these flowers, including the striking, tall delphiniums (Delphinium elatum, page 178), are perennials that will return every spring, saving time, work, and money.

CLOSER LOOK

What Is a Perennial?

A perennial is a plant that comes back year after year. In colder parts of the country, however, a few perennials must be grown as annuals because they can't withstand the cold or wet winter.

Sometimes you'll see perennials, such as flax, referred to as "short-lived perennials." These are perennials that last for only a few years and then die out. Other perennials, such as peonies, will last for decades.

Most perennials die out in the winter, but some (especially in warm climates) are evergreen or semi-evergreen, with foliage that needs just a little trimming, if even that, come spring.

What Is a Biennial?

A handful of our favorite flowers are biennials, plants that take two years to flower. The first year they grow foliage. The second year, they bloom and then die at the end of the season.

To flower gardeners, a biennial may not sound like a very desirable plant (all that waiting only for it to die!), but favorite biennials are so lovely they're worth the wait. Spectacular Canterbury bells *campanulas* (page 170) are an excellent example.

Some biennials, such as foxgloves and hollyhocks, are a bit erratic—in a good way. They often bloom their first year from seed and then reseed prolifically so that they seem like perennials.

Using Perennials

• Know when they bloom.
Some perennials, such as Oriental poppies, are glorious for a week and then fade out, looking ragged as they go. Others, such as coreopsis, bloom from midspring until frost. Orchestrate your garden so that something is always in bloom (see page 40 for achieving constant color).
Look at what's blooming in your neighborhood, parks, and public gardens. Make a list of a dozen or more perennials in a succession of bloom times.

• Deadhead! Trim spent blooms off regularly (see page 118), not only to keep the plant flowering but to keep your garden looking good.

• Don't be afraid to cut back.
If disease has felled a perennial, even if it's early summer, cut it back to just a few inches. It often will send out a flush of new foliage or even bloom. Also, this helps prevent the disease from spreading to other plants.

Long-Blooming Perennials

Bloom 10 or more weeks:

Name	Zones	Page
Aster	4–8	165
Aster spp. especially 'Moench,' 'September Ruby,' and 'Wonder of Staffa'		
Balloon flower	3–8	207
Platycodon grandiflorus		
Black-eyed Susan, perennial		209
Rudbeckia fulgida	3–9	
especially 'Goldsturm'		
Blanket flower, perennial	2–10	184
Gaillardia × *grandiflora* especially 'Baby Cole'		
Catmint	4–9	201
Nepeta especially 'Dropmore' and 'Six Hills Giant'		
Coreopsis	3–9	176
Coreopsis especially 'Sunray,' 'Early Sunrise,' 'Zagreb,' or 'Moonbeam'		
Daylily	3–10	189
Hemerocallis spp. especially 'Stella de Oro,' 'Happy Returns,' or 'Lemon Lollipop'		
Ever-blooming bleeding heart	3–9	179
Dicentra eximia		

Name	Zones	Page
Garden phlox	4–8	206
Phlox paniculata especially 'Eva Cullum' and 'Franz Schubert'		
Goldenstar	5–9	173
Chrysogonum virginianum		
Pinks, Sweet William	2–11	178
Dianthus spp.		
Russian sage	5–7	204
Perovskia atriplicifolia		
Salvia, perennial blue	4–8	210
Salvia × *superba* especially 'May Night'		
Scabiosa	3–7	210
Scabiosa caucasica		
Sedum	3–10	211
Sedum 'Autumn Joy'		
Thrift	4–8	163
Armeria		
Verbena bonariensis	7–10	214
Verbena bonariensis		
Veronica	3–8	214
Veronica spp. especially 'Sunny Border Blue'		
White gaura	5–9	184
Gaura lindheimeri		
Yarrow	3–9	159
Achillea spp. especially 'Fire King' or 'Apple blossom'		

This perennial flower bed is designed with a subtle blue and yellow color scheme. It also has silver foliage for contrast, no matter what else is in bloom.

DesignTip

Legacy Plants Are Memory Makers!

Legacy plants will fill your garden with memories of those you love. Commemorate birthdays, graduations, special holidays, any moment that's special to your family and friends. Sharing plants with neighbors and friends is also a great way to cement relationships and remind you of life's important moments.

Designing with Bulbs

■ *Choosing Spring-Blooming or Summer-Blooming Bulbs*

Say "bulbs" and most people think of spring bloomers such as tulips and daffodils. However, the term bulbs loosely used also include lilies, cannas, gladiolus, irises, and other less common summerbloomers.

Spring-blooming bulbs are planted in fall. They are hardy in even the coldest climates and need a cold period to bloom. In very warm climates, gardeners need to prechill spring bulbs, such as tulips and hyacinths, or purchase prechilled bulbs and plant them in very early spring.

Tulips are among the showiest of bulbs. Although they usually last just two or three years, their glowing beauty is worth it.

CLOSER LOOK

What Is a Bulb?

Some flowers we commonly think of as bulbs really aren't bulbs at all. True bulbs look a little like an onion with many layers. Lilies, hyacinths, amaryllis, and daffodils, for example, are true bulbs. Others are actually corms, tubers, or rhizomes (see page 136 for planting information). Don't let the terminology throw you, though. They're not treated any differently. Just follow the label directions.

As a rule, prechilled bulbs should be planted in Zones 9 and warmer, with the exception of the Northwest.

Tender summer-blooming bulbs often can't take much cold. In most gardens in Zones 7 and colder, these bulbs are usually planted in spring, and many need to be dug up in the fall and stored indoors (see page 136). If in doubt, check individual bulb listings on pages 216-225.

For more on growing bulbs, see page 78 for planting information and page 136 on digging and storing summer-blooming bulbs.

■ *Orchestrating A Bulb Display*

Bulbs have a wide variety of bloom times, heights, and planting depths, making it fun to orchestrate their blooms in long successions that explode with color among the perennials and annuals.

For a year of color from bulbs, check the list on the next page. From snowdrops to autumn crocuses, you'll have

Types of Bulbs

Bulbs must be planted with the correct end facing upward as shown below. If you are not certain which way is up, check with your local garden center.

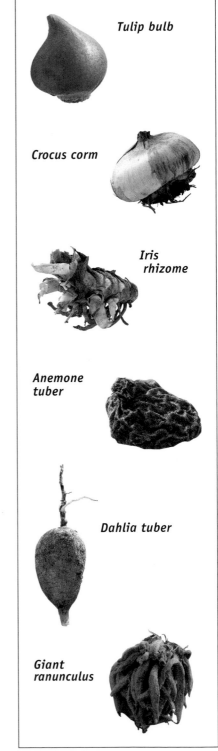

Tulip bulb

Crocus corm

Iris rhizome

Anemone tuber

Dahlia tuber

Giant ranunculus

bulbs that bloom all growing season.

Bulbs are magnificently space efficient because you can plant them in the same spot as other flowers and even on top of each other. For instance, you can plant several daffodils 6–8 inches deep, then plant crocuses above the daffodils.

Bulbs aren't greedy for food and water, so they don't interfere with other flowers when you plant them together. Most bulb foliage begins to brown after bloom, and the unattractive foliage must be left to replenish the flower for next year. Planting bulbs with other plants allows the emerging companion plants to cover the bulb foliage or at least allows you to push down the foliage so it's concealed by the second plant. The fresh, emerging foliage of daylilies, for example, will hide daffodils' dying foliage.

Design Tip

Bulb Companions

Plant bulbs with other plants that will cover the bulbs' ripening foliage. Sun-loving bulbs can be interplanted with shade-loving plants as long as they're under a deciduous tree that allows ample sun in spring before leaves are full but casts shade later.

- Daffodils (page 223) and hostas (page 190)
- Daffodils and daylilies (page 189)
- Daffodils and ferns
- Small bulbs, such as crocuses (page 219) or grape hyacinths (page 223), with vinca minor (page 241)
- Tulips and forget-me-not (page 200)
- Early tulips and columbine (page 162)
- Early tulips and creeping phlox (page 206)
- Any small bulbs under a deciduous shrub
- Tulips or hyacinths (page 222) with lady's mantle (page 164)
- Ornamental onion (page 217) and artemesia (page 164)
- Daffodils or tulips with hardy geraniums (page 185)

A Year of Bulbs

Name	Zones	Page
Late-winter/ early-spring Flowering		
Crocus	5–7	219
Crocus spp.		
Daffodil, early types	3–11	223
Narcissus spp.		
Ranunculus	8–10	224
Ranunculus asiasticus		
Snowdrops	3–7	221
Galanthus nivalis		
Squill	2–8	224
Scilla spp.		
Mid-spring Flowering		
Checkered lily	3–8	221
Fritillaria meleagris		
Daffodil, mid- and late	3–11	223
Narcissus spp.		
Freesia	2–11	220
Freesia spp.		
Grape hyacinth	3–8	223
Muscari spp.		
Trillium	4–8	224
Trillium spp.		
Tulip, mid-season types	3–11	225
Tulipa spp.		
Windflower	4–9	217
Anemone spp.		
Late-spring Flowering		
Agapanthus, early	2–11	217
Agapanthus		
Crown imperial	5–8	221
Fritillaria imperialis		
Gladiolus	2–11	221
Gladiolus hybrids		
Hyacinths	3–11	222
Hyacinthus orientalis		
Iris	3–10	191
Iris spp.		
Lily-of-the-valley	3–7	175
Convallaria majalis		
Tulip, late	3–11	223
Tulipa spp.		

Name	Zones	Page
Early-summer Flowering		
Agapanthus, late	2–11	217
Agapanthus		
Calla lily	3–11	225
Zantedeschia aethiopica		
Cyclamen, hardy	7–9	220
Cyclamen hederifolium		
Gladiolus	2–11	221
Gladiolus hybrids		
Lily, Asiatic	3–9	222
Lilium spp.		
Society garlic	8–11	225
Tulbaghia		
Mid- through late-summer Flowering		
Caladium	2–11	218
Caladium bicolor		
Canna	2–11	218
Canna hybrids		
Crocosmia	5–10	219
Crocosmia × crocosmiiflora		
Dahlia	2–11	220
Dahlia		
Gladiolus	2–11	221
Gladiolus hybrids		
Lilies, Oriental and Easter	3–11	222
Lilium spp.		
Magic lily	5–8	223
Lycoris squamigera		
Peacock orchid	3–11	222
Gladiolus callinathus		
Society garlic	8–11	225
Tulbaghia		
Tuberous begonia	2–11	218
Begonia tuberhybrida		
Autumn Flowering		
Autumn crocus	5–9	219
Colchicum autumnale		
Caladium	2–11	218
Caladium bicolor		
Canna	2–11	218
Canna hybrids		
Dahlia	2–11	220
Dahlia		
Gladiolus	2–11	221
Gladiolus hybrids		
Tuberous begonia	2–11	218
Begonia tuberhybrida		

Note: Exact bloom times will vary somewhat by region, especially in late winter and early spring. The sequence of bloom, however, is the same across the country.

Designing with Roses

Plant the right rose in the right spot and you'll have a plant that's as close as any flower comes to low maintenance. Roses, unfairly, have a reputation of being fussy, but if you provide good growing conditions and choose a low-maintenance rose, you'll see how ill-deserved that reputation is. (See pages 86-97 for rose selection and planting information. See pages 108-113 for information on pruning, diseases and pests, and winterizing roses.)

■ Choosing the Site

• **Bring on the rays.** Roses are sun-lovers. Plant them where they will get at least six hours of direct, unfiltered light a day. Less light invites pest and disease problems and results in fewer blooms.

• **Provide good drainage.** Although roses like moist soil, they don't like soggy soil. Choose a well-drained site and work in plenty of organic matter (page 63).

• **Let them breathe.** Many disease problems can be prevented by placing roses so air circulates freely around them and they aren't crowded too tightly with other plants.

• **Position for easy irrigation.** In arid climates, most roses will need regular water. A drip, bubbler, or microsprinkler system will need to be part of the design.

■ Choosing the Rose

• **Know your area's climate and gardening zone.** Many roses die out in the winter in colder climates, suffer from mildew and molds in others, or

Top Low-Maintenance Roses

Name	Zones	Name	Zones
Types of Roses		'Constance Spry'	4–9
David Austin roses	4–11	'Flower Carpet'	4–11
Meidiland roses	5–10	'Graham Thomas'	4–9
Rugosa roses	3–11	'Hansa'	3–9
		'Iceberg'	4–10
Specific Cultivars		'Lady Banks' rose	7–10
'Abraham Darby'	5–10	'Linda Campbell'	4–11
'Ballerina'	4–9	'Madame Hardy'	5–11
'Belle Story'	5–10	'Mary Rose'	4–11
'Betty Prior'	4–10	'Queen Elizabeth'	5–10
'Blanc Double de Coubert'	3–9	'Roseraie de l'Hay'	4–9
'Bonica'		'Royal Bonica'	4–9
'Carefree Beauty'	4–9	'Simplicity'	4–11
'Carefree Wonder'	3–9	'The Fairy'	5–10

This arrangement demonstrates the many colors and forms found among roses.

Work Smarter!

The Rose Experts

The American Rose Society sponsors a toll-free rose hotline for gardeners to field questions to rose experts. Call (800) 637-6534 with your rose questions. Also check out the ARS's extensive website, which is filled with rose recommendations and growing information: www.ars.org.

Design Tip

Roses by Height

Climber/rambling roses: 6-20 feet
Most shrub roses: 3-6 feet
Standard roses: 2-6 feet
Hybrid tca roses: 2½-5 feet
Floribunda roses: 2-3 feet
Polyantha roses: 2 feet
Groundcover roses: 1-3 feet
Miniature roses: 6-18 inches

(See pages 86-95 for more information on types, heights, and growing conditions.)

Rose Talk

Confused about all the terms rose fanciers use to describe a rose? Terms such as shrub rose, low-maintenance rose, and landscape rose are used interchangeably.

wither and die from drought in still others. There are hundreds of different roses. Choose the right rose for your region. (See pages 86-95 for further descriptions of roses; refer to the section on regional gardening starting on page 8 for roses recommended for your part of the country.)

• **Choose the right size.** Roses can grow anywhere from 1 foot tall and 1 foot across to 30 feet tall and 10 feet across. Read labels carefully.

• **Consider form.** Roses can be tall, sprawling climbers or grow in neat shrubs. Some have elegant "vase" shapes, while others are groundcovers. Know what you're getting and use it accordingly.

Also check flower form. Some roses are single; just a simple row of petals. Other roses are many-petaled with a cabbage-rose look. And roses such as hybrid teas have elegant oval, pointed buds that open into a classic rose shape.

• **Consider bloom patterns.** Roses bloom either just once in June or in flushes throughout the season. Again, read the label to know what you're getting.

• **Sniff out fragrance.** Roses range from no scent to lightly fragrant to intensely fragrant. Give a sniff when the rose is in bloom. Otherwise, read the label.

■ Using Roses In the Landscape

Roses can play a variety of roles in the garden. Get started with these ideas:

• **The rose garden.** If you love roses, a whole garden of them is a treat. Consider interplanting them with complementary perennials, such as lavender, campanula, and hardy geraniums. These plants not only add another dimension to the garden, but are believed to prevent rose diseases and pests.

• **Hedges.** Vigorous, tall roses such as rugosas or Meidiland roses make beautiful, informal flowering hedges. The roses can be powerfully fragrant, and the thorns make them impenetrable. Again, since you're planting so many roses together, they will be more prone to disease. It's a good idea to mix the types of roses and therefore prevent problems.

• **Roses for cutting.** You don't need to have a special cutting garden to gather armloads of roses from your yard. Roses like being cut (it's a form of deadheading, after all), so even a few shrubs—especially repeat bloomers—will provide a bounty of flowers. Hybrid teas make superb cut flowers. Avoid rugosas and David Austins for cutting as they shatter easily when cut.

• **Roses in a mixed border.** Roses associate well with annuals, perennials, herbs— even vegetables and other shrubs. Also, since roses, especially hybrid teas, tend to be rather leggy, underplanting them with other flowers is an attractive option. Just be sure to feed them liberally so they're not competing for nutrients.

Well-sited and properly supported, this climbing rose makes a pretty backdrop for garden accessories and other flowers.

Designing with Flowering Shrubs

Larger flowering shrubs are excellent in the back of large, tall beds.

Blooming shrubs produce maximum effect in your garden landscape for minimum work. (See page 114-115 for information on caring for shrubs.)

■ *How to Choose*

• **Select the right size.**
Flowering shrubs range in size from just a foot tall and a foot wide to 20 feet tall and 10 feet wide. Read labels and plant shrubs in the appropriate spot.

• **Check growing requirements.**
Flowering shrubs can be drought-tolerant, moisture-loving, or somewhere in between. Their other needs can vary from deep shade to full sun and poor soil to rich. If you're planting a shrub with other plants, including other shrubs, be sure that they

have similar growing and watering requirements.

• **When do they bloom?**
Nearly all shrubs bloom for just a few weeks. Read labels to determine the blooming time frame and plant other bloomers accordingly so you'll have flowers all season long. Some shrubs are evergreen in some climates but deciduous in others. Some azaleas, for instance, lose their leaves while others don't.

• **What insect problems and diseases are they prone to?**
Lilacs, for example, are notorious for their vulnerability to powdery mildew. Seek out disease-resistant cultivars. Read the entries in the Flower Encyclopedia beginning on page 156 before you buy the shrubs you're considering.

■ *How to Use*

• **Hedges.** Flowering shrubs make good informal hedges. Or plant just a few tall shrubs for a privacy screen. Good choices include lilacs, shrub-type rose of Sharon, forsythia, honeysuckle, mockorange, spirea, viburnum, and smokebush.

• **Specimens.** Many gardeners set showier shrubs apart from other plantings, letting them shine on their own in a lawn. If you do this, mulch several feet out from the base of the shrub to promote better health and to prevent damage from mowers and weed trimmers.

• **Mixed borders and beds.**
Mixed borders and beds are where annuals, bulbs, perennials, and shrubs all work together. Shrubs add height and structure to a flower garden, as well as keeping maintenance to a minimum.

Hydrangeas (Hydrangea spp., page 231)

✿ DesignTip

The Easiest Flower Bed Ever

Instead of a bed of flowers, consider one of just flowering shrubs. It's low-maintenance and costs a fraction of an equally showy perennial planting. Choose smaller flowering shrubs that don't need pruning, such as hydrangea (page 231), daphne (page 229), small Fothergillas (page 230), tree peony (page 202), azalea (page 233), potentilla (page 233), smaller spireas (page 234), 'Miss Kim' lilac (page 235), and small viburnums (page 235).

Designing with Flowering Vines

Flowering vines are inexpensive; yet with just a few square feet of garden soil and a good support, they soar up and provide a striking vertical element to your garden. (See page 116-117 for care.)

■ *How to Choose*
Consider the following when selecting a vine:
- **Will it reseed?** Some annual vines, particularly heirloom or nonhybridized vines, reseed freely. This is particularly true of morning glories, which can become a bit of a pest.
- **How tall does it grow?** Some vines top 40 to 60 feet. Read the label!
- **What kind of support does it need?** A large-flowered clematis will politely climb an attractive, light-wood, 6-foot trellis purchased at a garden center. Big climbers like wisteria and bittersweet form woody vines more akin to small trunks and can engulf even small trees. They need sturdy, well-constructed supports, pergolas, or porches to climb.
- **What is its climbing habit?** A twining vine may be all right for a trellis attached to wood siding. But a climber that attaches with stickfasts can be hard to remove when it comes time for painting.

■ *How to Use*
- **Camouflage an ugly fence.** Plant annuals such as morning glories, black-eyed Susan vine, or scarlet runner bean at the base of the fence. Also try perennials such as sweet autumn clematis, silver fleece vine, or cup-and-saucer vine.
- **Camouflage an ugly building.** For masonry, choose a self-clinging vine, such as climbing hydrangea, trumpet vine, jasmine, morning glory, star jasmine, or akebia. Use galvanized nails and wire as a trellis so you can remove the vine for painting.
- **Frame a window.** Build a permanent lattice up the sides and over the top of a window.

Homer's Hindsight

Sadder But Wiser
It pays to know your vines before you put them in the ground. The little wisteria I planted a few years ago has turned into a monster that's threatening to lift the shingles off my house. Next time I'll read the label!

Plant a relatively tame 12-foot annual, such as black-eyed Susan vine, or a perennial such as a large-flowered clematis, on either side for a living shutter.
- **Interplant with tall, vertical plants.** Large-flowered clematis are beautiful next to roses or tree peonies. They climb the larger plant and bloom atop it.
- **Keep the irrigation system free.** Don't plant vines in areas where they may block sprinkler heads at maturity.

This climbing hydrangea (Hydrangea petiolaris) cloaks the entire side of this house. Vines like these can easily top 60 feet and should be planted only on masonry or brick.

Designing for Fragrance in the Garden

■ *Finding Fragrant Flowers*

Even within the same species of flowers, some plants are fragrant and some aren't. Some viburnums, for example, have no scent (or even an unpleasant scent), while others may overwhelm you with their delicious fragrance. And there can be a huge range of scent within a single family of flowers. A rose, for example, might have

Some petunias have no scent while others are deeply fragrant. The only way to tell for sure is to take a sniff.

no scent at all, a light scent, or a heavy scent, depending on the cultivar. And even those with heavy scent can have different fragrances, each redolent perhaps of lemon, tea, honey, or a host of other scents.

How do you find these fragrant flowers? There's no test like the nose test. Whenever you smell a particularly fragrant flower, take note not only of the type of plant but also of its cultivar—the most specific part of the plant name that's often in quotes. For example, the Oriental lily 'Stargazer' is exceptionally fragrant, as is the hybrid tea rose 'Mr. Lincoln'.

Fragrant Plants

Name	Zones	Page
Annuals/Perennials		
Bee balm*	4–8	200
Monarda didyma		
Carolina jasmine	7–9	238
Gelsemium sempervirens		
Catmint	4–9	201
Nepeta spp.		
Clematis*	4–9	238
Clematis spp.		
Creeping thyme	5–9	240
Thymus spp.		
Datura	3–11	168
Brugmansia		
Daylily ('Hyperion' cultivar)	3–10	189
Hemerocallis spp.		
Flowering tobacco*	2–11	201
Nicotiana spp.		
Geraniums, scented types	2–11	203
Pelargonium spp.		
German bearded iris*	3–10	191
Iris × germanica		
Godetia*	2–11	174
Clarkia amoena		
Heliotrope	2–11	188
Heliotropium arborescens		
Honeysuckle*	3–9	239
Lonicera spp.		
Hosta (plantaginea species)	3–9	190
Hosta plantaginea		
Jasmine	6–9	239
Jasminum		
Lavender	5–10	192
Lavandula spp.		
Lavender cotton	6–9	210
Santolina chamaecyparissus		
Peony*	2–8	202
Paeonia spp.		
Pinks*	2–11	178
Dianthus spp.		

Name	Zones	Page
Star jasmine	8–9	241
Trachelospermum spp.		
Stock	3–11	198
Matthiola incana		
Summer or garden phlox*	5–7	206
Phlox spp.		
Sweet alyssum	2–11	196
Lobularia maritima		
Sweet pea	2–11	192
Lathyrus odoratus		
Sweet woodruff	4–8	184
Galium odoratum		
Violets* (odorata species)	7–9	215
Viola spp.		
Shrubs		
Azalea*	3–9	233
Rhododendron spp.		
Daphne	4–9	229
Daphne spp.		
Flowering quince	4–9	228
Chaenomeles speciosa		
Gardenia	8–11	230
Gardenia augusta		
Korean spice viburnum	2–9	235
Viburnum carlesii		
Lilac	2–8	235
Syringa spp.		
Mockorange	4–8	233
Philadelphus spp.		
Oleander*	5–7	232
Nerium oleander		
Roses*	2–11	88–95
Rosa spp.		
Summersweet	4–9	228
Clethra alnifolia		
Witch hazel*	5–9	231
Hamamelis spp.		

Name	Zones	Page
Bulbs		
Daffodil*	3–11	223
Narcissus spp.		
Freesia	2–11	220
Freesia spp.		
Hyacinth	3–11	222
Hyacinthus orientalis		
Lily*	3–9	222
Lilium spp.		
Magic lily	5–8	223
Lycoris squamigera		

* While some types of this plant are very fragrant, not all are. If the plant is in bloom, sniff it to see. If it's not in bloom, check the label.

■ *Using Fragrant Plants*

• Position near a sitting area.
Plant fragrant vines up the railing of a deck or porch. Fill pots with fragrant plants near sitting areas or in planters.

• Make an impression. Plant fragrant flowers along an entrance to greet visitors or near your back door to greet you when you get home.

• Plant at nose level. Especially with flowers that don't have heavy, wafting scents, it's important to get them up close in pots near nose level. The same holds true for many vines, including sweet peas.

• Plant along a window. This can be as simple as hammering a few nails and placing string on either side or as complicated as building a wood trellis around the window.

This spot in the garden is loaded with fragrant plants, including white heliotrope (Heliotropium arborescens, page 188), and pink petunias (Petunia spp., page 205.)

CLOSER LOOK

How to Smell a Flower

Flowers release their scents in different ways. Scented geraniums don't have fragrant flowers but fragrant leaves that release scent when brushed. If they're in a warm room, you'll get a wafting fragrance.

Others, such as types of nicotiana, are fragrant or most pronounced in the evening. Still others are most fragrant on warm, sunny days when the heat hits their open flowers.

Some flowers, such as lilacs, hyacinth, and daphne, fill the garden with fragrance. Others, such as stock, heliotrope, and some daffodils, must be sniffed up close. Finally, the scent of any flower is easier to smell on a still day rather than a windy one.

Designing for Outdoor Living

Create spaces for outdoor living—pleasant spots to sit and read a book, share a meal with family and friends, or simply relax.

Plan your outdoor spaces carefully. Well-conceived living areas are the most successful and will be the most used because they flow smoothly and satisfy your needs.

■ *Areas for Sitting And Lounging*

Group a few chairs and low tables in a comfortable spot. Porches, patios, and decks are the obvious places to create a sitting area. However, it's also a nice idea to tuck a few chairs away in a far corner of the yard. They invite visitors (and you!) to view the landscape from a refreshingly different angle. They also heighten the sense of getting away from it all, even if it's only 40 feet.

Choose seating that is large and inviting and has arms. Small, hard straight chairs seldom encourage people to sit for any length of time.

A simple table equipped with chairs turns nearly any area into a haven for outdoor dining.

One very big, very large chair, chaise, or hammock is fine if you are the primary user. Two chairs are more companionable. For entertaining, place four or more seats together. It's also nice to include at least one low table for drinks and snacks.

■ *Dining Areas*

All you need is a table and some sturdy chairs, and you have an outdoor dining area. Set it up on a porch or patio or place it right on the lawn for a romantic English effect. Purchase new patio furniture or use a coat of paint to spruce up garage sale and flea market finds. Even a card table can be put into service if you throw a water-resistant vinyl tablecloth over it first. Picnic tables are always a dining classic.

Move dining furniture around to suit the seasons. It's nice to have it in a sunny spot for lunch on a balmy spring day, but better to move it under a tree in summer when temperatures mount. Be aware, however, of setting up too close to shrubs and flowers that attract bees or yellow jackets—angry pests hovering around the table are rarely welcome.

Outdoor kitchens have been gaining in popularity in recent years. Create an inexpensive version by erecting a small roof attached to a garage or side of the house. Set up a grill with an attached burner or two. Add a small dorm fridge (with a GFCI outlet to prevent shocks) along with a rollaway cabinet to hold paper or plastic plates and cups.

Here's an Idea:

Play Areas for Kids

All the garden is a play area for children. And the garden will hold even more interest for them if you have at least one open area of lawn for tossing balls and running.

Children love clearly delineated paths to walk along, and paths are helpful for the garden because they direct small feet to the right places.

It's also easy to create little hideaways for children. Make a tepee out of several bamboo poles; then plant with morning glories. Or plant fast-growing flowering shrubs, such as lilacs or forsythia, near the corner of a fence to create a leafy hiding spot for children.

Garden Accessories

Garden accessories add character and personality to a garden. Chosen carefully, they create mini focal points in parts of the garden, drawing attention to certain areas of the garden.

■ *Functional Versus Decorative*

Garden accessories tend to fall into one of two categories: functional or decorative. Functional accessories do double duty. They're pleasant to look at but also serve a purpose. They include benches, birdhouses, butterfly houses, birdbaths, accent lighting, and sundials. Functional accessories have the benefit of looking as though they really belong in the garden. Purely decorative accessories, such as plaques, statues, fountains, gazing balls, or figurines can beautify a garden, too, but need to be used with caution and restraint since too many can make a garden look busy.

■ *Garden Style*

It's also important that garden accessories fit in with your overall garden style. Rustic,

Cluster garden-inspired collections, such as these birdhouses, to achieve maximum impact and prevent a cluttered look.

Garden accessories look most at home when they're also functional.

country accents are perfect for a rustic, country garden, for example, but may not look right in a formal garden. And the accessories should all go together. They don't have to match, but they do need to harmonize with one another. If in doubt, set all your garden accessories together and see if they look good as a group.

■ *A Focal Point*

If you have a lot of accessories, you can prevent a chaotic look by having one clear, large focal point, such as a striking fountain or fence. All accessories should be secondary to the focal point.

One strong focal point directs the eye, preventing a look that's kitschy.

DesignTip

Keep It Simple

Don't overdo it! When choosing garden accessories, it's good to follow that old adage about jewelry and clothing accessories: When in doubt, leave it out.

Designing Entry and Front Gardens

Whether it's your front door or the side door you use to come home from work every day, you can create a cheerful, welcoming approach to your home with a few simple touches and a wealth of flowers.

■ *Clean Up Your Act*

Set the stage for great flowers with a little home improvement. Steady any wobbly railings, give the front door a fresh coat of paint, put out a pretty doormat, and invest in an attractive mailbox. These small touches add to the beauty of your home.

■ *Go for Color*

Since the front entry is viewed first from far off, it's a smart strategy to use brilliant color there. Brightly colored flowers are eye-catching and help announce "This is the entrance." Red is an especially warm and welcoming color at a front entry; one of the reasons you see so many front doors painted red. Blue flowers are lovely but can get lost visually when viewed from a distance. Use them as elements that are part of a closer look.

An interesting front walk, thoughtful plantings, several potted plants, and a chair make this an irresistible entry.

Always Beautiful

Brighten entries in winter by inserting boughs of cut evergreens into the soil of window boxes and pots. They add a fresh, welcoming touch for months in cold climates.

■ *Use Containers Liberally*

A big pot or planter filled with flowers on either side of the door is a classic. Line the steps with pots, too. Use pots of varying sizes for interest, but the pots must also work together as a group. Give them a unifying theme, such as the material (clay, concrete, wood) or the color.

■ *Have Fun with Accessories*

An entry is the ideal place for practical and pretty accessories. A bench not only beckons visitors to come closer, it's also a practical place to set down a box or a bag of groceries. Small sculptures, wreaths, swags, decorative knockers, and other touches all say that the people who live here care about their home and have put some thought into welcoming you to it.

■ *Light up Your Life*

Low-voltage outdoor lighting is perfect for illuminating walks and plantings in your front yard. It lets you and your guests enjoy your flowers after dark, creates a dramatic effect, and softly lights up steps and paths to prevent falls. Look for uplighting to tuck into shrubs to light the sides of your home and footlights to line a path.

The classic yard light is also a good idea. It requires more elaborate wiring (you'll probably want to hire a professional), but it can make a walk much safer and more secure. It's also a great support for a small flowering vine, such as a clematis.

■ *Break out of the Mold*

So many flower gardens are only in the back, while the front has only staid foundation shrubs, a tree or two, and lawn.

A front yard often gets the most sun and makes sense as the location for an herb garden, wildflower garden, or cutting garden. Get experimental and plant more flowers in front. A good place to start is to line the front walk with flower beds, each at least 3 feet wide. With permission from the city, you can even turn that strip between the sidewalk and street into a delightful flower garden.

These homeowners have equipped a front patio with table and chairs, the perfect evening spot to say hello to neighbors and watch the world go by.

This splendid Texas porch is set off by beautiful annuals. Although most of these plants are relatively thirsty, they've been grouped together to minimize watering.

Chapter 3
Preparation and Planting

W hat could be better on a beautiful day than getting out in the garden, turning over the soil, and planting flowers? Planting is a simple process, however achieving great results year after year takes preparation and good soil. Your garden will thrive far better with less work and expense in the long run if you take time to educate yourself about proper soil preparation and good planting techniques.

On the following pages, you'll learn how to improve your soil, dig a flower bed, choose flowers, and site them in the optimum spot. It's knowledge that will make a pleasant task even better.

Delphiniums (Delphinium elatum, page 178) are beautiful plants that do well as long as you make sure they have very rich, perfectly drained soil.

Building Great Soil

The best way to know your soil is to grow things in it. Plant a small grouping of annuals and see how they struggle or thrive. Check by hand throughout the year to see how the soil feels when it's wet, dry, hot, or cold. Following are some some things you can do to build great soil.

■ Analyze Soil Structure

Ideal soil is loose and crumbly, but still holds together when you squeeze it in your hand. This texture allows water, air, and nutrients to percolate easily down to the roots, creating healthy, vigorous plants. Dig a hole about 18 inches to 2 feet deep in several places in your yard and see what you find. If the soil is dark and crumbly and you haven't hit rock, quietly give thanks because your soil is probably in pretty good shape.

Most gardeners, however, aren't that blessed. They work in soil that's laden with clay, filled with rock, a shallow layer above a concrete-hard sheath of hardpan, or sandy and loose.

Grab a handful when the soil is moderately moist. Squeeze it into a ball in your hand. If it crumbles, it's sandy soil. If it's a tight ball and slick, it's clay. If it forms a loose ball that's easy to break apart, it's loam—the ideal.

■ Test the Drainage

Further analyze your soil by testing the drainage. Fill an 18-inch-deep hole with water. If it drains within a half hour, you have well-drained soil, which supports a wide variety of garden plants. If it takes more than an hour to drain, your soil does not drain well. You'll either need to install drainage tiles—a tedious process—or build raised beds, a more practical alternative (see page 68). If the hole won't fill at all, your soil is quick-draining and you need to work in compost, sphagnum peat moss, and other soil amendments to improve its ability to retain moisture (see the opposite page).

■ Analyze Soil pH

It's also a good idea to know the pH of your soil; that is, how acid or alkaline (sour or sweet) it is. Invest a little money in a pH meter and test it. A high (alkaline) reading (above 7.5) or low (acidic) reading (below 6.0) will limit what you can grow successfully. You're looking for a neutral pH, which is a balance

TOOL TIP

pH Meter

A pH meter, which starts at around $15, can tell you instantly what your soil pH is. Since it's so fast, you can test several areas of your garden in just minutes.

between acid and alkaline. You can alter the pH with soil amendments (see chart opposite) to create that balance.

Acidic soil, common in the East and Pacific Northwest, is below 6.0. "Sweet" or alkaline soil, common in the dry West, Southwest, and some of the Midwest, is higher than 7.5. *(Continued on page 64)*

Soil Types

Sandy soil is very crumbly and won't hold its shape unless wet.

Loam, the ideal, will hold together somewhat but crumbles easily.

When slightly damp, clay soil will form a tight clump.

Soil Amendments

A soil amendment is anything you work into the soil to improve its fertility and texture. Some soil amendments also alter the pH. Check the following and decide which amendments you need:

Blood meal: Made of dried animal blood. A rich organic source of nitrogen. Slightly improves soil texture. Sprinkle lightly on the soil surface or follow package directions, and rake in.

Bonemeal: Source of phosphorous. Made of finely ground, steamed animal bones. Popular as a fertilizer for bulbs, but Bulb Booster or another bulb fertilizer is much more effective. Slightly improves soil texture. Work into planting holes, or sprinkle on the soil surface and rake in.

Compost: Nearly the perfect soil amendment. Improves soil fertility, breaks up clay, improves sand's ability to hold water, improves the texture of all soils, and encourages beneficial earthworms and microbes. It's nearly impossible to add too much. Add to planting holes, work compost into planting areas, mulch with 1–2 inches, or spread several inches on top of new beds and borders.

Garden sulfur: Lowers the pH of the soil, making neutral and alkaline soils better for acid-loving plants. Add according to package directions only if you're certain of your soil's pH.

Gypsum: Breaks up some clay soils, but its effectiveness is limited. Sprinkle on the soil surface and then dig in to a depth of several inches. Follow package directions exactly.

Lime: Made of ground limestone. Raises the pH of the soil. Should be applied only on acid soils to accommodate plants that need more alkaline conditions. Folk wisdom prescribes liming your soil each spring, but this creates pH problems unless your soil is very acid. Processed lime takes effect in a few weeks; dolomite takes a few months.

Manure: Usually sold as composted manure, not to be confused with regular compost. Fresh manure applied to the soil can burn plants. Allow fresh manure to compost or age for one year before applying. Composted (also referred to as aged or well-rotted) manure has a much higher concentration of nutrients. Too much can adversely affect plants. Improves soil texture as well as fertility. Usually has a slight odor that disappears in a week or two. Work into the top inch or two of the soil.

Sphagnum peat moss: Harvested from bogs and then dried. Acts like a sponge to help soils retain water. Also helps soil texture and slightly lowers pH. Good for sandy and clay soils alike, though it can worsen soil texture in some clay soils. Experiment in a small area first. It's also a problem if used too extensively because it's difficult to rewet once it dries out. Avoid products labeled simply "peat" because they are poor-quality products and environmentalists are concerned about peat harvesting.

Perlite: Made of tiny, heat-popped volcanic rock. Keeps soil loose and improves its ability to hold water. Good for both clay and sandy soils. Too expensive to use for projects much larger than containers. Work into the soil before adding to the container or into the top several inches of the soil.

Sand and gravel: Often worked in to break up clay soils. Sharp or builders sand or sharp gravel is best. Play box sand is too fine to be effective. Beach sand has too much salt and can damage many plants. In some clay soils, especially those with a greenish cast, the addition of sand can create something akin to concrete. Experiment with a small area first before using on a large scale. Work to a depth of 18 inches to 2 feet.

Soil conditioner: A loose term used for any material that improves the texture and/or fertility of the soil. Sometimes it's nothing more than compost, but materials can include anything from bark dust to crushed coral. Includes planter's mix, which is a blend of soil amendments. As with any product, read the package carefully. Work into the top 18 inches to 2 feet.

Preparation and Planting

Beach Bummer

One fine Saturday I went to the beach and loaded up the truck with sand to work into my garden's clay soil. Then I knocked myself out working it into my soil. The result? A lot of damaged and dead plants. Turns out, the sand was full of salt, and I burned half of what I'd planted.

■ Improving Your Soil

All of your soil may need minor additions of soil amendments—especially compost. **Compost** adds fertility, encourages microbial action, and creates texture. Other soil amendments—**sphagnum peat moss**, **perlite**,

sand, **leaf mold**—all contribute to balanced soil.

Sometimes, however, the soil is so hopeless that more dramatic action is needed in the form of **raised beds** or **berms**. Raised beds can be anywhere from just an inch or two high to a foot or more. They're built on top of the poor-quality soil and then filled with a mixture of compost, soil amendments, and high-quality topsoil.

Berms are a close relative of raised beds. Just pile compost and topsoil on top of your existing soil to form a mound a few inches to a few feet above the existing soil.

■ Maintaining Your Soil

The most important way to maintain your soil is to continually add soil amendments. Some gardeners make it a rule that every time they plant, they add compost to the planting hole or the area they're planting. Others mulch their flower beds with an inch or two of compost each spring. Still

others periodically renovate their flower beds, digging out all the perennials, working in abundant compost or other soil amendments, and then putting the perennials back in.

Gardeners also maintain their soil by working it only when it's moist. If the soil is too wet, as it so often is in spring, or if it's dry, as it is in late summer, digging in it will make it clump, creating lumpy soil that may take years to break up properly.

Mulches other than compost also help maintain soil. Grass clippings, pine needles, chopped leaves, bark mulches, and other organic mulches that break down slowly feed the soil over the years, adding to its fertility and texture.

Sphagnum peat moss is an excellent soil amendment for nearly all soil types except acidic soil.

Soil Troubleshooting

Problem	Symptoms	Solution
Heavy clay	Difficult to work either wet or dry; water puddles rather than soaks in; soil usually has a red or orange cast; plants fail to thrive.	When soil is lightly moist (never when very wet or dry), spread with 4–6 inches of compost, sand, gravel, and/or sphagnum peat moss and work in to a depth of 18 inches. However, since sand and sphagnum peat moss can create soil texture problems in some clays, experiment on a small area first and wait at least four weeks before proceeding with the rest of the area. A power tiller is useful in some clay soils because it saves work and more thoroughly works in the soil amendments. Each year, continue to add compost in planting holes, and mulch the entire bed with 1–2 inches of compost each spring. A raised bed or berm is often the best solution (page 68).
Sandy	Very loose whether wet or dry; water drains quickly; difficult to keep plants well-watered.	Spread 2 to 3 inches of compost and/or sphagnum peat moss over the top of the soil and work it in to a depth of 18 inches to 2 feet. Continue to add compost to planting holes and mulch with 1–2 inches of compost each spring.
Poor, light, dry	Most plants don't thrive, while a handful, such as lavender and thyme, do well; soil is light in color.	Spread 2 to 3 inches of compost over the top of the soil and work in to a depth of 1 foot. Continue to work in compost in planting holes, and mulch with 1–2 inches of compost each spring.
Boggy, wet	Usually damp even during dry spells, usually in a low-lying area; may give off a marshy smell; flowers planted there often have yellowing foliage.	Consider draining soil by installing drainage tile in a bed of gravel. Otherwise, build raised beds (page 68) and/or plant moisture-loving flowers.
Hardpan	Soil is workable on top. However, a few inches or a foot or so down, there's a hard, rocklike layer.	Experiment with the depth of the hardpan by removing topsoil from a small area and trying to chip away at it with a small pickax. If the hardpan breaks easily, proceed. If not, build a raised bed or berm (page 68).
Rocky soil	Difficult to dig; spade hits many rocks, large or small.	If rocks are reasonably small and sparse, old-fashioned digging and removal are called for. If the rocks are more numerous, consider constructing a rock garden or raised bed (page 68).
Soil filled with tree roots	Difficult to dig; spade hits tree roots.	As much as possible, plant between roots. Cut out small (less than 1 inch in diameter) roots with a small ax 1–2 yards out from the base of the tree. Extensive cutting of roots can damage trees, so proceed with caution. Raised beds (page 68) should be no higher than 2 inches; more can harm the tree's roots.

Preparation and Planting

Digging a Flower Bed

There are a number of ways to dig a flower bed. The *"lazy bed" method,* below, involves minimal labor but can take weeks to months. *Double-digging* is labor intensive, but you can't beat it for thoroughly loosening and enriching the soil. It's most feasible in small areas. *Combining tilling and digging* falls between the two. A power tiller, which can go down no more than a foot, works the top layer of soil and saves labor. Then hand digging allows you to go down the 18–24 inches ideal for most flower gardens.

No matter what method you use, if possible, dig the flower bed on a day when the soil is lightly moist. If the soil is dry, turn on the sprinkler and soak it. Then let the water trickle down for several hours. If the soil is wet, put off digging until it doesn't clump and ruin the texture.

Mark the area to be dug with spray paint, flour, a garden hose, or lime.

In most cases, you can leave the existing sod in place. It will break down and enrich the soil. Just pluck out or rake away any tufts or clods that may be on the surface when you're done. However, if you have Bermuda grass or another invasive grass, you should kill it first with a non-selective herbicide or remove it altogether.

Your digging tool is a matter of preference. Some gardeners swear by a round-point shovel or a flat-edged spade, both of which slice through the soil and lift it up as well. Others like a spading fork, using it to loosen and sift through the soil without much lifting.

When you're done digging, smooth the soil with a broad hoe. Then follow with a ground rake to break up clumps and make a finer soil.

STUFF YOU'LL NEED

✔ Spade or spading fork
✔ Soil amendments (page 63)
✔ Wheelbarrow
✔ Newspapers (tarp optional)
✔ Power tiller
✔ Garden gloves
✔ Sturdy shoes or boots

What to Expect

Digging is arduous work and tough on the back. For large beds, plan on digging just a small section at a time over a period of a few days.

Digging a Bed: The Lazy-Bed Method

1 **Smother grass or weeds** by covering with several layers of newspaper. Top with soil amendments (page 63), preferably a few inches of compost or high-quality topsoil. Allow to break down at least two months or preferably over a season, such as winter.

2 **Dig it under.** When the newspaper has broken down, turn the whole thing under to a depth of 12–18 inches. It's fine if there are still a few chunks. Leave them in to further break down. Rake the surface smooth, removing larger bits of paper or sod as needed.

Digging a Bed: The Double-Digging Method

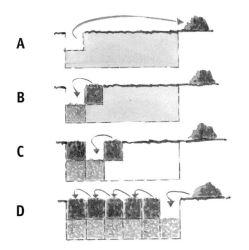

A

B

C

D

1 **Start by digging a trench** 8–12 inches deep across the length of the bed. Set aside this better-quality topsoil in a wheelbarrow or on a tarp.

2 **Work soil amendments** (page 63) into the lesser-quality subsoil to a total depth of 16–24 inches. Then, in a sort of soil shell game, remove another "row" of topsoil alongside the first. Toss it atop the newly improved subsoil. Repeat until the bed is complete, filling the last trench with the reserved topsoil from the first row.

Digging a Bed: The Tilling/Digging Method

1 **Spread soil amendments** (page 63) on top of the soil and till in as deeply as possible, usually 8–12 inches. Be sure to wear sturdy shoes or boots to protect your feet.

2 **Use a spading fork or a spade** to loosen the soil further to a total depth of 16–24 inches. This creates soil that's well loosened, allowing flower roots to reach down deep.

Building Raised Beds

Raised beds are the great cure-all for any type of soil problem. You can even build them right on top of concrete!

They create a perfect garden environment of good soil and excellent drainage.

■ Designing Raised Beds

How high you make your raised beds and what you make them of depends on several things:

• **How bad is the soil?** If your soil is fairly workable, you can get away with raised beds just 3 to 8 inches high. However, if the soil is completely unworkable—the kind of soil that can hardly be dented by a spade—make the raised beds 1 to 3 feet high.

• **What will you grow in your raised beds?** Annual flowers, herbs, and vegetables need about 1 foot of good soil to grow in, while perennial flowers, fruits, herbs, and vegetables need about 18 inches. Shrubs have deep roots but can tolerate less-perfect soil, so give them about 18 inches of good topsoil.

You'll have to guesstimate how much good topsoil you'll have in your raised beds. If the underlying soil is adequate and you build a 6-inch raised bed on top, you can estimate that you have about a foot of good-quality soil, enough to grow annuals. If the underlying soil is terrible, you'll need to make beds raised at least 18 inches if you want to grow perennials.

• **What materials should you use to build the raised beds?** As much as possible, use local materials, which are less expensive. Possibilities include fieldstone collected from local ditches and fields (get owner permission first and never collect from public land) as well as river rock, small boulders, plain concrete blocks, concrete and retaining wall blocks, landscape timbers, wooden boards, and scrap lumber. As long as lumber is rot-resistant and won't seep harmful chemicals (the way creosote-treated railroad ties might), you can use it in a raised bed. Any wood you use should either be naturally rot-resistant (cedar, redwood, and others) or have been pressure treated to prevent decay.

■ Preparing the Soil for Raised Beds

If the soil is at all workable, it should be loosened and improved (see page 66). Ideally, it should be turned over and compost or other soil amendments worked in to a depth of a foot or more.

■ Filling the Raised Beds

If you're lucky, you may have the ideal source for filling the raised beds on your property—an

Raised beds can be made from most materials, including local stone.

overflowing compost heap or good-quality topsoil elsewhere on your property.

If not, you'll need to purchase topsoil and compost to fill the beds. Purchase the best quality you can, making sure you see any topsoil before you buy it so you don't end up with poor quality "fill dirt" (see "Tip-Top Topsoil" on page 64). For all but the smallest projects, it's more economical to purchase topsoil and compost in bulk and have it dumped on your driveway.

You can work in other soil amendments, such as sphagnum peat moss, but good topsoil and compost are the most economical with the best results.

■ Building a Berm

A variation on the raised bed, a berm has most of the same advantages—excellent soil and drainage. A berm is simply a large mound anywhere from 1 to 4 feet high (the taller the berm, the wider you must make it so the soil doesn't wash away).

Most berms are oval or kidney-shaped so they look more natural.

To build a berm, work the soil underneath as best you can, preferably to a depth of 6 inches or more. Then pile on compost, topsoil, and soil amendments (page 63) as desired and shape with a shovel and hoe. Allow to settle a week or so before planting. Mulch immediately after planting to minimize erosion.

Dirt-Cheap Dirt

Save having to buy and haul topsoil by salvaging some from your own yard. Dig out good-quality topsoil from behind large shrubs, from a little-used side of the house or garage, or from any other out-of-the way place. Then use the resulting pit as a place to dump leaves, grass clippings, branches, and other yard waste.

This is actually a form of in-ground composting. Depending on the size of the pit, it's likely to fill up in a year or two. Keep it filled; then dig the rich compost and use elsewhere in your yard.

Building a Wood Raised Bed

STUFF YOU'LL NEED

✔ Rot-resistant lumber, such as cedar or pressure-treated pine (Don't use pressure- or creosote-treated wood if you'll be growing edible plants.)
✔ Saw
✔ Galvanized screws or nails
✔ Screwdriver or hammer
✔ Spade
✔ Topsoil and soil amendments
✔ Rake

What to Expect
With this construction method, the height of the bed is limited by the width of the board.

1 **Screw or nail together pieces of rot-resistant lumber.** Use galvanized nails or screws. Nails are easier and faster, but screws are stronger and longer lasting.

2 **Dig a trench** an inch or two deep where you want the raised bed to rest. Position the frame on the trench and make it level by adding soil or digging out a little more. (Continued on page 70)

3 **Work the soil.** Loosen to a depth of 6 inches to 1 foot if possible, working in soil amendments as needed (see page 63). There's no need to remove turf (except for Bermuda grass) or most weeds; they'll break down and feed the soil.

4 **Fill with high-quality topsoil and rake smooth.** The topsoil can be purchased or moved from elsewhere on the site.

Design Tip

Scale is Everything

Make the size of your flower beds fit the size of your yard. It's a common mistake to make flower beds too small, and as a result, they get lost in the landscape. In a medium-size yard, a flower bed at least 6 feet wide and 14 or more feet long would not be out of place.

Digging Tips

- Keep your shovel sharp.
- Lift with your legs, not with your back.
- Invest in good work gloves. They'll save many blisters.
- Sturdy work boots will make digging easier.

Cut stone stacked a few rows high also makes a good raised bed and is easy enough for a beginner to execute.

Gardening for Everyone

◼ Universal Design Tips to Make Gardening Easier For Everyone

The concept of universal design—which takes into account a family's needs as they get older or if family members are physically challenged—isn't just for kitchens and bathrooms; it can apply to gardens as well.

Whether you're getting older, are physically challenged, or just don't like all the bending and lifting involved, you can minimize effort, maximize productivity, and make gardening a pleasure.

Consider the following:

• **Build raised beds** (see page 68). These are a terrific starting point for minimizing bending and lifting. They raise the garden, making it more easily accessible. Although most of these raised beds are shown at a height of a foot or two, raised beds can easily be made countertop height.

• **Add an edge to lower raised beds**, those just 18 to 24 inches high. They will be more user-friendly if you create an edge appropriate for sitting. Make the rim of stone or masonry raised beds wide enough to sit on comfortably. Wood raised beds can be outfitted with a seat on top that's 8 to 12 inches wide.

• **Try long-handled tools.** Many of your shorter favorites, such as hand cultivators and trowels, which usually have handles just a few inches long, also come in versions with handles up to 18 inches long. They make working the soil from a wheelchair or a walker much easier because you don't have to bend as much.

• **Try ergonomically designed tools.** Larger, cushioned handles make gripping easier and more comfortable for older gardeners or those with joint problems.

• **Create easy access.** Depending on your needs, a grass path to key beds and borders may be fine. Wheelchairs or walkers will require a firmer, more even path wide enough for the chair to make a 360-degree turn, made of material such as brick, concrete, or smooth flagstone set into concrete. Add ramps with railings, as needed, to decks and stair areas. They'll be a nice addition to existing decks, patios, and porches.

• **Have a seat!** If it's difficult to be on your feet for long periods of time, check out the new garden carts equipped with seats and wheels. There are also padded tops sold for 5-gallon buckets. Team them with cloth tool organizers that attach to the buckets. Or try a small, lightweight plastic step stool that will let you settle in for a good weeding or planting session in comfort. Set up a bench or two in the garden to create accessible spots for frequent breaks. (Strategically placed, these benches can also provide a support for less steady gardeners to keep their balance.)

• **Make watering easier.** Look for narrower, lighter-weight hoses that don't require as much strength to maneuver. Also check out the many devices that extend and raise a hydrant so you don't have to bend to turn water off and on.

• **Get a lift.** Look for the kneeling pads that have built-in supports on other sides so you can use your arms to help you get up and down. Some pads adjust for both sitting and kneeling.

• **Create shade.** Full sun can tire older or physically challenged gardeners more easily than light shade. Plant small-leaved trees, such as locusts or desert willow, that create cool havens underneath their branches for people, yet let through enough sun for most plants.

Raised beds help physically-challenged gardeners enjoy the pleasures of working in their garden.

The Right Plant in the Right Place

Situate a flower where it's well suited to the sun, soil, and moistures, and it will thrive, rewarding you with plenty of blooms and color. Learning a plant's needs takes a little time and patience, but it's well worth the effort.

■ *Watch the Sun*

What may seem at first like full sun might actually be part shade. Full sun is direct, unfiltered light for at least six hours a day. Watch the patterns of light and shadow in your garden at different times of the day as well as at different times of the year. (See page 74 for more information.)

■ *Read Up on Other Needs*

Before planting (or preferably even before buying) any plant, read about it and its soil, water, light, and drainage needs as

If a plant isn't thriving, try moving it to another spot better suited to its light, soil, or moisture requirements.

well as recommendations for regions of the country where it will thrive.

■ *Experiment with Containers and Annuals*

The best way to find out more about your garden's growing conditions is to just get growing. Grow plants in containers and move them around your garden to see where they do best. Move them to a brighter or shadier spot as needed.

Annuals are a good, inexpensive way to find out

more about soils and conditions. Their performance will give you clues on how hot and dry or dark and damp a spot is, as well as an idea of what pests and diseases you need to be aware of before investing in more permanent and expensive perennials.

■ *Move Plants Around*

Within reason and with care, you can move most perennials and small shrubs if they aren't thriving. Do so only after at least one year. The best time is in

Read the Label

I couldn't figure out why my rosebush wasn't doing very well. It kept getting diseases and wouldn't bloom much. Then I checked the label. It said it needed full sun, and here I had it in a shady spot. If I'd just read the label carefully in the first place, I could have saved myself a lot of trouble.

spring or fall. Most important, make sure the plant is not in bloom when you move it.

Choose a cloudy, overcast day—never a hot, sunny, windy day. Dig up as much of the root ball as possible and keep the plant well-watered in its new home for the next two to four weeks.

■ *When To Say Goodbye*

Some plants won't do well in your garden no matter how much attention you lavish on them or how many times you move them around. These are the plants that just limp along, year after year, looking ratty and unhappy.

Tough as it is to do, dig them up and write them off as a learning experience.

Poor drainage is a leading cause of sick plants. This rock garden on a slope is designed to assure ideal drainage.

Annuals in containers, such as these shade-loving impatiens (Impatiens, page 190), are a good way to find out more about light levels in your garden so you can put permanent plants in the best possible spots.

CLOSER LOOK

Top 10 Signs a Plant Isn't Thriving

❿ Chronic yellowing or dropping leaves, especially on the bottom portion of the plant

❾ Failure to bloom or poor, sparse blooms

❽ Slow to restart growth in spring, especially roses

❼ Chronic disease or insect problems

❻ Pale, spindly new growth

❺ Overall leggy plant growth

❹ Wilting between waterings, even when soil seems somewhat moist

❸ Pale or white spots on shade-loving plants that may be a sign of sunscald

❷ Overall small size and lack of fullness

❶ And finally . . . it's dying.

Open areas require plants that can thrive in direct sun for most of the day. Morning rays are less intense than midday or afternoon sun.

LITTLELEAF PERIWINKLE

Vinca minor

SUN
FULL SUN to
PARTIAL SHADE
Zones 4-8

Sun and Shade

Understanding the sun and shade requirements of your plants is important. The symbols for sun and shade on plant tags tell you how much sunlight a plant needs to thrive. To find the right plants for your yard, learn to interpret the label. If you find a label with all three symbols, the plant can grow successfully in any light condition.

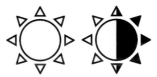

■ *Full sun*

A label with a circle or sun shape that isn't blackened indicates a plant that will tolerate a full day of hot, direct sun. The hottest climates are a possible exception; protection from the sun might be necessary during the hottest part of the day. The intensity and heat of the sun diminishes as you move into northern zones. Plants that have only the full-sun symbol on their label will not grow as well in partially shaded spots; flowers and foliage may be reduced.

■ *Part shade*

A circle half shaded and half open indicates that partial shade is the optimum condition. Morning sunlight followed by afternoon shade is best for these plants. The term partial shade also describes areas where the sun is filtered by overhead canopies, allowing some rays to penetrate during the day. Plant labels describe this condition as dappled or filtered shade. Both terms mean the same thing and are different types of partial shade.

■ *Full sun/part shade*

Though plant labels don't differentiate between morning and afternoon sun, you can still decide what a plant needs by looking for combinations of symbols. Tags with both full-sun and part-shade symbols indicate a plant can grow in conditions ranging from sunny all day to sunny for just part of the day. Choose plants with both of these symbols to grow in areas of your yard that are sunny all day or sunny in the afternoons. In hotter climates,

To learn about light in a given area, plant an impatiens, a red salvia, and a marigold. Impatiens thrives in part to full shade, the salvia in part shade to full sun, and the marigold in full sun only.

Homer's Hindsight

Six Hours

I knew roses needed a lot of sun, but I wasn't sure how much. After seasons of skimpy blooms and puny foliage, I cut my rose plants back, dug them up, and moved them to a brighter location. Now I know that unless a particular kind of rose is known for its shade tolerance, I need to find a spot in my yard that gets at least six hours of direct sun each day to grow.

intense midday and afternoon sun can be deadly to plants requiring some shade. If the plant label has a full-sun symbol, the plant should tolerate a half day of hot afternoon sun. Remember, the part-shade symbol tells you the plant can thrive with less than a full day of sun.

If you have dappled shade areas that receive some direct sunlight during a portion of the day, look for plants that include both the full-sun circle and the part-shade symbol on their labels.

Analyze Your Sunlight

Light levels in your landscape vary during the day and during the year. Areas in full sun early in the spring may turn to deep shade when your oak and maple trees leaf out. Chart the light levels over the entire growing season.

Stop, Look, and Listen

Plants can't talk, but they will tell you when something is wrong. Look for signs that plants aren't seeing the right kind of light. After allowing a few months for them to establish, the only solution is to move your plants to where the light better suits them.

Too much sun: Leaves wilt (even shortly after watering) and quickly become brown and crispy as though they've been fried.

Too much shade: Growth is tall, weak, and spindly; stems lean toward the light; foliage and flowers are sparse.

■ *Part shade/deep shade*
Plants that need some sunlight filtered through other plant canopies but that should stay deeply shaded most of the day have both the deep-shade symbol and the partial-shade symbol. These plants thrive in conditions that range from almost no direct sunlight to a half-day's sun. Morning sun is usually best for plants with these symbols, though the weaker rays of an afternoon winter sun will likely be OK.

■ *Deep shade*
If you need plants where there is little or no direct sunlight, look for plants with a solid dark circle on their tags. These plants thrive with low light levels—though nothing grows in the dark. In hotter climates, it's important that plants labeled for deep shade do not receive any midday or afternoon sun, especially during the hottest months of the year. Too much sun is fatal for deep-shade-loving plants.

Planting Basics

■ *Choosing the Right Time*

Different plants do best when planted at different times of the year. Some thrive in cool conditions, while others like it hot.

It's important to know your region's frost date (if any), found on page 13. It's from this date that most planting is calculated.

• **Cool-season annuals:** Include plants such as pansies, calendula, and snapdragons. These like to be planted in spring, several weeks before your region's last frost date. In warm-climate regions, plant cool-season annuals in the fall for winter color.

• **Warm-season annuals:** Include marigolds, celosia, petunias, and impatiens. These plants do not tolerate frost, so they can be planted anytime after your region's last frost date in spring.

• **Perennials and shrubs:** These flowers last through the winter, so they can tolerate some cold at planting time. Plant in spring, summer, or fall, as long as the weather won't be too cold (not getting below freezing for a few days), too sunny and hot, overcast, or the temperature is above 85°F (29°C).

• **Roses:** Plant bare-root roses up to a month before your region's last frost date in spring and container roses up to a week before. In Zones 6 and warmer, container roses can also be planted in the fall.

■ *Preparing the Soil Well*

Whether you're planting just one shrub or 50 annuals, it's important to prepare the soil. This is true even if you're planting in an existing flower bed. Prepare new flower beds correctly (see page 66). In existing flower beds, work a few spadefuls of a soil amendment, such as compost, into the area you'll be planting.

If planting annuals, also work a slow-release fertilizer into the ground. Annuals are hungry, fast-growing plants that thrive when given plenty of nutrients.

■ *Putting It in the Ground*

Before planting, make sure your plants are well-watered and not wilting. If they are indeed looking droopy, water them in their existing pots and wait a day for them to recover. If a plant is bare-root, soak it in cool water for several hours before planting.

To plant, remove the plant gently from its pot. If the roots are wrapped around in circles or they are thick and knotted, loosen them with your fingers.

Work Smarter!

When to Plant

There's a myth that you can plant only in the spring. Actually, you can plant almost any time during the summer as long as high temperatures aren't above 80 degrees. (Any warmer and plants will wilt and possibly die.) The best days to plant are those that are cool and cloudy, when strong sun won't stress the plant. If it's threatening to rain, new plants will benefit from the moisture.

In Zones 6 and warmer, fall is also a good time to plant. Cool temperatures and plentiful rainfall establish plants quickly and give you a jump start on spring.

Position the plant so the soil level is the same as it was in the pot. If the plant is bare-root, plant it at the depth specified on the package.

Tough as it may be to do, pinch or trim off any flowers. They're sucking energy that would be better put into establishing the plant's root system for bigger, better, and more flowers later on.

■ *Watering*

Water the plant very well. If it's a shrub or a rose, put a hose at the base just barely at a trickle and let it run for a half hour or more. For annuals and perennials, water so the soil is soaked a foot down.

Keep the plants well-watered for the first two weeks, checking them daily for soil moisture and signs of wilting. Once they're established, they'll need less water.

When planting, pinch off flowers to divert energy into the plant's roots. You'll lose one pretty bloom, but you'll be rewarded with a healthier and longer-blooming plant.

STUFF YOU'LL NEED

✔ Plants
✔ Soil amendments/compost
✔ Spade
✔ Mulch
✔ Hose/watering can
✔ Root-stimulating fertilizer

What to Expect

Plants often go into "transplant shock" for a day or two after planting. The larger the plant, the longer it lasts. Minimize this by planting on a cool, cloudy day and keeping plants well-watered.

1 **Dig the hole.** In most cases, make it a few inches wider and deeper than the plant's pot. If the soil is heavy clay, make the hole twice as deep as the pot to improve drainage.

2 **Amend the soil.** Even if you've improved the soil in past years, work in the equivalent of a spadeful or two of compost or other soil amendment. Then remove the plant from its pot.

3 **Loosen roots as needed.** If the roots are knotted or circling around the pot, loosen them with your fingers to stimulate them and encourage them to spread out in the soil.

4 **Set the plant in the ground.** The plant should be level with the surrounding soil. Then make a small moat around the plant with your hands or a spade to help water puddle around the plant.

5 **Mulch, then water thoroughly.** When possible, soak the ground and not the plant, but with small plants it's almost impossible not to douse the whole plant. Keep soil especially moist for the next several weeks.

Planting Bulbs

Be on the look out for bulbs at your garden center and buy early to assure the best selection. Choose full, firm bulbs that don't appear to be withered.

■ *When to Plant*
• **Plant spring-blooming bulbs in October or November,** usually for up to four weeks after your region's first average frost date (see page 13).
• **Plant summer-blooming bulbs in the spring,** anytime after your region's last average frost date (see page 13).
• **If in doubt, check with garden center staff.**

■ *How to Plant*
• **Plant bulbs as soon as possible after purchasing.** Some bulbs shrivel quickly. All other bulbs can be kept in a cool, dry place for a few weeks.
• **Provide excellent drainage.** Bulbs are prone to rot, so loosen the soil several inches deeper than the bulbs and work in a little compost.
• **Cluster bulbs in groups.** The smaller the bulbs, the larger the group. Group small bulbs, such as crocuses, in clumps of 30 or more. Group larger bulbs, such as daffodils and tulips, in clumps of 15 to 20 or more. If you plant singly or in straight rows, the result will look unnatural.
• **Use a fertilizer made specifically for bulbs.** While bonemeal is a popular fertilizer for bulbs, it doesn't contain all the necessary nutrients and it may attract rodents if used too close to the surface. Use compost or a commercial bulb fertilizer.
• **Plant at the right depth.** The depth listed in the planting instructions is from the bottom of the bulb and includes any mulch you're applying (just don't apply more than 3 inches). In Zones 5 and colder, plant bulbs about 1 inch deeper than specified.
• **Plant the right side up.** As a general rule, the pointed side goes up, with the exception of ranunculus and dahlias, where any pointed parts face down.

Preparation and Planting

BUYER'S GUIDE

Bulbs in Warm Climates

Most spring-blooming bulbs, such as tulips, crocuses, hyacinths, and daffodils, need the cold temperatures of winter to bloom. If you live in a warm climate (Zones 9 to 10 with the exception of the Northwest; see page 12), you'll need to make sure the bulbs have received a chilling period.

Purchase prechilled bulbs or chill regular bulbs in the vegetable drawer of your refrigerator for 12 to 16 weeks. Keep the bulbs separate from fruits, since the ethylene gas given off by ripening fruit can kill the bulbs.

Plant the bulbs outside in December or early January. They'll bloom just one year, but you'll love the show!

Planting Spring Bulbs

STUFF YOU'LL NEED

✔ Bulbs
✔ Compost/bulb fertilizer
✔ Spade
✔ Hose/watering can
✔ Plant labels
✔ Tape measure

What to Expect
Soil can be dry and hard in late fall. Water the area the day before you plant to soften the soil.

1 **Dig the hole.** It's best (and easiest) to cluster bulbs in large groups. Dig the hole to the recommended depth, working in compost and bulb fertilizer as necessary.

2 **Position the bulbs.** Put them at the depth recommended by the grower. In most cases, the pointed parts should face up. Then fill the hole and water well. Label the area so you won't dig up bulbs accidentally.

Starting Flowers from Seed

■ *Achieve Success with Seeds*

Stick to those flowers that are very easy to start from seed. Then follow package directions *exactly*. Don't start too early in the season, or seedlings will get leggy.

Nearly any container punched with drainage holes will do—an egg carton, clear plastic produce containers, or paper cups, for example.

■ *Choose the Right Soil*

Choose only a mix made specifically for seed (never regular potting mixes or soil from the garden). Otherwise, seeds can rot or become prone to diseases.

■ *Water Carefully*

Tiny seeds are easy to wash out. To prevent this, set the container in a tray filled with water halfway up the sides of the container. Water will slowly seep up from the bottom. Remove the seed container after a half hour or so.

■ *Keep Seeds at the Right Temperature*

Hold the seeds at the temperature suggested on the seed packet. "Warm" usually means 70 to 80 degrees while "cool" means 55 to 65 degrees. Set a room thermometer next to the seeds to make sure they're at the right temperature.

■ *Let There Be Light*

As soon as seeds start to sprout, remove the plastic bag (See Step 2, right.) and put them in a very bright south-facing window or directly under a grow light. Better yet, combine the two. Too little light is a leading cause of sickly seedlings.

Easiest Flowers to Start From Seed

Name	Zones	Page	Name	Zones	Page
Annuals/Perennials					
Annual sunflower *Helianthus annuus*	2–11	187	Pansy *Viola* spp.	2–11	215
Bachelor's button *Centaurea cyanus*	3–10	171	Purple coneflower *Echinacea purpurea*	3–9	180
Black-eyed Susan *Rudbeckia* spp.	3–10	209	Shasta daisy *Leucanthemum × superbum*	4–9	193
Celosia *Celosia* spp.	2–11	170	Snapdragon *Antirrhinum majus*	2–11	162
Cosmos *Cosmos* spp.	2–11	176	Sweet pea *Lathyrus odoratus*	2–11	192
Hollyhock *Alcea rosea*	3–11	160	Yarrow *Achillea* spp.	3–9	159
Marigold *Tagetes* spp.	2–11	212	Zinnia *Zinnia* spp.	2–11	215
Morning glory *Ipomoea*	2–11	239			

STUFF YOU'LL NEED

✔ Seed-starting mix
✔ Flat container with drainage
✔ Tray of water
✔ Seeds
✔ Room thermometer
✔ Plastic bag
✔ Grow light (optional)

What to Expect

If seeds take more than a few days to germinate, soil may dry out. Check daily and water just enough to keep soil moist.

Starting Seeds

1 **Fill an egg carton** or a flat, well-drained container with a mix made for starting seeds. Sprinkle with seeds. Cover with more mix as directed. Set the container in a tray of water to moisten.

2 **Slip the container into a plastic bag** to keep it warm and moist. Use a room thermometer nearby to make sure the temperature is correct. Remove the bag as soon as the seeds germinate.

3 **Provide light** as soon as the seeds germinate. Use either a very sunny south-facing window, a plant light just a few inches above the plants, or both. Raise the light as plants grow.

Well-grouped containers are gardens in themselves. This lavish arrangement uses containers both at ground and eye level for maximum impact.

Containers: Choosing and Positioning

◼ Types of Containers

There are nearly as many types of containers as there are plants to put in them. If it will hold soil, it can hold plants.

Innovative gardeners plant in everything from gigantic grand urns to old sneakers. Other unusual ideas include watering cans, metal buckets, bushel baskets, wicker baskets (line them with moss first), wheelbarrows, horse troughs, old ceramic bowls and pitchers, cereal bowls, and teacups.

The material of the container also comes into play. Clay pots are beautiful but are also very porous and tend to dry out. Plastic, resin, and fiberglass

TOOL T P

Masonry Bits

A simple masonry bit can turn ceramic, clay, or pottery containers without holes into pots with good drainage. Simply drill a hole or two with the bit. (Wear safety glasses.) Some containers may crack even with a masonry bit, so drill a test hole in a pot that's already cracked or damaged.

pots are inexpensive, hold moisture well, and are lightweight. But they aren't always as beautiful as some other containers. Wood containers, including whiskey barrels and window boxes, hold moisture well but are prone to rotting. Metal containers have few drawbacks, other than weight and price.

◼ Container Size And Shape

The size of the container also plays a role. Large containers can be heavy and expensive but hold moisture well and make a real impact. Smaller containers are less expensive but dry out quickly. Also, left on a front step, they can be snatched by unethical admirers.

The shape of the container also dictates what plants will go into it and how it will be used. Low, shallow containers do best with low, trailing plants. Taller, larger containers cry out for tall plants that capitalize on the container's generous size.

◼ Positions for Containers

There are seemingly endless ways to position containers around your yard, but here are ideas to get you started:

• **Making a garden of their own.** Group three or more containers that have like characteristics (such as all clay or all wood) together. Or fill different containers with plants that fit together into a theme, such as all herbs or all red blooms.

• **Flanking a door or a path.** Position two larger containers on either side of a front or back door—or even a garage door. Or set them so that they're on either side of an entry or a path.

• **Lining steps.** Set pots alongside a railing or running up a set of outdoor steps.

• **Hanging or mounted.** Baskets of plants look great hanging from a porch or flanking a doorway. Try them mounted along a tall, bare fence to break up the expanse. Mount securely; they'll be heavy when wet.

• **Creating a focal point in a border.** If you have a flower bed that lacks interest, position a large (18 inches or wider) pot in it and plant with colorful annuals or a striking shrub.

Containers: Plant Selection

■ *Choosing Plants for Containers*

Nearly any plant can be grown in a container, but some definitely perform better than others.

Annuals are favorites because they bloom quickly and for months at a time. However, long-blooming perennials also make a good choice for containers, as do small shrubs and even trees.

Many gardeners think they have to mix plants in

A leaky birdbath gets new life as a clever container.

containers, but some of the most striking plantings are of just one type.

What makes a good container flower? It should have the following:
• Foliage that is attractive for months at a time
• Blooms that last a long time, at least several weeks
• Roots that don't mind being crowded
• Form that makes it fit in well with a container, such as a pretty trailing habit or useful upright habit that's good for backs or centers of plantings.

■ *Combining Plants in Pots*

If you choose to combine plants in pots, you won't go wrong if you follow this formula: Plant at least three different plants— one tall and spiky, one low and trailing, and one medium-height as a filler.

Follow a color scheme with your pots, just as you would when decorating a room in your home or when planting an entire bed of flowers.

It's also important to combine plants with like growing needs. Plant a full-sun plant with other full-sun plants. Plant something that likes it on the wet side with other plants that need moisture. And plant drought-tolerant plants with other drought-tolerant plants.

Good Plants for Containers

Name	Zones	Page
Tall and Spiky		
Annual salvia	2–7	209
Salvia farinacea		
Bells-of-Ireland	2–11	200
Moluccella laevis		
Canna	2–11	218
Canna hybrids		
Celosia	2–11	170
Celosia spp.		
Delphinum	2–7	178
Delphinium elatum		
Flowering tobacco	2–11	201
Nicotiana spp.		
Snapdragon	2–11	162
Antirrhinum majus		
Spider flower	2–11	174
Cleome hassleriana		
Midheight Filler Plants		
Ageratum	2–11	160
Ageratum houstonianum		
Dusty miller	2–11	171
Centaurea cineraria (Senecio cineraria)		
Flowering cabbage, kale	2–11	168
Brassica oleracea		

Name	Zones	Page
Geranium, upright forms	2–11	203
Pelargonium spp.		
Globe amaranth	2–11	186
Gomphrena globosa		
Heliotrope	2–11	188
Heliotropium arborescens		
Impatiens	2–11	190
Impatiens spp.		
Marigold	2–11	212
Tagetes spp.		
Pansy	2–11	215
Viola spp.		
Tuberous begonia	2–11	218
Begonia tuberhybrida		
Verbena, upright forms	2–11	214
Verbena spp.		
Vinca	2–11	170
Catharanthus roseus		
Wax begonia	2–11	166
Begonia × semperflorens-cultorum		
Wishbone flower	4–11	213
Torenia fournieri		
Zinnia	2–11	215
Zinnia spp.		

Name	Zones	Page
Low and Trailing		
Dahlberg daisy	2–11	213
Thymophylla tenuiloba		
Edging lobelia	2–11	195
Lobelia erinus		
Fan flower	2–11	211
Scaevola aemula		
Fuchsia	2–11	183
Fuchsia spp.		
Geranium, ivy type	2–11	203
Pelargonium spp.		
Lantana	2–11	192
Lantana camara		
Nasturtium	2–11	214
Tropaeolum majus		
Petunia	2–11	205
Petunia spp.		
Swan River daisy	2–11	167
Brachycome iberidifolia		
Sweet pea	2–11	192
Lathyrus odoratus		
Verbena, trailing forms	2–11	214
Verbena		

A lush combination of tall, trailing, and filler plants makes for a gorgeously planted container.

CLOSER LOOK

Spring Bulbs in Pots

Spring bulbs, such as daffodils and tulips, make a gorgeous show in pots, planters, window boxes, and other containers.

In temperate regions with moderately cold winters (most of Zone 7 and including the Pacific Northwest and parts of the South), plant bulbs directly in large pots in fall.

In warm climates (warmer parts of Zones 8–11) plant prechilled bulbs (or chill your own; see page 78) in late autumn or early winter.

In very cold climates (Zones 4–5) bulbs will freeze solid over the winter. If you want bulbs in these climates, plant preforced bulbs into containers in early spring.

Containers: Planting and Care

■ Planting Containers

Planting a container is easy if you follow a few simple tips:

• Start with high-quality potting soil—purchased or made on your own.

• If the container is very large, put in an inverted plastic pot to minimize weight and soil.

• If you want a heavier pot, add a few bricks or rocks in the bottom.

■ Caring for Containers

Keeping containers watered is essential. Check the pots daily, and in hot, windy weather you may need to water twice a day. Completely soak the pot every time you water.

Container plants also need plenty of nutrients because you're continually flushing them out with each watering. Work in compost at planting time or add a slow- or timed-release fertilizer, or feed the plants every one to two weeks with a liquid fertilizer.

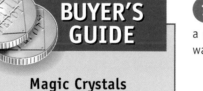

BUYER'S GUIDE

Magic Crystals

You can cut watering of containers almost in half by using polymer crystals. When dry, they look like rock salt. But when wet, they swell up several times their size into soft, spongy particles that hold water in the soil. Some potting mixes have them already added.

Follow package directions exactly, because adding too many can cause root rot or force plants from the soil.

Here's an Idea!

Perfect Potting Soil

Choose your potting soil carefully. Never use soil straight out of the yard—it's not suitable for pots. Instead, use purchased potting soil. Commercial potting soils vary greatly, so read the label carefully. Some are billed as soilless and are a combination of soil amendments (see page 63). Others have fertilizers and polymer crystals (see below) worked in. Don't select potting soils by weight only; some have a lot of heavy sand, and some lightweight potting mixes are excellent.

How to Plant a Container

STUFF YOU'LL NEED

✔ Pot
✔ Newspaper or clay shard
✔ Smaller plastic pot or plastic soda bottle with lid (optional)
✔ Top-quality potting soil
✔ Assorted plants
✔ Slow-release fertilizer (optional)
✔ Water-conserving polymer crystals (optional)

What to Expect

Containers dry out quickly. Be prepared to water them daily if needed.

1 **Cover the hole** at the bottom of the pot with newspaper or a clay shard to prevent soil from washing directly out.

2 **If the pot is large,** save soil and lighten the load by inverting a plastic pot or a large plastic soda bottle with a lid at the bottom.

3 **Knock plants from the pot and loosen roots.** Position in the pot and fill with soil (add fertilizer or polymer crystals); being sure to leave 1 inch of room at the top for water to pool.

Changing Plantings with the Season

Spring: Plant with cool-season annuals such as pansies and violas (page 215), stock (page 198), spring-blooming bulbs (page 49), lobelia (page 195), and snapdragons (page 162).

Summer: Replace in early summer with heat-loving annuals such as marigolds (page 212), impatiens (page 190), petunias (page 205), vinca (page 170), and ageratum (page 160).

Autumn: Replace with cold-loving flowering cabbages or kale (page 168), mums (page 173), or yet more pansies (page 215). Pumpkins or gourds make a nice accent.

Setting Up Drip Irrigation in Containers

STUFF YOU'LL NEED

✔ A kit for a drip-emitter system or:
✔ ½-inch tubing for supply line
✔ ¼-inch tubing, plus connectors
✔ Drip-emitter heads
✔ Drip-emitter ring for large containers (optional)
✔ Hose-end clamp
✔ Clamps to attach tubing to wood
✔ Timer (optional)

What to Expect
Even the best-made irrigation systems can spring leaks or experience clogs. Check regularly.

1 **Run the ½-inch supply line** among the containers as needed. Attach lengths of ¼-inch tubing to the larger tubing, using connectors, to lead to individual containers. Attach drip-emitter heads where desired, using a ring emitter on larger plants.

2 **Close the end of the supply line** with the end clamp. Clamp the supply line to the walls or railings. Attach to timer, if desired, and start.

The Right Rose For You

Chosen well, roses are actually low-maintenance plants. The key is planting the right roses for your climate and lifestyle. Below is a listing of roses to get you started. Availability in garden centers will vary; ask garden center staff for other roses that have similar characteristics.

When shopping, look for good-quality roses. Grade 1 is the best and most expensive but will take off fastest in a new home, followed by grades $1\frac{1}{2}$ and 2.

Patented roses are usually fairly new on the market. The patent means that the rights to reproduce the rose are protected for the breeder.

Roses are available either already growing in containers (see page 96) or dormant as bare-root (see page 97).

Bare-root is the preferred way to start roses in early spring before your region's last frost date, while container roses are the way to plant after all danger of frost is past or in the fall in warm-winter regions.

Roses this healthy are no accident. They've wisely been chosen with consideration to their site conditions.

■ Very Cold-Hardy Roses

Whether your roses make it through the winter depends on several variables, including how much protection from buildings and trees your roses get, how well drained the site is, how much snow falls (more snow protects roses), and how harsh a particular winter is. These roses tolerate cold better than others:

Name	Page
'Ballerina' (hybrid musk)	90
'Blanc Double de Coubert' (rugosa)	91
'Carefree Beauty' (other shrub)	91
'Carefree Wonder' (other shrub)	91
'Country Dancer' (other shrub)	91
'F.J. Grootendorst' (rugosa)	91
'Frau Dagmar Hastrup' (rugosa)	91
'Hansa' (rugosa)	91
'Iceberg' (floribunda)	90
'Linda Campbell' (rugosa)	91
'Max Graf' (rugosa)	91
'Morden Blush' (Canadian)	88
'Morden Ruby' (Canadian)	88
'Sally Holmes' (other shrub)	91
'Therese Bugnet' (rugosa)	91
'William Baffin' (climbing)	93

■ Roses for Light Shade

Roses always do best with six or more hours of direct, unfiltered sunlight. However, there are some that may do well with just four or more hours of sunlight.

Name	Page
'Angel Darling' (miniature)	94
'Ballerina' (hybrid musk)	90
'Belinda' (hybrid musk)	90
'Bobbie James' (rambler)	93

Name	Page
'Buff Beauty' (hybrid musk)	90
'Cardinal de Richelieu' (gallica)	90
'Carefree Wonder' (other shrub)	91
'Cecile Brunner' (polyantha)	91
'Dainty Bess' (hybrid tea)	92
'Flower Carpet' (other shrub)	91
'Frau Dagmar Hastrup' (rugosa)	91
'Gruss an Aachen' (floribunda)	90
'Irish Fireflame' (hybrid tea)	92
'Lady Banks' rose (rambler)	93
'Lady X' (hybrid tea)	92
'Limelight' (hybrid tea)	92
'Madame Alfred Carriere' (climbing)	93
'Playgirl' (floribunda)	90
'Red Cascade' (miniature)	94
Rosa wichuraiana (climbing)	93
'Sally Holmes' (other shrub)	91
'Simplicity' (floribunda)	90
'Sir Thomas Lipton' (rugosa)	91
'Souvenir de la Malmaison' (bourbon)	88
'Tear Drop' (miniature)	94
'The Fairy' (polyantha)	91
'Zephirine Drouhin' (bourbon)	88

'Hansa'

'Therese Bugnet'

■ Drought-Tolerant Roses

No rose will do well with minute amounts of water, but many do fine with moderate water. Many of the old roses and the Rosa wichuraiana ramblers do especially well with moderate water.

Name	Page
'Alberic Barbier' (climbing)	93
'Dorothy Perkins' (rambler)	93
'Fortune's Double Yellow' (china)	89
'Gloire des Rosomanes' (china)	89
'Harrison's Yellow' (other shrub)	91
'John Hopper' (hybrid perpetual)	90
'La Reine Victoria' (bourbon)	88
'Lady Banks' rose (rambler)	93
'Madame Alfred Carriere' (climbing)	93
'Marie Pavie' (polyantha)	91
'Marie Van Houtte' (tea)	89
'New Dawn' (climbing)	93
'Paul Ricault' (centifolia)	89
'Penelope' (hybrid musk)	90
'Silver Moon' (climbing)	93

'Sun Flare'

■ Roses Resistant to Mildew and Other Fungal Diseases

Some roses do better in damp or humid conditions that foster fungal disease. Most of the rugosas, the David Austins, and the Meidilands are resistant to fungal diseases. So are many roses that have shiny, glossy foliage. Some specific cultivars to go for include:

Name	Page
'Ballerina' (hybrid musk)	90
'Belinda' (hybrid musk)	90
'Blanc Double de Coubert' (rugosa)	91

When planted in a mass, any type of miniature rose can be used as a groundcover for a small area.

Name	Page
'Bonica' (other shrub)	91
'Buff Beauty' (hybrid musk)	90
'Class Act' (floribunda)	90
'Dainty Bess' (hybrid tea)	92
'Escapade' (floribunda)	90
'French Lace' (floribunda)	90
'Iceberg' (floribunda)	90
'Intrigue' (floribunda)	90
'Linda Campbell' (rugosa)	91
'Olympiad' (hybrid tea)`	92
'Playboy' (floribunda)	90
'Playgirl' (floribunda)	90
'Roseraie de l'Hay' (rugosa)	91
'Sarah van Fleet' (rugosa)	91
'Sexy Rexy' (floribunda)	90
'Simplicity' (floribunda)	90
'Sun Flare' (floribunda)	90
'Sun Sprite' (floribunda)	90
'Topaz Jewel' (rugosa)	91

■ Roses Tolerant of Salt Spray and Other Coastal Conditions

Rugosa and species roses, two types of roses close to the wild, as well as a handful of other tough roses, are what do best on the coast. Many of the Canadian Explorer series also do well. Specifically, check out:

Name	Page
'Agnes' (rugosa)	91
'Betty Prior' (floribunda)	90
'Blanc Double de Coubert' (rugosa)	91
'Frau Dagmar Hastrup' (rugosa)	91
'Fruhlingsgold' (other shrub)	91
'Hansa' (rugosa)	91
'Linda Campbell' (rugosa)	91

Name	Page
'Robusta' (rugosa)	91
Rose wichuraiana (climbing)	93
'Roseraie de l'Hay' (rugosa)	91
'Therese Bugnet' (rugosa)	91
'Topaz Jewel' (rugosa)	91

■ Groundcover Roses

Whether you're looking for a solution for a slope or just want a low, sprawling rose, one of these roses is sure to please.

Name	Page
'Alba Meidiland' (other shrub)	91
'Bonica' (other shrub)	91
'Carefree Beauty' (other shrub)	91
'Max Graf' (rugosa)	91
'Paulii' (rugosa)	91
'Red Cascade' (miniature)	94
Rosa wichuraiana (climbing)	93
'Scarlet Meidiland' (other shrub)	91
'White Meidiland' (other shrub)	91

'Bonica'

Shrub Roses

The term "shrub rose" encompasses many different roses. It can include the old garden "antique" roses, those bred a hundred years or more ago. It can also mean the same thing as a "landscape" or "low-maintenance rose." It is also an umbrella term for a number of more specific types of roses, such as David Austin or Buck roses or Meidiland roses.

As you can see from these pages, different types of shrub roses have slightly different needs. But as a group, all are fairly easy to grow and will thrive in your garden for years.

Availability of the roses listed here will vary by region and source. If you can't find a particular rose, ask the retailer about other roses in that category with similar characteristics.

Alba Roses

Among the oldest in cultivation, alba roses have been grown for nearly 1,000 years—

'Queen of Denmark'

definitely one of the old roses. They are noted for their rich fragrance and showy rose hips in fall. They grow 4–6 feet and bloom in early summer.

Good used in the back of beds, along borders, or as informal hedges. Also can be trained as climbers.

Requirements: Full sun to light shade. Rich to poor soil; moderate moisture. As a rule, does well in Zones 3–9.

Special instructions: Little pruning needed, but remove old canes on mature shrubs every year immediately after flowering for best blooms. Easy to grow and fairly disease-resistant.

Varieties:
'Amelia'
'Celestial'
'Felicite Parmentier'
'Queen of Denmark'
'Semi Plena'

Bourbon Rose

'Zephirine Drouhin'

Classified as old roses, Bourbon roses continue blooming throughout the summer. Victorian favorites, they are usually very fragrant and usually grow 2–6 feet in a habit that can be either bushy and upright or spreading.

Good in the back of the border, as specimens by themselves, or as hedges. Those with long, trailing stems flower best trained on trellises or other supports.

Requirements: Full sun. Rich, well-drained soil. Plentiful moisture. Generally Zones 6–9.

Special instructions: Prune mature shrubs when dormant in late winter or very early spring, shortening main branches by one-third and smaller branches by two-thirds. They bloom on old wood grown the previous year, so don't get too carried away with spring pruning. But do cut out old wood at ground level every few years. Far more prone to black spot than other roses.

Varieties:
'Boule de Neige'
'Celestial'
'Konigin Von Danemark'
'La Reine Victoria'
'Louise Odier'
'Madame Ernst Calvat'
'Madame Isaac Pereire'
'Souvenir de la Malmaison'
'Souvenir de St. Anne's'
'Variegata di Bologna'
'Zephirine Drouhin'

Canadian Roses

'Morden Blush'

Bred to withstand cold and tough conditions, Canadian roses bloom prolifically through the summer and early autumn. They are sometimes sold as Morden or Canadian Explorer roses. Good choices for cold regions in Canada and the United States, this group is primarily shrub roses but includes some climbers. The shrubs grow from 3–8 feet.

Requirements: Full sun. Rich, well-drained soil. Plentiful moisture. Mulch. Hardy in Zone 2 in protected sites; otherwise generally Zones 3–8.

Special instructions: Purchase only Canadian roses grown on their own roots so they will resprout from the roots if the tops die. No winter protection needed. Very resistant to black spot and mildew.

Varieties:
'Cuthbert Grant'
'Henry Hudson'
'J.P. Connell'
'Morden Armorette'
'Morden Blush'
'Morden Ruby'

Centifolia Roses

Another old rose, it is sometimes also called a cabbage rose for its lush, whorled petals. Blooming once in early summer, centifolias are very fragrant and grow 4–6 feet. They're good in the middle and backs of beds and borders. Taller types can be trained up fences and trellises.

'Fantin-Latour'

Requirements: Full sun. Rich, well-drained soil. Ample moisture. Mulch. Generally hardy Zones 3–9; winter protection in Zones 3–4.

Special instructions: Flowers best on older wood. To prune, right after flowering cut out as much old wood as is practical.

Varieties:
'De Meaux'
'Fantin-Latour'
'Juno'
'Paul Ricault'
'Petite de Hollande'
'Tour de Malakoff'

Damask Rose

'Celsiana'

Noted for their famous fragrance, these old roses usually grow 4–6 feet high. Most bloom just in early summer.

Requirements: Full sun. Rich, well-drained soil. Plentiful moisture and mulch. Generally hardy Zones 4–9; winter protection Zones 4–5.

Special instructions: Prune by thinning old canes every few years immediately after blooming. To rejuvenate, cut back hard—to just about a foot—every 5 years or so. Those over 4 or 5 feet bloom best if trained on a low fence, wall, or other support.

Varieties:
'Autumn Damask'
'Celsiana'
'Comte de Chambord'
'Hebe's Lip'
'Ispahan'
'La Ville de Bruxelles'
'Leda'
'Madame Hardy'
'Madame Zoetmans'
'Marie Louise'
'Omar Khayyam'
'Petite Lisette'
'Rose d'Hivers'
'York and Lancaster'

China and Tea Roses

'Sombreuil'

Introduced to Western gardeners from Asia in the late 18th and 19th centuries, these old roses flower through the summer and early autumn. They aren't very cold-hardy but do well in Texas, southern California, and the Deep South, where they may also bloom through most of the winter. Most grow 2–6 feet.

Requirements: Full sun. Rich, well-drained soil. Drought-tolerant. Generally China roses hardy Zones 6–10; tea roses Zones 7–10.

Special instructions: Prune mature shrubs by cutting back by one-third in late winter, very early spring, or another time when not blooming. Prune to shape and remove dead wood. Disease-resistant. Deadhead diligently to promote long bloom time.

Varieties:
'Burbank'
'Echo'
'Fabvier'
'Fellenburg'
'Fortune's Double Yellow'
'Gloire des Rosomanes'
'Louise Phillipe'
'Madame Laurette'
'Maitland White'
'Marie van Houtte'
'Monsieur Tillier'
'Old Blush'
'Papa Gontier'
'Sombreuil'

English or David Austin Roses

Introduced in the 1970s by British breeder David Austin, these roses (also known as English roses) combine the best of the new and old roses. From the old roses, they retain fragrance, charming flower form, attractive shrubby foliage, as well as some hardiness and disease resistance. From modern roses, they get a bloom time from early summer through frost and a wide color range. Most grow 3–6 feet with attractive, shrubby foliage.

'Graham Thomas'

Requirements: As a rule, protected areas in Zones 4; otherwise Zones 5–9.

Special instructions: Prune in late winter to early spring, removing weak, old, unproductive wood. Cut back by one-third to one-half. Deadhead regularly to promote long bloom.

Varieties:
'Abraham Darby'
'Belle Story'
'Bibi Maizoon'
'Constance Spry'
'Cottage Rose'
'English Garden'
'Fair Bianca'
'Fisherman's Friend'
'Gertrude Jekyll'
'Glamis Castle'
'Graham Thomas'
'Heritage'
'L.D. Braithwaite'
'Lilac Rose'
'Mary Rose'
'Othello'
'Pretty Jessica'
'Sharifa Asma'
'The Herbalist'
'The Pilgrim'
'The Prince'
'Winchester Cathedral'

Floribunda and Grandiflora Roses

Long stems and long-lasting flowers make both floribundas and grandifloras excellent for cutting. Floribundas grow just 2–3 feet and grandifloras grow 3–6 feet.

'Gold Medal'

Requirements: Full sun. Rich, well-drained soil. Plentiful moisture. Mulch. Hardy Zones 5–9, with winter protection in Zones 5–6.

Special instructions: Prune in late winter or early spring (see pages 108–109). Fertilize once or twice a month, but stop one month before your region's first frost date in fall. More disease-resistant than hybrid teas, but black spot, aphids, Japanese beetles, slugs, and other pests are still significant problems.

Floribunda varieties:
'Angel Face'
'Anthony Meilland'
'Apricot Nectar'
'Bahia'
'Betty Prior'
'Centernaire de Lourdes'
'Class Act'

'Escapade'
'Europeana'
'Fashion'
'Fragrant Delight'
'French Lace'
'Gene Boerner'
'Gold Badge'
'Gruss an Aachen'
'Iceberg'
'Intrigue'
'Lavaglut'
'Love Potion'
'Pink Parfait'
'Playboy'
'Playgirl'
'Sexy Rexy'
'Simplicity'
'Singin' in the Rain'
'Sun Flare'
'Sunsprite'

Grandiflora varieties:
'Gold Medal'
'Queen Elizabeth'

Hybrid Musk Roses

These musk-scented roses have large clusters of flowers, each a minibouquet. They bloom heavily in late spring or early summer, with a few scattered flowers throughout the rest of the year. They grow 4–6 feet tall, with taller types making good short climbers. They tend to sprawl, which can be a useful characteristic on a slope or with a retaining wall.

'Ballerina'

Requirements: Full sun. Rich, well-drained soil. Plentiful moisture. Mulch. Deadhead diligently.

Special instructions: Fertilize once or twice a month, halting at least one month before your region's first frost date. Fairly disease-resistant. Most are hardy Zones 6–9, with some being hardy to Zone 5.

Varieties:
'Ballerina'
'Belinda'
'Bloomfield Dainty'
'Bubble Bath'
'Buff Beauty'
'Cornelia'
'Daybreak'
'Felicia'
'Kathleen'
'Nymphenburg'
'Penelope'
'Prosperity'

Gallica Roses

'Charles de Mills'

Grown by the Greeks and Romans, these fragrant roses blooms in early summer on old wood produced the previous year. They grow 3–5 feet tall. Good as a low hedge or in beds and on borders.

Requirements: Full sun. Tolerates poor, sandy, or gravelly soil. Rich soil is best. Generally hardy Zones 4–9.

Special instructions: To prune, thin out old wood on mature plants immediately after bloom time to encourage new growth for flowers the following year. No need to

trim spent blooms. Disease- and pest-resistant.

Varieties:
'Belle de Crecy'
'Cardinal de Richelieu'
'Charles de Mills'
'Empress Josephine'
'Gloire de France'
'Rosa Mundi' (the Apothecary's Rose)

Hybrid Perpetual Roses

In Victorian times these old roses were all the rage because, unlike other roses of that time, they bloomed not just in the early summer but a second time in the autumn. They're highly fragrant with classic old rose form. Plants grow fairly upright to 4–5 feet, making them good for hedges as well as beds and borders. If desired, you can train taller types along a fence or trellis.

'Baron Girod de l'Ain'

Requirements: Full sun. Rich, well-drained soil. Generally hardy Zones 4–9. Very prone to black spot.

Special instructions: Needs a hard spring pruning (see pages 108–109) but also a second pruning after their first flowering to encourage repeat bloom in fall.

Varieties:
'American Beauty'
'Baron Girod de l'Ain'
'Duke of Edinburgh'
'Ferdinand Pichard'
'Frau Karl Druschki'
'General Jacqueminot'
'Henry Nevard'
'John Hopper'
'Marchioness of Londonderry'
'Marchioness of Lorne'
'Reine des Violettes'

Moss Roses

'Crested Moss'

Named for the interesting mossy spines on the flower buds and stem tips, these old roses have a rich fragrance. Most bloom once in early summer. Plants grow upright to 6 feet tall.

Requirements: Full sun. Rich, well-drained soil. Ample water and mulch. Generally does well in Zones 4–9.

Special instructions: Flowers best on older wood. To prune, right after flowering cut out as much old wood as is practical.

Varieties:
'Comtesse de Murinais'
'Crested Moss'
'Henri Martin'
'Hunslet Moss'
'Marechal daVoust'
'Perpetual White Moss'
'Rene d'Anjou'
'Salet'
'Soupert et Notting'
'Striped Moss'
'White Bath'
'Wichmoss'
'William Lobb'
'Zenobia'

Rugosa Roses

The toughest of all roses, these natives of the Northeast coast truly thrive on neglect, doing poorly if pruned, sprayed, or fertilized much. They're also extremely cold-hardy, and most will produce a few flowers throughout the summer after a big flush in

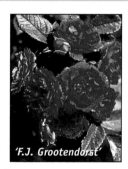
'F.J. Grootendorst'

early summer. Their flowers have a somewhat wild look and aren't very good for cutting, but many types are very fragrant.

Growing 3–6 feet tall and wide, they're excellent for low-maintenance and naturalistic gardens and as informal hedges.

Requirements: Full sun. Tolerates poor, dry soil. Generally hardy in Zones 2–9 but does best in Zones 2–7.

Special instructions: Do not spray. Appreciates a spring fertilizing with compost or a slow-release fertilizer. No need to deadhead; faded flowers will form lovely hips. Disease-resistant. Hard pruning is discouraged; looks best with natural shape. Cut out any suckers and a few large canes each fall.

Varieties:
'Agnes'
'Blanc Double de Coubert'
'F.J. Grootendorst'
'Frau Dagmar Hastrup'
'Hansa'
'John Hopper'
'Linda Campbell'
'Max Graf'
'Paulii'
'Robusta'
'Roseraie de l'Hay'
'Sarah van Fleet'
'Sir Thomas Lipton'
'Therese Bugnet'
'Topaz Jewel'

Polyantha Roses

Low and spreading, but still lush and full, polyantha roses work beautifully in the front of beds and borders. Growing about 2 feet tall and 2–3 feet wide, these old roses have sweet, tiny clusters of small roses that come in waves. Their leaves are small, and the plants are fairly disease- and pest-resistant. They're excellent for cutting.

'Cecile Brunner'

Requirements: Full sun. Rich, well-drained soil. Ample water and mulch. Significant winter protection in Zone 4, otherwise generally Zones 5–9.

Special instructions: Prune in early spring (see page 108). Cut back branches by about one-third. Fertilize once every 2–4 weeks to assure repeat bloom; halt fertilizing about one month before your region's first frost date.

Varieties:
'Cecile Brunner' (the Sweetheart Rose)
'China Doll'
'Happy'
'Kathleen'
'Margo Koster'
'Marie Pavie'
'Nathalie Nypels'
'The Fairy'

Other Shrub Roses

'Country Dancer'

There are a number of other shrub roses that are easy-care and well worth growing. They include the cold-hardy and disease-resistant Griffith Buck roses, Harkness roses, "pavement" roses, Romantica roses, and Meidiland landscape roses.

Requirements: Full sun. Rich, well-drained soil. Ample moisture and mulch, though many will tolerate dry soil.

Special instructions: An annual spring application of compost or 9-month, slow-release fertilizer is usually enough. Disease- and pest-resistant. Generally hardy Zones 4–9.

Varieties:
'Bonica'
'Carefree Beauty'
'Carefree Wonder'
'Colette'

'Country Dancer'
'Country Fair'
'Country Lady'
'Country Life'
'Country Music'
'Earth Song'
'Flower Carpet'
'Frontier Twirl'
'Fruhlingsgold'
'Harrison's Yellow'
'Hawkeye Belle'
Meidiland, all colors
'Michelangelo'
'Royal Bonica'
'Sally Holmes'
'Sevillana'
'Toulouse Lautrec'

Hybrid Tea Roses

Hybrid tea roses such as this one are renowned for glossy green leaves and classically shaped flowers ideal for cutting.

Hybrid Tea Roses

Introduced by a French breeder in 1867, hybrid teas were a real breakthrough. Not only were the flowers a lovely high-centered shape—what we now think of as the classic rose shape—but they also bloomed an astonishingly long time, all season long. Even today, the flowers are unsurpassed for cutting, blooming atop long stems.

Hybrid teas became the darling of rose breeders, and today hundreds of cultivars are available in every color but true blue. Some are highly fragrant, others lightly so, and some have no scent at all. Flowers bloom atop plants 2½ to 5 feet tall.

Availability of the roses listed here will vary by region and source. If you can't find a particular rose, ask the retailer about other roses with similar characteristics.

Requirements: Full sun. Rich, well-drained soil. Plentiful water. Mulch. Most hybrid teas are significantly less cold-hardy than other roses, needing wrapping of the stems with burlap and mounding in Zones 5-6; otherwise just mounding will suffice in Zones 7-9 (see page 113). Northern gardeners should expect to regularly replace hybrid teas. Even in warmer climates, most last no more than several years.

Special instructions: Most cultivars are prone to aphids, black spot, Japanese beetles, powdery mildew, rust and other rose diseases. They can be grown organically, but every 2-4 weeks follow a regular program of prevention and fertilizing. (See page 110 for tips on disease and pest control.) Prune in late winter or early spring. (See page 108 for instructions.) Deadhead diligently to promote longer flowering.

Varieties:
'Billy Graham'
'Brandy'
'Brigadoon'
'Caroline de Monaco'
'Chicago Peace'
'Chrysler Imperial'
'Dainty Bess'
'Desert Peace'
'Diana'
'Double Delight'
'Elizabeth Taylor'
'First Prize'
'Fragrant Cloud'
'Fragrant Lace'
'Fragrant Rhapsody'
'French Perfume'
'Garden Party'
'Granada'
'Grand Impression'
'Irish Fireflame'
'John F. Kennedy'
'Just Joey'
'King's Ransom'
'Lady X'
'Limelight'
'Marijke Koopman'
'Medallion'
'Melody Parfumee'
'Midas Touch'
'Mikado'
'Mister Lincoln'
'Olympiad'
'Paradise'
'Pascali'
'Peace'
'Perfect Moment'
'Perfectly Red'
'Perfume Beauty'
'Precious Platinum'
'Pristine'
'Rio Samba'
'Royal Highness'
'Sheer Bliss'
'Taboo'
'Tiffany'
'Touch of Class'
'Tropicana'

Preparation and Planting

Climbing and Rambling Roses

Nothing makes a statement as dramatic and romantic as an explosion of roses up an arbor, wall, or large trellis. Heights vary from a petite 6 feet to more than 20 feet; flowers range from 2 to 6 inches. Some bloom heavily in late spring or early summer with few, if any, flowers later, while others have a heavy flush of bloom followed by intermittent blooms and then a final flush of bloom in the early autumn. All climbers need full sun and moderate water, as well as a sturdy support that can accommodate their full height.

Availability of the roses listed here will vary by region and source. If you can't find a particular rose, ask the retailer about other roses with similar characteristics.

■ Climbing Roses

Also called large-flowered climbing roses, these are a bit better behaved than ramblers, seldom reaching more than 15 to 20 feet in height. Climbers have long, flexible stems (canes) that need to be tied or gently intertwined with their support. They usually bloom heavily just once in late

'Joseph's Coat'

spring or early summer and then intermittently in fall once temperatures drop.

They need regular feeding and are prone to all the usual rose pests and diseases. Keeping them looking good requires some attention. (See pages 108–109 for pruning tips; pages 110–111 for pest and disease information.)

Name	Zones	Height
'Alberic Barbier'	6–9	20 feet
'Aloha'	6–10	10 feet
'Altissimo'	6–9	10 feet
'America'	6–10	12 feet
'Belle Portugaise'	8–9	20 feet
'Blaze Improved'	5–10	14 feet
'Climbing Cecile Brunner'	6–9	12 feet
'Climbing Etoile de Hollande'	6–9	18 feet
'Climbing Iceberg'	6–9	15 feet
'Climbing Peace'	6–9	20 feet
'Don Juan'	6–9	10 feet
'Dortmund'	6–9	10 feet
'Dublin Bay'	6–11	10 feet
'Fourth of July'	6–11	14 feet
'Golden Showers'	6–9	8 feet
'Henry Kelsey'	4–8	7 feet
'John Cabot'	4–8	6 feet
'Joseph's Coat'	5–10	12 feet
'Madame Alfred Carriere'	7–9	18 feet
'New Dawn'	5–9	20 feet
'Pink Pillar'	6–9	10 feet
'Rhonda'	6–9	8 feet
Rosa wichuraiana	6–10	10-20 feet
'Silver Moon'	7–9	18-20 feet
'White Dawn'	6–9	12 feet
'William Baffin'	3–8	8 feet

■ Rambler Roses

If you have space and a very sturdy support, rambler roses will thrive, blanketing a large arbor, wall, fence—or even a whole tree—in bloom. They bloom for several breathtaking weeks in early to midsummer.

But they definitely need a large and strong support because few grow less than 20 feet and some can reach 50 feet. They can easily pull down any support that's not large enough to accommodate their sprawl and weight, including modest-

CLOSER LOOK

What Makes a Rose a Climber?

Some roses are definitely climbers, with stems 10 feet or longer. But the line is blurrier with shorter roses. Prune them high in spring and they'll hit 8 feet or more. Prune them low and they'll stay in shrub form.

Then there is the so-called pillar rose, a sort of cousin of the climbing rose. It has fairly long (6 foot or so), marginally flexible stems that do best when tied upright onto a pillar or rose tuteur (a pyramidal, freestanding trellis).

sized trees. Ramblers are usually tied to their supports, though their large thorns sometimes help them scramble up trees. They bloom on wood grown the previous year, so prune immediately after blooming. (See pages 108–109.)

They're fairly pest-resistant but are particularly prone to mildew if air circulation is poor or humidity is high.

Name	Zones	Height
'Bobbie James'	4–9	30 feet
'Dorothy Perkins'	6–9	10-12 feet
'Dr. W. Van Fleet'	5–9	20 feet
'Etain'	4–9	15 feet
'Felicite Perpetue'	6–9	20 feet
'Lady Banks' rose	8–9	20 feet
'Leontine Gervais'	5–9	20 feet
'Paul's Himalayan Musk Rambler'	4–9	30 feet

'New Dawn'

Preparation and Planting

Miniature Roses

Even though the flowers of miniature roses can be as small as a half-dollar, their subtlety of coloration is amazing, as 'Rosy Dawn' demonstrates.

Miniature Roses

Sweet little downsized versions of the larger roses, miniature roses grow just 6–18 inches tall with small flowers to match. They're wonderful massed in flower beds, dotted along paths, or tucked into containers or window boxes. They work well almost anywhere.

Availability of the roses listed here will vary by region and source. If you can't find a particular rose, ask the retailer about other roses with similar characteristics.

Requirements: Full sun to very light shade. Rich, well-drained but moist soil.

Special instructions: Mulch to conserve moisture and minimize disease. Fertilize every 2-4 weeks, halting 1 month before your region's first average frost date in fall. Trim spent blooms to promote long blooming.

In Zones 8–10 no winter protection is needed. In Zones 5-6 mound the base with a few inches of soil or compost and cover roses as shown on page 113. In late winter or early spring, prune by removing all but five to seven of the strongest stems, evenly spaced around the base. Then cut those back by half (see pages 108–109 for tips on where to make cuts).

Varieties:
'Angel Darling'
'Candy Mountain'
'Cupcake'
'Fire Princess'
'Gypsy Dancer'
'Happy Trails'
'Lady of the Dawn'
'Little Bo Peep'
'Orange Sunblaze'
'Popcorn'
'Red Cascade'
'Rise 'n' Shine'
'Rosy Dawn'
'Sun Sprinkles'
'Sweet Dream'
'Tear Drop'

Miniature roses like these brilliant yellow 'Sun Sprinkles' come in as many colors as their larger cousins.

Standard Roses

Standard roses thrive in pots and are easier to take indoors for the winter if needed.

Standard Roses

Like something out of a fairy tale, standard roses (sometimes called tree roses) seem too lovely to be real. But they're simply more traditional roses, pruned and grafted as a ball atop an elongated stem.

Tree roses vary in size with 2 feet and 3 feet being the most common. However, some places sell standards of 4 and even 5 feet.

Standard roses grow well around the garden but do especially well in pots. Availability of the roses listed here will vary by region and source. If you can't find a particular rose, ask the retailer about other roses with similar characteristics.

Requirements: Full sun. Rich, well-drained soil (potting soil if in a container). If not already staked, attach a stake the length of the trunk.

Special instructions: Mulch; never allow to dry out. Fertilize every 2-4 weeks, halting 4 weeks before your region's first average frost date in fall. Trim spent blooms to prolong bloom.

Where temperatures get below 28°F (-2°C) (Zones 8 and warmer), protect plants in pots by storing in a garage or basement. In Zone 7, try wrapping the tree rose with burlap outdoors. In Zones 6 and colder, if you can't bring the rose indoors, you'll need to do the "Minnesota tip" shown below.

In spring, when danger of frost has passed, tuck the tree back into place. Prune out old, dead, and weak canes and remove any suckers at the base. Then prune selectively to maintain ball shape.

Highly prone to the usual rose diseases and pests (see page 110).

Varieties:
(Standard versions of other roses)
'Bill Warriner'
'Candelabra'
'Double Delight'
'Fame!'
'French Lace'
'Honor'
'Intrigue'
'Melody Parfumee'
'Mister Lincoln'
'Opening Night'
'Pat Austin'
'Peace'
'Rio Samba'
'Sun Flare'
'Ultimate Pink'

Work Smarter!

The Minnesota Tip: Winter Protection for Standard Roses

In Zones 6 or colder, overwinter tree roses by slicing through the soil on one side of the roots and tipping the tree rose to the ground—a process called the Minnesota Tip. Secure with stakes and cover with soil and leaves. You may need to dig a second hole to accommodate the top.

Planting Roses

Roses are packaged as bare-root or in containers. Bare-root roses can be planted in early spring and tend to be less expensive. Container roses can be planted later in the season and usually cost a little more. Either way, be sure to take the time to get them started right.

■ Bare-Root Roses

Often sold in cardboard cartons or foil or plastic bags. (Be sure to remove from the container before planting!) Look for bare-root roses with firm, sound-looking stems and no shriveling. It's all right if a few leaves are starting to sprout. If the rose is sending out new stems and leaves longer than 3 or 4 inches, it has probably been sitting around too long and will have more problems getting established in your garden.

Choose a site for your roses in full sun—a spot receiving at least

BUYER'S GUIDE

Planting-Time Pruning

Most bare-root roses are sold "prepruned"; that is, they have no more than three to six stems, each just a foot or two long. Check the package to make sure. If still in doubt, use your good judgment on the general shape of the rose. Remove any damaged canes. Then evaluate it: It should have three to six stems cupping outward into an open vaselike shape, and the branches should each be about 8 to 12 inches long. If not, prune (see page 108).

6 full hours of direct light a day. The site also should have excellent drainage because roses don't like soggy roots.

Prepare the soil by digging a hole about a foot deeper and wider than the roots of the plant. Work in several spadefuls of compost to enrich the soil, improve drainage, and feed the roses.

If desired, also work in a slow-release granular fertilizer, following package directions. Some fertilizers are made specifically for roses and also contain a systemic pesticide.

After planting, mound the rose (see page 113) to prevent the graft union from drying out at its base. Water well and keep moist for the next few weeks, then gently hose or push away the mound.

■ Container Roses

In Zones 5 and colder, plant container roses in the spring only so they have enough time to get established before winter hits. In Zones 6 and warmer, you can plant roses in either the spring or the fall.

Choose sturdy-looking plants with healthy green leaves and no wilting, spotted, yellow or chewed leaves.

Planting a Container Rose

1 **Remove the rose from its pot.** You may need to step on the side of the pot once or twice to loosen the root ball. Dig a hole about 6–10 inches deeper than the rose's roots, working in abundant compost.

2 **Position the rose in the hole** so the soil is level with the surrounding soil. Mound soil slightly around the base so water will puddle around the rose. Give a good watering. Allow water to soak in; water two or three times more to make sure the water reaches all roots.

Preparation and Planting

STUFF YOU'LL NEED

✔ Bare-root rose
✔ Large bucket
✔ Bypass hand pruner
✔ Spade
✔ Compost
✔ Watering can or hose

What to Expect

New growth in the form of red shoots should start a week or two after planting.

Work Smarter!

How Deep?
Where to Plant the
Graft Union

The graft union (also called the bud union) is the knobby part of the plant where the top has been grafted onto the roots. In most climates, plant the bud union 1 to 2 inches above the soil level. In cold-winter regions Zones 5 and colder, plant it at soil level or up to 2 inches below the soil. If in doubt, follow the instructions that come with the rose.

1 **Prune the rose**, if it hasn't already been prepruned by the seller. Cut off any damaged branches and thin it (ideally) to three to six healthy branches at least as thick as a pencil.

2 **Soak the rose** in a bucket for about 12 hours. This helps hydrate the rose so it doesn't dry out once you've planted it in the ground. Then prepare a hole for the soil, working in several spadefuls of compost to improve drainage and feed the rose.

3 **Position the rose** in the hole so the bud union is the correct height. Spread out the roots. Cover the plant and mound the soil in a small moat around the rose so water will collect at its base.

4 **Water well,** allowing water to soak in; repeat two or three times. After watering, mound soil about 6 inches over the base of the plant to prevent it from drying out. Remove the excess soil after two or three weeks.

Chapter 4
Maintenance

O nce you've planted your garden, it's time for maintenance: weeding, watering, fertilizing, and deadheading. All are routine chores essential for a flourishing garden.

In this chapter, you'll find the best, the easiest, and the fastest ways to care for your growing flower garden. First there is a discussion of smart watering techniques, then details about the basics of mulching and fertilizing. There's also special-care information on roses, shrubs, and vines, as well as tips on weeding, staking, dealing with diseases, dividing perennials, storing summer bulbs, and much more.

The goal is to make the time you choose to spend in your flower garden as enjoyable as possible. After all, that's what flower gardening is all about.

Grape hyacinths (Muscari, page 223) are delightfully low-maintenance plants, needing almost no attention after planting.

Watering Basics

Watering plants according to their specific needs is essential to a successful garden. And if you learn to water right, you'll spend less time at it. As a bonus, your plants will grow better and cost less to maintain.

■ Don't Let 'Em Wilt

Many gardeners wait until their flowers are drooping to water them. This is a mistake. Wilting severely stresses flowers, causing dropped flowers and discolored leaves. Also, a wilted plant instantly becomes more susceptible to insect and disease problems.

Instead, look for early warning signs, such as leaves becoming less glossy or soil appearing hard and crusted. Do what experienced gardeners do. Keep an eye on the impatiens! They're usually the first flowers to wilt during dry conditions. If they're looking dry, turn on that hose.

■ Water Early in the Day

Start your sprinkler as early in the day as possible (4 in the morning is not too soon!). By watering early, you'll avoid the heat of the day and prevent evaporation. Early watering also allows plants to dry off well before nightfall, when fungal diseases take root.

In some parts of the country, watering early also prevents leaf burn. Leaf burn occurs when droplets of water fall on leaves in the heat of the day, acting like tiny magnifying glasses and burning the leaf or flower beneath them.

■ Water Deeply

Plants do best when you give them a deep soaking once in a while rather than a shallow watering often. Deep watering encourages plants to send their roots far into the soil. These deep roots help plants find moisture during dry spells, making them more resilient in difficult weather.

Most plants do best with approximately 1 inch of water a week. If you haven't had an inch of rain for a week, apply an inch of water from the hose.

If you're watering by hand, thoroughly soak the plants. If you're watering a shrub, for example, set the hose so that it just barely dribbles and let it drip there for an hour or more. If you're watering with a spray attachment or watering wand, let the water soak in and then come back in a half-hour or so and repeat the watering. It's much better to do a small area well than to just "mist" a large area.

■ Water the Ground, Not the Plant

Many leaves and flowers resent getting wet, making them more prone to disease. Some flowers, such as petunias, rebel by closing. Of course, sometimes you'll need to use a sprinkler, and getting the leaves and flowers wet will be unavoidable. But when using a hose or watering can, water just the

Here's an Idea:

Dryness Test

The easiest way to see how dry soil is? Feel it! Wiggle your finger or poke a stick 2 to 3 inches into the ground. If it's bone dry all the way down, it's time to water.

soil. Your flowers will be happier for it, and it saves water.

Better yet, consider investing in a drip-emitter system, micro-sprinklers, or black soaker hoses. Each slowly applies water exactly where you want it. And because water is not dispersed through the air, these systems are highly efficient, using minimal water.

Although fancy metal pipe systems are available through professionals, there are many easy do-it-yourself water systems available at your garden center.

Measuring Water

As a rule, your garden needs 1 inch of water a week. How can you tell how much water you've applied?

Set out an old cake pan or other shallow, flat container where the sprinkler will hit it. For best accuracy, position it midway between the sprinkler and the farthest point the water falls.

CLOSER LOOK

Super Soaker
When it is time to water your garden, you may not realize that you need to leave the sprinkler on for a long time.

Depending on the type of sprinkler you have and your water pressure, it can easily take 4 to 6 hours of steady watering to provide ample water to a modest-sized backyard.

TOOL T P

Using Technology to Help
Irrigation systems and watering aids have become much more sophisticated in recent years. Here are some of the most useful features:

Timer
A timer allows you to stop and, in some models, start watering whenever your want, even when you're gone. Fancier models allow you to set programs for several days.

Leaky or soaker hose
Often made from recycled tires, these flexible black hoses have thousands of tiny pores that seep water slowly. Wind them through or bury them in flower beds, hedges, or other plantings.

Drip emitters
Position these thin lines from a main hose at the base of trees, shrubs, containers, or other large plants where they'll slowly drip water. Water plants spaced far apart or hook them up to several containers.

Microsprinklers
Unlike their larger counterparts, microsprinklers can be positioned to deliver water in the precise areas needed. They also furnish water slowly to prevent runoff. Set up a series through a flower or shrub bed, or over groundcovers.

Bubblers
These are ideal for positioning at the bases of shrubs and roses. They create mini floods right where the plants can utilize the water most.

Conserving Water

No matter where you live, following basic water-smart gardening practices will save you money and time.

Sometimes referred to as "xeriscaping", water-conserving gardening doesn't mean your garden needs to look like a desert. Instead, it means making the most of your watering time and dollar. Here's how:

■ *Reduce Lawn Space*

This is an easy one for flower lovers. Flowers, with their deep roots, tend to need less water than turf grass. Create big beds of perennials, annuals, and flowering shrubs to replace grassy areas. Turn grassy slopes into rock gardens. Forget about grass in shady areas under trees and instead plant them as woodland gardens full of low, flowering groundcovers such as vinca minor, forget-me-not, or hostas.

■ *Prepare Soil Well*

Create the darkest, most moisture-retentive soil you can. Good, crumbly soil helps water trickle down deeper, helping plants develop deep, strong root systems that can get moisture to the subsoil more readily. (See page 62.)

■ *Mulch Well*

Mulch in summer suppresses weeds and keeps the soil cool and moist, minimizing your need to water. Flower beds do

Like so many drought-tolerant plants, this artemisia (Artemisia, page 164) sports beautiful silvery foliage.

Maintenance

Even annuals can be drought-tolerant. This planting of purple globe amaranth (Gomphrena globosa, page 186), annual blue salvia (Salvia farinacea, page 209), geraniums (Pelargonium, page 203) and marigolds (Tagetes spp., page 212) needs minimal water.

A Walk on the Dry Side

Another terrific way to conserve water is to choose drought-tolerant plants. Plants that don't use much water tend to have at least one of the following characteristics:

- Silver leaves
- Hairy or furry leaves
- Thick, waxy, succulent leaves
- Thorns
- Very small, fine-textured leaves

best with 1 to 3 inches (no more—you'll suffocate them!) of mulch (see pages 104–105 for more information).

■ Group Plants

Save yourself work by grouping together those plants that need more water. These include hydrangeas, impatiens, lungwort, azaleas, astilbe, and hibiscus. Put plants that need less water together as well.

■ Use the Shade

If you're in a particularly hot region, especially Zones 7 and warmer (see page 12), plants will appreciate more shade than they do in other parts of the country. They like afternoon shade. This is especially important for plants in pots, window boxes, and other containers.

■ Add a Zone

If you've got an underground irrigation system in place, consider adding a soaker zone for your flower beds. You can also install a drip irrigation system that is dedicated to the flowers.

Drought-Tolerant Plants

Note: Some flowers will perform as annuals or perennials depending on your zone and local growing conditions in your garden. For more information on the plants below, check the Flower Encyclopedia beginning on page 156 and consult with associates at your local garden center.

These are flowers that can do with little watering, depending on your region of the country.

Name	Zones	Page
Annuals/Perennials		
Annual sunflower *Helianthus annuus*	2–11	187
Baby's breath *Gypsophila paniculata*	3–9	186
Blanket flower *Gaillardia* spp.	2–11	184
Butterfly weed *Asclepias tuberosa*	4–10	164
California poppy *Eschscholzia californica*	2–11	181
Catmint *Nepeta* spp.	4–9	201
Clump verbena *Verbena canadensis*	6–10	214
Coreopsis *Coreopsis* spp.	3–9	176
Cosmos *Cosmos* spp.	2–11	176
Gayfeather *Liatris spicata*	3–9	193
German bearded iris *Iris × germanica*	3–10	191
Lamb's-ears *Stachys byzantina*	4–8	212
Lavender *Lavandula* spp.	5–10	192
Love-in-a-mist *Nigella damascena*	2–11	202

Name	Zones	Page
Marigold *Tagetes* spp.	2–11	212
Moss rose *Portulaca*	2–11	207
Pot marigold *Calendula*	2–11	169
Russian sage *Perovskia atriplicifolia*	5–7	204
Sedum *Sedum* spp.	3–11	211
Snow-in-summer *Cerastium tomentosum*	2–9	172
Spider flower *Cleome hassleriana*	2–11	174
Strawflower *Helichrysum bracteatum*	2–11	187
Swan River daisy *Brachycome iberidifolia*	2–11	167
Thrift *Armeria*	4–8	163
Verbena *Verbena* spp.	2–11	214
Yarrow *Achillea* spp.	3–9	159
Zinnia, creeping and narrow-leaved types *Zinnia* spp.	2–11	215

Maintenance

Mulch Basics

Mulch does so many things. It conserves moisture, prevents weeds, slows the spread of disease, adds organic material to the soil, protects plants from weather extremes, and encourages beneficial earthworms.

Mulch is used in two different ways. In warm weather it's laid around the base of plants in a thin layer to cool them. In cold weather it's mounded up around the base of plants to protect them.

■ *Warm-Weather Mulch*

Warm-weather mulch keeps the soil cool so that it holds moisture better. It suppresses weeds by shading them out before they can start. Warm-weather mulch serves as a barrier between the soil and the plant so soil-borne diseases don't splash on the plant during rain or watering. It absorbs water readily, preventing runoff and allowing the soil to better take in water. Organic mulches (those that break down) improve the soil's texture.

Apply warm-weather mulch at about the time all the tulips have stopped blooming. Spread it 1 to 3 inches thick—never thicker or you'll risk rotting or suffocating and invite diseases and pests, such as rodents. Keep the mulch about a half-inch away from the base of plants as much as is practical.

When mulching trees or shrubs set in the lawn, mulch out as far as the branches reach. This prevents competition for food and water from hungry grass and also protects the trunks from string trimmers and mowers.

Apply warm-weather mulch

in the spring for best results, but you can apply it almost any time of year.

■ *Winter Mulch*

In colder regions of the country, Zones 7 and colder, winter mulch is used to protect plants from winter's extremes. Even in warmer parts of the country, plants that aren't particularly cold hardy to that region should be protected with a winter mulch.

Mulch in winter prevents frost heave as well as the eruption of the soil as it freezes and thaws in late winter, which damages many perennials.

Plants well adapted to a region (with the exception of roses in most parts of the country, see page 86) need little or no winter mulch. If you do plant to winterize your roses see page 113.

Apply winter mulch in fall after your region has had 48 hours of below-freezing temperatures. Remove and discard winter mulch in the early spring, just as perennials are starting to send up fresh growth.

STUFF YOU'LL NEED

✔ Hand shears
✔ Lightweight mulch, such as chopped autumn leaves, pine needles or boughs, or wood chips
✔ Garden gloves
✔ Leaf rake

What to Expect
The mulch may blow a little in the wind. If so, weight it down with large branches.

① **Cut back perennials** to just a few inches in late fall or early spring. Pull up annuals.

② **Apply several inches of lightweight mulch,** such as chopped autumn leaves, pine boughs, hay, straw, sawdust, or wood chips. Rake into place.

TRIP SAVER

Rake and Save
Use what you already have! Autumn leaves make an ideal winter mulch as long as you chop them to prevent blowing and matting on the plants. Use your mower to chop them or run them through a shredder or a blower-shredder.

Maintenance

Which Mulch for You?

Cocoa hulls: Adds nutrients. Chocolate aroma for a short time. May mold or attract rodents or blow off. Can be expensive for large areas. Attractive with dark color.

Leaves: When chopped or shredded, greatly improves soil texture and fertility. May blow. Thick, heavy layers of leaves that aren't shredded may mat, suffocating plants. Oak leaves make soil more acidic only if used for many, many years and even then only slightly so.

Compost: Greatly improves soil texture and fertility; very attractive. If making your own homemade compost, use only "hot" compost (see page 120) for mulching since cold compost contains weed seeds.

Pine needles: Available only in certain regions, but they are inexpensive and plentiful. Lasts two to four seasons. Can be a fire hazard where used extensively.

Grass clippings: A great way to dispose of lawn waste. Adds organic matter. Use no more than 2 inches, or it may mold.

Straw/Hay: Fluffy and therefore good as a winter mulch. Not very attractive or compact enough for a warm-weather mulch. Often contains weed seeds.

Gravel and stone: Best for arid and rock gardens. White or light-colored rock reflects sunlight and heat onto plants.

Wood bark, nuggets: Longer-lasting than wood chips. Large nuggets suppress weeds better than smaller ones, though smaller look more attractive. Needs to be aged or will rob nutrients from the soil.

Landscape fabric: Also called weed block. Made of a porous material that allows water to trickle into soil but reduces the number of weeds. Cover with another loose mulch to disguise it. Use only in permanent plantings where you won't need to work the soil, such as around shrubs and trees.

Wood chips: Needs to be aged at least one year or will rob nutrients from the soil. Cedar, redwood, and cypress chips last the longest.

Maintenance

Maintenance   105

Fertilizing Basics

■ Fertilizer is Food

There are no cut-and-dried rules for feeding plants effectively. Some need more fertilizer and others less depending on the season, region, weather, soil, and gardener. Experienced gardeners constantly refine their fertilizing regimes. And remember that fertilizer is a food, not a medicine. Don't expect it to cure a sick plant all by itself.

■ Organic vs. Synthetic

Organic fertilizers are derived from minerals, animals, and plants. They tend to release their nutrients slowly and often improve the texture of the soil. Synthetic (also called chemical or nonorganic) fertilizers are more concentrated, and the plants use them more quickly. They leach from the soil more quickly so there's danger of applying too much, burning plants, upsetting the nutrient balance, or stimulating too much of one type of growth.

■ Fertilizer Basics

The main plant nutrients in chemical fertilizers are **N** (nitrogen—for green, leafy growth), **P** (phosphorus—for root development, flowering, fruiting, and seed formation), and **K** (potassium—for disease-resistance and general growth).

Different proportions of these nutrients provide different results. The proportion of these nutrients is on fertilizer packages (see below) in the same order as their chemical symbols, **N-P-K**.

An easy way to remember their functions is: "Up (N), down (P), all around (K)."

A Fertilizer Glossary

Following is a glossary of terms you'll find on fertilizer boxes or bags:

Balanced: Roughly equal proportions of the major three nutrients—nitrogen (N), potassium (P), and phosphorus (K)—and therefore a good general-purpose fertilizer. Package may read, for example, 10-10-10 or 5-10-5.

Complete: Contains all three primary plant nutrients (N, P, and K).

Foliar: To be sprayed on the plants, which quickly absorb the nutrients through their leaves. Usually used as a supplement to more conventional fertilizer.

Granular: Looks like tiny pellets or sand. Easy to apply; can use your hand, a measuring cup, or a spreader. Balance of N-P-K may vary by application, such as 11-40-6.

Liquid: May come as a liquid concentrate, or as a water-soluble powder. Liquid fertilizers work well for heavy soils where a granular form may dissolve but not be absorbed well. Fish emulsion is one of the few commercial organic liquid fertilizers available.

Slow-release: A fertilizer that releases its nutrients slowly over a period of months. It can be organic (as with compost, bonemeal, and blood meal) or synthetic.

Soluble: Dissolves in water or after watering. Usually, a substance labeled soluble can be applied as a liquid fertilizer, but it can also mean the fertilizer is activated when it comes in contact with water. Check the label to be sure.

Specialty fertilizers: Some fertilizers are designed for the specific needs of a particular plant, such as an African violet or a rose. Others go beyond fertilizing, with added benefits of built-in insecticides or of changing the pH for acid-loving plants. Still others are designed for the specific needs of a plant at a particular time, such as a fertilizer rich in phosphorus (P) to help newly planted flowers establish their roots. Read the package carefully or ask garden center staff to make sure the fertilizer is right for your needs.

Timed-release: Fine-tuned to release nutrients at various times of the growing cycle to match plants' changing needs.

How to Fertilize Different Types of Flowers

Perennials: Work in plenty of compost at planting time to improve soil fertility and texture. Each spring, work a slow-release fertilizer into the top inch or two of soil to feed plants slowly over the season. You may need to reapply later in the growing season; check the label. Otherwise, put 1 inch of compost on top of the soil each spring to feed perennials.

In arid regions where foliage tends to yellow from iron chlorosis or for top performance in other regions, give a foliar feeding in late summer to green up plants and promote growth and flowering.

Annuals: Feed as for perennials. However, because annuals are fast growers, they benefit from periodic "snacks" throughout the season. Consider an application of a liquid or foliar fertilizer to annuals several times during the growing season. Follow package directions. Don't overapply.

Containers: At planting time, work in a slow-release fertilizer or add plant spikes. Use a liquid fertilizer several times, as often as every two weeks during the growing season, to replace the nutrients that are continually washed out with watering.

Roses: At planting time, work in a slow-release fertilizer. Continual bloomers like an additional fertilizing several times during the growing season with a liquid fertilizer, as often as every two weeks. Slow-release rose fertilizers with built-in systemic insecticides are also available.

Shrubs: Newly planted shrubs or those that completely regenerate foliage each year, such as butterfly bush or some hibiscus, benefit from an application of compost or a slow-release fertilizer. However, in most cases, flowering shrubs do not need additional fertilizing. In arid regions where foliage tends to yellow from iron chlorosis, consider an occasional foliar feeding to green up plants.

Bulbs: When planting bulbs, add a bit of compost to the bottom of the planting hole. Also add a granular fertilizer made specifically for bulbs, following package directions. You may use bonemeal, but it attracts animals and needs to be combined with blood meal for a more complete fertilizer.

Work Smarter!

When to Stop

Stop all fertilizing late in the growing season, two months before your region's first average frost date (see page 13). Otherwise, fertilizer is likely to encourage tender new growth that will get zapped by frost and winter's cold.

Homer's Hindsight

Doctor's Orders

My azaleas were looking sick the other day, so I gave them some fertilizer. It didn't help. Then I saw a sign at my garden center that made the light bulb go on: "Fertilizer is a food, not a medicine." The azalea ended up biting the dust. Next time, I'll look up the disease in a book or bring in a few of the plant parts to show the staff at the garden center. That way, I'll be treating the actual problem rather than just dumping on fertilizer.

Work in compost or slow-release fertilizer in the spring. It feeds the plants all season long.

Pruning Roses

Pruning roses is easy if you follow a few time-tested rules. The basic principle for all roses except climbers is to direct all growth outward in a regular and even fashion, keeping the attractive center of the rose open so air can circulate to prevent disease.

■ When to Prune
You can cut out diseased or dead (black) wood any time of year. But roses need a major pruning in the late winter or early spring when they're just starting to send out new growth. The new growth is usually little red buds or shoots that will turn into new leaves and stems.

■ What to Use
You need sharp bypass shears for most jobs. Dull shears crush and damage wood and damaged wood invites disease. You may need a pair of loppers (long-handled shears for larger

branches) as well. Loppers easily cut through wood thicker than a half-inch. For heavy pruning jobs, you could use a small saw, but that's unusual for roses.

A pair of heavy gloves is a must. Rose thorns can cause nasty gashes and cuts, and smaller thorns have an unpleasant habit of staying imbedded in your skin. Long sleeves are also a good idea.

Keep rubbing alcohol or a weak bleach solution and paper towels on hand to sterilize the blades between plants, to avoid spreading disease.

■ What to Prune
The first step in an early-spring pruning job is to cut out all completely dead wood which is black. When you cut into it, the center (called the pith) is also black or gray. Wood is still alive if it's green, even if the outside is black—as long as the pith is white and firm. It's just not as vigorous as green wood.

Next cut out any branches that are rubbing against each other, crossing each other, or damaged or diseased.

Then choose three to six canes as your "keepers." These canes should not be too thin—at least as thick as a pencil—nor too thick and old. They should also spread outward from an open center.

Remove other thin, spindly growth. Then cut the canes you are going to keep to a height of from 1 to 3 feet, depending on how high you want your rosebush. This is no exact science; but as a rule, cut the rose canes about one-fifth as high as the desired mature height of the rose stalks.

Make the cut at the top of the

Maintenance

cane so it's at a 45-degree angle ¼ inch above an outward-facing bud (see opposite page). This assures that new growth will be outward and upward, creating a healthy, pretty shape.

There's no need to paint or dab any substance on the cuts. They'll heal nicely by themselves.

■ *How to Prune Climbers*

Climbing roses get a different treatment than bushier roses.

Climbing roses are divided into two types: ramblers and large-flowered climbers.

Ramblers usually have smaller flowers and grow rampantly, up to 20 feet in a season. If you don't prune them, they'll become a thorny, overgrown thicket. Also, ramblers flower on old wood grown the previous season. If you're unsure what type of rose you have, observe the way it flowers to tell if it's a rambler or a large-flowered climber.

Ramblers bloom just once a year. After they're done blooming, cut the canes back to just a foot or so. This encourages fresh, rapid growth the next year. Tie this new growth to a fence or a trellis.

Large-flowered climbers are less vigorous. In their first year, you must train them up the arbor or the trellis they're planted on. Tie them with soft twine or strips of cut pantyhose. Sometimes you can also carefully weave the pliable stems in and out of the support.

In the following two to four years, you won't need to prune them much at all, other than to remove dead or damaged wood. As the rose grows, prune as needed to shape it and control its height.

Pruning Roses

1 **Cut away the dead growth.** Cut out any dead (black throughout), rubbing, or damaged wood first. Then assess the plant.

2 **Trim the rest.** Trim any spindly growth thinner than a pencil. Leave just four or five thick, healthy canes 1 to 3 feet tall.

Pruning Once-Blooming Climbing Roses

1 **Prune in early spring.** Cut out old branches (canes) that flowered the year before.

2 **Cut out all dead, weak, or thin canes,** leaving four to five strong, new ones.

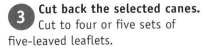

3 **Cut back the selected canes.** Cut to four or five sets of five-leaved leaflets.

4 **Tie the selected canes** to the support with soft twine or strips of pantyhose.

Rose Diseases and Pests

If you plant the right rose in the right place and follow up with good maintenance, it will be gorgeous. Roses aren't fussy unless you neglect them. Here's how to have the healthiest roses on the block:

• **Choose an easy rose.** Roses vary radically in disease and pest resistance. When shopping for roses, look for terms such as "low-maintenance," "shrub," "carefree," or "landscape" in the description. Or refer to the list of disease-resistant roses on the next page.

• **Give it plenty of sun.** Roses need at least six hours of full, direct light. With less sun, they're far more prone to pests, diseases, and poor flowering.

• **Water wisely.** Roses love just their roots watered, not the whole plant. Avoid watering them after noon, or the wet leaves will encourage fungal diseases as evening hits.

• **Spray with dormant oil.** In winter or early spring, spray with this organic product before new growth begins. It prevents disease problems.

• **Trim off diseased flowers and plant parts.** This will often slow, or even stop, the spread of the disease. Be sure to sterilize your shears with rubbing alcohol or a weak bleach solution between plants to prevent the spread of disease.

• **Mulch.** Apply 1 to 3 inches (no more!) of mulch around the base of the plant to prevent soil-borne diseases from splashing onto the plant.

• **Prune smart.** Keep the center of the plant open and the canes spaced evenly apart to encourage good air circulation, and prevent disease.

Healthy roses don't just happen. You must watch for diseases or pests and treat them promptly.

• **Feed regularly.** Roses are hungry plants that need regular fertilizing. Apply a slow-release granular rose fertilizer with a systemic insecticide once or twice during the growing season. Well-fed plants resist disease.

• **Remember that some bugs are good.** Ladybugs, lacewings, praying mantises, and bees help your garden. Sprays and powders to kill harmful insects are likely to kill beneficial insects, too, even if the product is organic.

■ *Aphids*

Aphids are easy to spot as tiny white or pale green ovals that attach themselves to buds and tender new growth. If the problem is small, just hose them off and then swab the area liberally with a half-and-half solution of liquid dish soap and water. For more serious problems, spray with an insecticide specifying control of aphids, or use a systemic insecticide early in the season the next year to prevent a recurrence.

aphid

■ *Black Spot*

Black spot is one of the most common rose diseases. In fact, by summer's end, only the most disease-resistant roses have no black spot at all. Black spot starts, logically enough, with the appearance of tiny black dots on leaves. The leaves eventually turn yellow and brown and fall off. Black spot is a fungal disease that likes moist conditions and is therefore less common in arid regions or in a dry year. Planting roses in full sun will lessen this problem. Prevent spread of the disease by picking up fallen leaves and trimming off as many of the affected leaves as is practical. Water the roots of the plant only, not the leaves. If the problem is severe, spray with a fungicide.

■ Japanese Beetle

Japanese beetles are a common rose problem east of the Mississippi. They eat all parts of the plant (although the flowers are their favorite), leaving holes where they've chewed. Small infestations can be controlled by picking off the slow-moving beetles and dropping them into a can of water with a thin film of oil on top. If the problem is severe, spray as soon as you notice them with a spray specifying control of Japanese beetles. Japanese beetle traps may also be effective.

■ Mildew

Mildew is a disease that shows up in mid- to late summer, primarily in regions with cool, humid evenings. Gray or white splotches appear on leaves and stems. Leaves eventually yellow, then brown, then fall. Planting roses in full sun will lessen this problem. Prevent spread of the disease by picking up fallen leaves and trimming off as many of the affected leaves as is practical. Water the roots of the plant only. Severe problems can be controlled by spraying in the spring before the problem becomes visible with a

fungicide, following package directions exactly. This usually means repeating the application until weather gets up to 75°F (24°C) or so.

■ Rust

Rust likes warm, damp conditions and becomes evident in early summer in the form of bright orange spots on undersides of leaves. Spots turn brown, then black. Planting roses in full sun will lessen this problem. Prevent spread of the disease by picking up fallen leaves and trimming off as many of the affected leaves as is practical. Water the roots of the plant only. Severe problems can be controlled by spraying in the spring before the problem

becomes visible, using a fungicide and following package directions. This usually means repeating the application until weather gets up to around 75°F (24°C).

■ Thrips

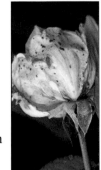

Thrip are tiny brown insects that love hot, dry weather. They become evident in discoloration and deformation of flower buds and flowers, especially in light-colored roses, as the small insects nibble the flower. Repeat spraying with a chemical specifying thrip control as one option, but even

this has limited effectiveness. If thrips are a problem year after year, use a systemic insecticide early in the season to stop this pest before its damage can be seen.

Disease-Resistant Roses

Certain roses are disease-resistant as a group. They include gallica, hybrid musk, rugosa, romantica, Meidiland, Griffith Buck, and David Austin roses.

In particular, the following cultivars of these and other groups of roses are also disease-resistant.

Name	Page
'Ballerina' (hybrid musk)	90
'Belinda' (hybrid musk)	90
'Belle Story' (English)	89
'Betty Prior' (floribunda)	90
'Bonica' (other shrub)	91
'Buff Beauty' (hybrid musk)	90
'Carefree Beauty' (other shrub)	91
'Carefree Wonder' (other shrub)	91
'Cecile Brunner' (polyantha)	91
'China Doll' (polyantha)	91
'Country Dancer' (other shrub)	91
'F.J. Grootendorst' (rugosa)	91
'Flower Carpet' (other shrub)	91
'Frontier Twirl' (other shrub)	91
'Graham Thomas' (English)	89
'Lady Banks' rose (rambler)	93
'Mary Rose' (English)	89
'Max Graf' (rugosa)	91
'New Dawn' (rambler)	93
'Othello' (English)	89
'Pretty Jessica' (English)	89
'Prosperity' (hybrid musk)	90
'Sally Holmes' (other shrub)	91
'Sir Thomas Lipton' (rugosa)	91
'The Fairy' (polyantha)	91
'Therese Bugnet' (rugosa)	91

Maintenance

Fertilizing Roses

Ask 10 expert rose gardeners about fertilizing and you'll probably get 10 different answers. That's because fertilizing is as much of an art as a science and varies according to region, overall gardening practices, and just plain personal philosophy.

The only thing that everyone agrees on is that roses need nutrients. Here are some ways to provide them:

■ *The Organic Approach*

Make sure your roses are well fed by working in a spadeful or two of compost around the base of the rose each spring.

Once a month thereafter, fertilize your roses with a liquid organic fertilizer, such as manure tea or fish emulsion.

If you want to really pamper your roses, each spring, make a batch of the following "spring tonic" for your roses. Mix together in a 5-gallon bucket the following: 2 cups alfalfa meal, 2 cups Epsom salts, 2 cups fish meal, 2 cups greensand, 2 cups gypsum, and 1 cup bonemeal. Work approximately 1 cup of this spring tonic into the top inch or so of the soil for smaller rosebushes, using a trowel or hand cultivator. Very large rosebushes (those 6 feet or taller) need 3 to 4 cups.

■ *The No-Brainer Approach*

At planting time and in early spring each year following, sprinkle a slow-release, granular combination fertilizer-insecticide at the base of the roses. It feeds and protects your roses for weeks and even months. Reapply as the package directs, usually every six weeks.

■ *The Intense Approach*

If you want the biggest and best roses, fertilize with a liquid fertilizer every two to three weeks. It will give them a quick, easily absorbed snack. Mix into a watering can or attach a spray feeder to your garden hose.

Here's an Idea:

The Percolator Effect

Roses really love rich, loose soil. Loose soil allows nutrients to percolate deep into the soil, reaching the rose's roots and giving nutrition where it's needed.

Provide this soil by working in abundant compost at planting time. After a rose is planted, you can further improve the soil each spring by working a gallon or two of compost into the surface of the soil around the rose.

Feeding Roses

One of the fastest, easiest ways to feed roses—as well as prevent insect problems—is to apply a systemic rose fertilizer a few times throughout the growing season. Follow package directions exactly.

Cut It Out

I thought I was doing my roses a favor, fertilizing them right up until frost. But what I didn't know is that you're supposed to stop fertilizing your roses one month before the first frost date (see page 13). Otherwise, they keep sending out lots of new growth. So mine got one dandy case of winter-kill, and the bush was half-dead by spring.

Winterizing Roses

How much winter protection you give your roses depends on your climate and the rose. It also varies depending on the severity of each winter. But in general, do the following:

■ Zones 5 and Colder

In late fall, before the first snowfall, mound all roses with soil or compost to a height of 10 inches to 1 foot. In Zones

4 and 5, the hardiest roses, such as rugosas, Morden, Canadian Explorer, and most David Austins, will survive normal winters without additional protection. But hybrid teas and other borderline-hardy roses need their top protected as well (see illustrations below). And in Zones 3, all roses need their top protected.

Remove the top protection when daytime temperatures regularly are in the 50s, usually in March or so. Gently hose or push away the mounded soil two or three weeks later.

■ Zones 6 to 8

In late fall, after the ground freezes, mound roses with 4 to 8 inches of soil, compost, or mulch. Remove in late February or early March.

■ Zones 9 and Warmer

No mounding or mulch is needed except for the least cold-hardy roses, such as hybrid teas, during the coldest winters. Even then, they'll need only 3 to 4 inches of mulch around their bases.

Most David Austin roses are fairly winter hardy, requiring minimal winter protection.

Maintenance

Winter Protection for Roses

Mounding. In all but the warmest climates (Zones 9 and warmer), roses need to be mounded in late fall with soil or compost 6 to 12 inches high.

Tying canes. In higher-wind areas, it's a good idea to tie together tall bushes to prevent damage from canes whipping in the wind.

Wrapping. In Zones 5 and colder, less hardy roses should be wrapped with burlap and twine for further protection. Remove the covering in early spring, about the time the snow melts permanently.

Caring for Flowering Shrubs

As long as you choose the right shrub for your region and position it well, a flowering shrub will last for years and deliver armloads of flowers with very little—if any—work on your part. Shrubs' deep root systems tend to make them more drought-tolerant than other flowers, and they usually demand little feeding, pruning, or fussing.

■ *Feeding Flowering Shrubs*

After the first year or two, most flowering shrubs don't need much additional feeding. When they're first planted, most appreciate plenty of compost worked into the planting hole and perhaps an application of a "root booster" plant fertilizer to stimulate root growth and get them off to a good start. After that, with a couple of exceptions, most flowering shrubs thrive with, at most, one annual application of a slow-release fertilizer.

One exception is those flowering shrubs, such as buddleias, which in some conditions regenerate their foliage every year. These plants have a large growth each year and need one application of a slow-release fertilizer in the spring or a repeat application of a liquid fertilizer every few weeks throughout the growing season.

Another exception can be acid-loving shrubs, such as azaleas and rhododendrons. If your soil is neutral to alkaline, they'll do best with a regular application of a fertilizer that makes the soil more acidic.

In warm-climate areas (Zones 9 and warmer), where plants grow nearly year-round, a boost once or twice a year with foliar fertilizer is helpful.

■ *Watering Flowering Shrubs*

The water needs of flowering shrubs vary as much as the shrubs themselves. Some, such as hydrangeas, are thirsty while others, such as potentilla, are drought-tolerant. Check the listing of water needs of shrubs on the opposite page and refer to the shrub section of the Flower Encyclopedia starting on page 226 to check the water needs of other specific shrubs. Otherwise, water the shrub whenever its leaves begin to lose gloss, feel limp, or otherwise show signs of drought-related stress. Be sure to water shrubs slowly and thoroughly so water can percolate down a foot or more. Do this by laying a hose at the base of the plant and turning the hose to a tiny trickle. Let the water run for an hour or more. (Drip-irrigation systems are excellent for this.)

It's important that shrubs go into winter well watered. If the autumn has been dry, shrubs may become water stressed

Some very vigorous, fast-growing shrubs such as fuchsia and forsythia can be rejuvenated by cutting them off to only a few feet high.

Here's an Idea:

Shrubs in Containers

Shrubs are wonderfully different in containers. They add height, foliage, and structure that's hard to find in more common container plants.

You can leave most shrubs in their containers in Zones 8 and warmer and sometimes in Zones 7 and warmer. In colder areas, bring the pots into a garage or other protected area that seldom gets much below freezing.

An alternative is to double-pot the containers (see page 81) in spring. In fall, just lift out in the plant, still in its plastic inner pot, and dig a trench deep enough to hold the pot. Mulch well, including the lower foot or so of the shrub. Repot in spring.

Different shrubs have different pruning needs. Refer to the shrubs section of the Flower Encyclopedia beginning on page 226.

and die during the winter.

Mulching is an excellent way to conserve water around shrubs. Apply a 2- to 3-inch layer of mulch out as far as the branches reach to maintain cool, moist soil and prevent damage from string trimmers and mowers. (Never allow a string trimmer to nick the base of a shrub, or a mower to bump into it. The resulting injury invites disease and other problems.)

■ *Pruning Flowering Shrubs*

Most flowering shrubs thrive with little pruning. As long as you've planted the shrub in a place where it has enough room, all you'll need to do is periodically remove dead or damaged wood and foliage.

Flowering shrubs are most attractive when pruned lightly, if at all. Pruning usually distorts their natural shape as well as cutting off blooms.

Some flowering shrubs benefit from a thinning each year after

Work Smarter!

When to Prune

Prune **spring-flowering shrubs** in late spring, right after they've flowered.

Prune **summer-flowering shrubs** in very early spring.

Prune **shrubs with late-summer or fall flowers** or berries in early spring.

flowering. Forsythia, weigela, and lilacs produce many new stems or canes from their bases each year, quickly creating a thicket if not thinned out. Each spring, remove up to one-third of the old foliage by cutting the oldest, thickest stems at the base of the shrub.

If the shrub is fast growing and overgrown, consider cutting it back to only a few feet to rejuvenate it.

Shrubs by Water Needs

Name	Zones	Page
Flowering Shrubs that Need Plentiful Water		
Azalea	3–9	233
Rhododendron spp.		
Camellia	6–11	228
Camellia spp.		
Gardenia	8–11	230
Gardenia augusta		
Glossy abelia	6–9	227
Abelia × *grandiflora*		
Hydrangea	4–9	231
Hydrangea spp.		
Japanese rose	5–9	232
Kerria japonica		
Pussy willow	3–9	234
Salix spp.		
Rhododendron	3–9	233
Rhododendron spp.		
Summersweet	4–9	228
Clethra alnifolia		
Winterberry	4–9	232
Ilex verticillata		
Witch hazel	5–9	231
Hamamelis spp.		
Moderate-Water Flowering Shrubs		
Butterfly bush	5–10	227
Buddleia spp.		
Daphne	4–9	229
Daphne spp.		
Forsythia	4–8	230
Forsythia intermedia		
Purple beautyberry	5–8	227
Callicarpa spp.		
Rose of Sharon	5–11	231
Hibiscus spp.		
Smokebush	5–8	229
Cotinus coggygria		
Spirea	3–9	234
Spiraea spp.		
Viburnum	2–9	235
Viburnum spp.		
Drought-tolerant Flowering Shrubs		
Broom	6–10	229
Cytisus spp.		
Flowering quince	4–9	228
Chaenomeles speciosa		
Lilac	2–8	235
Syringa spp.		
Mock orange	4–8	233
Philadelphus spp.		
Oleander	5–7	232
Nerium oleander		
Potentilla	2–7	233
Potentilla fruticosa		
Weigela	4–9	235
Weigela florida		

Caring for Flowering Vines

Vines, especially perennial types, need minimal care. Plant them and watch them grow, often with amazing speed. In fact, the biggest challenge, especially with tall perennial types, is to keep them in bounds with an occasional pruning.

■ Training New Vines

Vines need little encouragement to send them on their way up their support. Rapidly growing vines, such as wisteria or honeysuckle, need you only to guide them onto the support, and they will rapidly climb it. More timid vines, such as clematis, benefit from being tied to their support, at least at first. Do this with soft twine or strips of pantyhose.

As your vine grows, ensure that it has the right support. Many vines such as wisteria, honeysuckle, trumpet vine, and

Mandevilla (Mandevilla, page 240)

climbing hydrangea can top 40 feet with heavy, woody stems. They need large, sturdy, well-built supports such as walls or pergolas. The type of support you provide also depends on the vine's climbing habit. A vine that attaches itself by twining needs a trellis or a pole. A vine that attaches with stickfasts needs masonry or brick. The wrong vine on the wrong support needs to be transplanted at the earliest opportunity.

■ Pruning/Cutting Back

Annual vines need no pruning or cutting back. In all but the warmest regions, they die when frost hits and are pulled or cut down from their supports. Perennial vines, however, need more management. They need an occasional bit of dead wood pruned out and often need to be cut back to prevent them from creeping into places you don't want them.

The best time to prune most vines is in late winter or very early spring, just as the vine is leafing out. At this point you can tell dead wood from live, yet can still see its structure easily. Cut out any dead wood, using hand shears, loppers, or a small saw for large stems.

Follow each branch back to its origin at a main branch. Cut back side branches from a few inches to 2 feet from the main trunk. Then remove any suckers from the base.

Clematis are a special case. Refer to page 238 for more information on pruning clematis correctly.

Training a Vine

STUFF YOU'LL NEED

✔ Trellis or other support
✔ Strips of pantyhose or stretch tape

What to Expect

Timid vines will take a week or two to catch on and start twining by themselves. More vigorous vines will need less assistance but may start to wander. Keep tucking in or tying down straying branches to keep them in check.

1 **When the vine is small,** twist it gently once or twice around the support. Stiffer vines might need the help of stretch tape or strips of pantyhose, which stretch with the vine.

2 **Keep tying.** Every week or two, check the vine and continue to tie it as needed. It will soon climb without much further assistance.

CLOSER LOOK

Let It Climb!

Climbing vines don't hurt the masonry of buildings, as long as the masonry is already sound. Nor will they trap moisture against a house.

Aggressive vines that attach with suckers or stickfasts can create problems on siding that needs to be painted, tearing off loose shingles and trim as well as leaving bits of the plant to be scraped or sanded off when you move the vine out of the way.

■ *Feeding*

Annual vines, such as morning glory and scarlet runner bean, appreciate being well fed during their rapid growth. Work in a spadeful or two of compost at planting time. Then work in a slow-release fertilizer or apply a liquid fertilizer every few weeks.

Perennial vines thrive with minimal care. Most do well without any fertilizing, but work a slow-release fertilizer into the soil each spring, if desired.

■ *Watering*

Annual vines tend to be thirsty plants, often wilting in the late-afternoon heat. Plant them in moisture-retentive, compost-rich soil and apply a liquid fertilizer every few weeks. Be careful not to overfertilize or they'll produce too much green growth at the expense of flowers.

Perennial vines, with their deeper roots and woodier stems, are far more drought-tolerant. With the exception of smaller vines, those 12 feet and under, most perennial vines do well without additional water in all but the most arid regions.

Some large, fast-growing vines such as this bittersweet (Celastrus scandens, page 237) need a hard pruning each spring to keep them from growing out of control.

Maintenance

Deadheading

Deadheading—simply, removing fading blooms—not only keeps your garden looking tidy, it also encourages many plants to continue flowering longer.

A plant's job is to set seed and reproduce. Seeds are produced from flowers. When you remove the flowers, the frustrated plant goes into overtime, producing blooms in an effort to set seed.

If you don't deadhead it is very likely that the plant will stop producing as many blooms.

■ *Which Flowers Need It*

Annuals benefit the most from deadheading. With proper deadheading, many will produce more than double the flowers they would without.

Many perennials also benefit from deadheading, but some are unaffected. Perennials usually bloom for just a few

When deadheading a shrub, reach into the plant. That way, the stub resulting from the cut will be hidden by the foliage.

weeks, but some perennials will continue to bloom for months with diligent deadheading. Others will respond with a second flush of bloom, sometimes as late as fall.

Bulbs and shrubs tend to be the least responsive to deadheading, but some will bloom longer with diligent trimming of spent blooms. (Be sure to leave the bulb foliage to help it rejuvenate the next year.)

■ *How to Deadhead*

The method of deadheading depends on the flower. Tall, tough stalks such as those on daylilies and irises need to be removed individually at the base of the plant. Use pruning shears, though sometimes the flower stalks will fade and can be pulled off easily by hand.

Other flowers such as marigolds can be pinched off. If just a flower or two in a large cluster is fading, pinch or cut it off to allow the others to develop better.

Some plants look awful when first deadheaded but fill out again in a week or two. Also, when deadheading individual flowers, reach into the plant as much as possible to minimize unattractive stubs.

You can deadhead with a variety of tools. Sometimes your hands are all you need to pinch or snap off a fading flower. At other times, a scissors is useful as well. Woodier plants will require hand shears. Soft, bushy plants sometimes are easiest to do with a sharp pair of grass clippers or hedge shears.

Homer's Hindsight

Leave It Up

I got carried away and deadheaded some plants I wish I would have left alone. Thinking I was doing a good cleanup job in the fall, I cut back my ornamental grasses, sedum, and other plants. Turns out, these flower and seed heads dry right on the stalk and look great. So all winter long I had to enjoy my neighbor's perennials instead of my own.

Work Smarter!

Deadhead Early and Often

Deadheading regularly is important for maximum flowering in your garden. Although it's best to deadhead daily, if you can get out there at least once a week, that should be sufficient.

Cutting Back

Some annuals and perennials get messy near the middle or end of the season and benefit from a hard cutting back. Cut back the plant by one-third to two-thirds with hand shears. The plant will look ragged for a week or two but will soon regenerate with fresh foliage and a new burst of bloom.

Good candidates for cutting back include petunias (page 205), many bellflowers (page 170), coreopsis (page 176), perennial blue salvia (page 210), balloon flower (page 207), golden marguerite, lobelia (page 195), hardy geraniums (page 185), gaura (page 184), and verbena (page 214).

How to Deadhead

Roses: If only a few flowers on a cluster have faded, pinch or trim them off. If the whole cluster is fading, cut it off at the first leaflet with five leaves (see page 108 for details).

Perennials with tall stalks: Cut off the stalk as near to the base as possible. In some cases, the stalk dries up enough that you can gently tug it off.

Perennials and annuals with partly faded flower clusters: Cut or pinch off only the faded flower. When the entire cluster fades, remove the whole stem.

Bushy annuals and perennials with many small flowers: It's difficult to get only the faded flowers, so when most flowers have faded, give the plant a haircut by shearing back about one-third and removing all the blooms.

Maintenance

Compost

Compost is called black gold for a good reason. It's an almost-miracle substance that greatly improves your garden.

The list of what compost can do for your garden goes on and on: It feeds plants, improves drainage, retains moisture, makes weeding easier, helps distribute fertilizer, attracts beneficial earthworms, promotes biological activity in the soil, prevents disease in some cases, and provides micronutrients.

Composting is not only important, it's easy. Pile up materials and let them break down. In fact, composting makes daily work in the garden easier because it's a convenient way to dispose of leaves, grass clippings, and other yard wastes. No more bagging!

Although they're on the market and easy to install, you don't need a fancy bin to compost. Wire fencing works fine. It's nice to have 3 bins (one for finished compost, one for partly composted materials, and one for fresh materials). But it's not necessary, especially for the beginning composter. Once you have a bin, add materials as you gather them in the ordinary course of your yard work. You'll have compost in several months, usually at the bottom of the pile.

■ Cold Compost vs. Hot Compost

• **Cold compost,** the easiest method, is made by piling up materials and letting them break down for a year or two with an occasional turn if possible. Add cold compost to the bottom of a planting hole, but don't mulch with it or otherwise use it on the soil surface if you've added weeds or plants that will volunteer (such as tomatoes or hollyhocks). Weed and volunteer seedlings in the compost sprout and create problems.

• **Hot compost** comes from a compost pile constructed with

a balance of nitrogen-rich and carbon-rich materials that are turned regularly, at least once every week or two. It is also kept evenly moist with occasional watering. Hot compost becomes very hot to the touch, and the heat kills weed seeds and many disease pathogens.

■ Tips for Faster, Better Compost

• **Keep the pile a manageable size.** Make it no more than 4 feet across and 3 feet high so you can turn it easily.

• **Turn the compost regularly,** as often as every few days, with a spading fork or pitchfork. Any turning is helpful, but more is

These beautifully designed compost bins are the ideal way to provide an ongoing supply of black gold for a garden.

Maintenance

better because active compost piles need oxygen.

• **Cut up or shred materials.** The smaller the materials, the faster they'll break down.

• **Layer nitrogen-rich materials,** (green materials), with carbon-rich materials, (brown materials.) If a pile has too much nitrogen, it will get slimy. If it has too much carbon, it won't break down quickly.

• **Keep it moist.** During dry spells, soak the compost heap with a hose.

Materials to Compost

Nitrogen-Rich (Green) Materials to Compost:

Alfalfa hay
Fruit and vegetable scraps
Grass clippings
Green leaves and weeds
Manure
Seaweed

Carbon-Rich (Brown) Materials to Compost:

Dried leaves
Shredded newspaper
Straw
Woody stems and sticks

Other Materials to Add:

Coffee grounds/tea leaves
Eggshells
Pine needles
Wood ash

Do Not Compost:

Bones
Cat, dog, or other pet wastes
Diseased or invasive plants
Meat or meat products
Oils, fats, greases
Seed heads

STUFF YOU'LL NEED

✔ Compost bin
✔ Materials to compost
✔ Spading fork or pitchfork

What to Expect

Be patient! Cold compost can take up to two years to formulate. However, as soon as you start adding materials, they begin to break down and pack down, creating more space day by day.

If you don't want to wait that long, keep the heap moist by watering it occasionally and turning it more frequently. That speeds the process.

Building a Compost Heap

1 **Erect your compost heap.** A wire bin is shown, but concrete blocks stacked several feet high will also work. The ideal set-up has three bins to hold compost in various states of decomposition, but one bin is sufficient.

2 **Alternate materials if possible.** You can dump materials into the pile; but for the fastest, hottest compost, layer one part nitrogen-rich materials to three parts carbon-rich materials. If the weather is dry, further speed the process by watering the pile.

3 **Turn as often as possible.** The more you turn the pile, the faster and hotter your compost will be. Turning once or twice a week is ideal. If you never turn your pile you still get compost, but the decomposition takes much longer.

Weeds

■ Using an Ounce of Prevention

Save hours of work by attacking weeds early. Weeds that have been allowed to get large are harder to pull or hoe out and can set seed, dispersing seeds into your garden. Here's how to prevent weeds from becoming a problem:

• **Never let a weed get more than 1 inch long or wide.** They compete less with other plants, are easier to remove, and won't set seed if you get them early. In fact, there's an old saying, "One year of seeds means seven years of weeds."

• **Use a preemergent herbicide when needed.** Sold under a variety of brand names, these granular herbicides are sprinkled onto the ground to prevent weed seeds from germinating. They don't work on existing weeds, but are useful in early spring (about the time forsythia is blooming) when weeds get their start.

To minimize chemical use, apply a preemergent only when weeds have been a severe problem. Hoeing, pulling, cultivation, and mulching are still the best ways to deal with weeds.

• **Mulch.** Mulch blocks light from weed seeds so they can't germinate. Lay a 1–to–3 inch layer of mulch around flowers in mid-spring, after the soil begins to warm up—about the time the daffodils stop blooming.

■ Dealing with Weeds After the Fact

Try these solutions for weeds that have gotten too large or out of control:

• **Go first for the weeds that are flowering.** Do everything you can to prevent them from setting seeds, creating a new generation of problems later on.

• **Know when to pull or hoe.** Hoeing is best for getting broad sweeps of small weeds in open areas, while pulling is better when weeds are in tight areas or are large. Pulling is also the only method for getting those weeds that spread and resprout if chopped up by a hoe (see chart on opposite page).

• **Renovate when things get out of hand.** If weeds badly infest a perennial planting, causing the weeds and the flower to become hopelessly interplanted, the

Work Smarter!

Easier Weeding

Follow these tips and weeding may be a joy.

• **Weed when the soil is moist.** If you can do it right after a rain, terrific. If not, first give the bed a thorough soaking with the sprinkler.

• **Weed on a dry, sunny day.** The weeds you behead with the hoe or drop onto the ground after pulling will shrivel in the sun, never to be heard from again. On cool, overcast, moist days, weeds sometimes re-establish themselves where they lie.

• **Wear well-fitting gloves.** Regular garden gloves can be too bulky for weeding, but your hands still need protection. Use tough, well-fitting latex gloves. They may be found in the garden center, but if not they're often sold in automotive or paint sections.

• **Invest in a kneeling pad or knee pads.** These pads make work more comfortable and keep you cleaner.

best solution is to wait until fall or spring and then dig up the whole mass or clump. Break the perennial apart, picking out the weeds. Add a spadeful or two of compost or other soil amendment to the area to enrich the soil. Cut the tops of the perennials back by two-thirds and replant the sections in the original spot.

• **Know annual weeds from perennial.** This will help you figure out which ones are most pressing to remove. If it's right before a frost and your annual weeds are a problem (but not flowering!), you can leave them alone. They'll die in a week or two anyway. Perennial weeds, however, will only get bigger. Do not leave them for the frost.

• **Use chemicals as a last resort.** Herbicides are somewhat effective on mature plants. Some herbicides attack grasses only and are good choices for flower beds. Other herbicides are "nonselective"; that is, they kill everything they touch. Be careful! These herbicides are sprayed on, and sometimes they drift onto plants you want to keep. Repeat applications may be necessary to kill mature weeds.

A preemergent herbicide applied in spring stops many weeds before they start.

Maintenance

Weed Chart

Bindweed: Perennial. This relative of the morning glory has deep roots that are hard to eradicate. Roots or pieces of roots left from  pulling or hand tilling resprout easily. Pull small (under 3 inches) bindweed as soon as you see it. Dig up at least the top 6 inches of the roots of larger bindweeds. Repeat removal may be necessary. In severe infestations, repeat application of a nonselective herbicide may be necessary.

Chickweed: Annual in all but the warmest parts of the country. Shallow roots make this weed easy to pull.  Remove plants from the garden because they can easily reroot.

Clover: Perennial. Pull clover as soon as you see it. Remove plants from the garden because they can easily reroot.

Dandelion: Perennial. This weed must be dug up. Get at least the top two inches of its long, slender taproot, or it will return.

Ground ivy: Perennial. It is also called creeping Charlie and cat's-foot. Shallow roots make it easy to pull.  Weeds left lying on the ground can reroot. It's good to put it in the compost heap because of it's high iron content.

Knotweed: Annual in all but the warmest regions. It has a long taproot, so it's best to pull this weed when the soil is moist. Be sure to  sever the crown from it's roots, or it will resprout. After weeding, work compacted soil lightly to prevent further invasion.

Lamb's-quarters: Annual in all but the warmest regions. A sturdy stalk and shallow roots make this easy to pull. Small plants are easy to hoe.

Plantain: Perennial. Remove at least the top inch of taproot to kill. After weeding, work the compacted soil lightly to prevent further invasion.

Purslane: Annual. Most common in the Northeast, least in the Pacific Northwest, it is easy to pull. Do not hoe into pieces or allow  stems to break off and lie on the ground, or it will spread.

Weed grasses: Can be annual or perennial. This includes crabgrass (as shown at right), Bermudagrass, goosegrass, and  quackgrass. Dig out plant with roots, or it will regrow. It reroots from bits of stem left in ground or bits of plant left lying on the ground.

> See inside front cover for reference to a variety of weeding tools.

Maintenance

Staking Flowers

Gardeners who know how to stake and support their plants will have well-groomed gardens.

■ Know When to Stake

The best staking is done while the plant is no more than 1 foot or so high. That way the plant can grow tall and straight with the stake. But there are times when you may have to stake after the plant has begun to sprawl and spread. The effects are less graceful, but staking is still helpful because staking keeps plants off the ground where moisture invites disease.

■ Don't Show Your Work

The best staking is nearly invisible. Whenever possible, choose staking materials in dark neutrals or deep greens rather than shiny metal or white. If shiny or white is all you have, a coat of dark green spray paint takes care of the problem. Materials for tying should be soft and stretchy to prevent damage. Good choices include cut strips of pantyhose, rags, or soft twine.

Stakes can be sticks or branches salvaged from the yard (keep a pile in the garage) or bits of scrap lumber. Bamboo rods are classic. There are also a number of metal supports now available. Some are rounded grids for plants to grow through, while others create a fence to provide support.

Taller lilies (Lilium, page 222) tend to lean. Cleverly designed stakes keep them attractive and upright.

Maintenance

Staking mature flowers. Often the need for staking isn't apparent until after the plant has begun to bend or lean. In that case, tie the plant to a stake or two for additional support.

Staking young flowers. Taller individual flowers, such as delphiniums and many lilies, need sturdy stakes. Install natural-colored stakes when the plants are only a few feet high. As the plants grow, tie them to the stakes using soft twine, stretch tape, or strips of pantyhose.

Natural support. Bushy plants that tend to sprawl, such as sweet peas and bush morning glory, will twine easily around a shrubby branch or two pushed into the ground. Branches make free, natural-looking supports!

Grid support. Bushy flowers, such as peonies, yarrow, and asters, benefit from a gridlike plant support. Position the grid over the plant in spring and allow it to grow through.

Maintenance

Managing Reseeders

Reseeders, properly tended, can be a gardener's great friend. Hollyhocks, cleome, sunflowers, bachelor's buttons, larkspur, California poppies, ox-eye daisies, and others sow themselves around the garden, multiplying rapidly each year.

At first, these reseeders are welcome, adding a charming, unexpected element to the garden. But after a few years, they can become a headache if not well managed, cropping up everywhere and gaining weed status. Here's how to make the most of self-sowing flowers:

■ Designate an Area

Unless you're going for a tousled wildflower look, designate one spot for allowing a particular reseeder, such as larkspur, to thrive, and then mark it. Ruthlessly pull out or hoe reseeding larkspur in other areas. If you're going for a more groomed look, this method displays reseeders to their best advantage.

■ Thin as Needed

Many reseeders self-sow thickly and crowd out other plants. When the reseeding plants are a few inches high, thin them so there is at least a few inches between each. Refer to the Flower Encyclopedia beginning on page 156 for ideal spacing.

Conversely, dig up small (under 1 inch) reseeded plants and transplant them elsewhere for better effect.

■ Deadhead or Cut Back

Reseeders can't reseed if you don't let the flowers ripen into seeds. Keeping spent flowers pinched or trimmed off reduces reseeding considerably. Conversely, let the flower heads dry if you want to encourage reseeding. When removing or cutting back dead plant material, scatter the seeds.

■ Compost with Caution

Don't throw old flower heads on the compost pile unless you're making hot compost, which kills seeds. Cold compost will spread the reseeders, creating weed headaches later.

■ Exercise Tough Love

If a reseeder becomes a weed problem, get tough and pull it out. Keep pulling out new shoots to eradicate it from your garden.

Self-Sowing Plants

The following flowers reseed prolifically, depending on the cultivar and the climate:

Name	Zones	Page
Bachelor's button *Centaurea cyanus*	3–10	171
Bee balm *Monarda didyma*	4–8	200
Blue flax *Linum perenne*	4–9	195
California poppy *Eschscholzia californica*	2–11	181
Coreopsis, some types *Coreopsis* spp.	3–9	176
Cosmos *Cosmos* spp.	2–11	176
Dahlberg daisy *Thymophylla tenuiloba*	2–11	213
Flowering tobacco *Nicotiana* spp.	2–11	201
Hollyhock *Alcea rosea*	3–11	160
Larkspur *Consolida ambigua*	2–11	175
Love-in-a-mist *Nigella damascena*	2–11	202
Marigolds, some types *Tagetes* spp.	2–11	212
Nasturtium *Tropaeolum majus*	2–11	214
Poppies, annual types *Papaver* spp.	2–11	203
Purple coneflower *Echinacea purpurea*	3–9	180
Spider flower *Cleome hassleriana*	2–11	174
Sunflower, annual *Helianthus annuus*	2–11	187
Sweet alyssum *Lobularia maritima*	2–11	196
Violas, some types *Viola* spp.	2–11	215

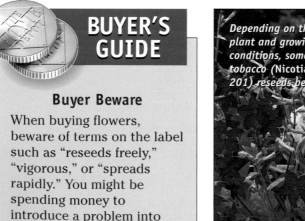

BUYER'S GUIDE

Buyer Beware

When buying flowers, beware of terms on the label such as "reseeds freely," "vigorous," or "spreads rapidly." You might be spending money to introduce a problem into your garden.

Depending on the type of plant and growing conditions, some flowering tobacco (Nicotiana, page 201) reseeds beautifully.

Maintenance

All in the Family

Don't expect reseeded plants to look exactly like their parents. Colors, disease resistance, and overall vigor might be quite different.

Low-growing, colorful nasturtiums (Tropaeolum majus, page 214) are wonderful along gravel and other paths.

This exuberant flower garden is filled with Queen Anne's lace and various types of colorful annual poppies (Papaver spp., page 203), many of which will reseed.

Maintenance

Diseases and Pests:

Keeping Your Garden Healthy

A healthy garden is not only possible, but fairly easy as long as you follow some basic principles.

■ Choose Disease-Resistant Cultivars

Read labels and plant descriptions carefully for mentions of disease resistance. These flowers have been bred to fight off diseases that normally would fell their less tough counterparts. For example, several cultivars of garden phlox have minimal problems with powdery mildew and several roses are resistant to black spot.

■ Avoid Monocultures

Monocultures—extensive plantings of the same thing can be too much of a good thing. A garden planted only with roses is a huge flashing neon sign welcoming Japanese beetles, aphids, and black spot pathogens. However, if you break up the rose plantings with perennials, annuals, and flowering shrubs, it's tougher for diseases and pests to move from plant to plant.

■ Practice Good Gardening Practices

Keep plants weeded and watered and give them the soil and sun they prefer. They'll have far fewer disease problems. Wilted or otherwise stressed plants become a magnet for pests and are vulnerable to diseases.

■ Provide Good Circulation

This prevents fungal and other diseases from getting a foothold. Space plants according to label directions and avoid placing plants up against walls or fences.

■ Mulch

Mulch prevents soil-borne disease pathogens from splashing onto stems and leaves. Just keep mulch to 1 to 3 inches.

■ Water the Soil, Not the Plants

Whenever possible, water the soil rather than the plant, keeping leaves and stems dry and preventing fungal disease.

■ Water in the Early Morning

If you have to water from overhead, do it as early in the morning as possible. The sun dries plants quickly.

What to Do When Diseases and Pests Strike

When you notice that a flower is ailing, there are some quick, inexpensive, and earth-friendly things to do:

• **Look it up.** Check garden books and ask your garden center staff to figure out what the problem is. (Take a portion of the diseased plant in with you to the garden center for staff to look at.) You may be able to take simple, specific measures to stop the problem.

• **Spray it with water.** A good, hard spray of water often will knock off even tiny insects, reducing their population and giving the plant a chance to recover. Keep an eye on the plant and repeat spray every day for several days.

• **Get rid of it.** Trim off diseased plant parts to prevent spread. (Sterilize tools with rubbing alcohol between plants.) If the entire top of the plant is diseased and it's a perennial, cut it back to a few inches above the soil. If it's an annual, consider pulling it out to prevent the spread of the disease. (Don't put these plants in the compost heap unless you make hot compost—see page 120—or you'll further spread the disease with the compost.)

A hard spray of water can slow down many pest problems.

Trimming off diseased plant parts prevents further spreading of the problem.

Aphids

Symptoms: Minute pale yellow, pink, or black insects appear on soft stems, new leaves, and flowers. Leaves curl and new growth is stunted. Sometimes a sticky honeydew and a sooty mold are produced. Ants may be crawling on the honeydew.

Recommended controls: Organic: Give plants a hard spray of water once a day every 10 or more days. Chemical: Use insecticidal soap or pyrethrin. For roses and shrubs, if the problem is chronic from year to year, use dormant oil spray in early spring to control overwintering eggs.

Grasshoppers

Symptoms: Large, chewed holes in leaves; many grasshoppers present. Worst in dry weather and arid regions.

Recommended controls: Use acephate, spraying as soon as you see grasshoppers. Grasshoppers usually move into gardens from fields or weedy areas. The first few act as scouts and alert the rest about the available food in your garden.

Japanese beetles

Symptoms: Shiny blue-green beetles present; holes in leaves and flowers, especially roses.

Recommended controls: Organic: Pick off beetles in early morning and drown in water. Use pheromone traps. Apply milky spore disease (available at some garden centers) to lawn to control grubs, which are Japanese beetle larvae. Spray plants with rotenone.

Mealybugs

Symptoms: Clusters of insects create cottonlike, white masses on stems and leaf axils. Can slow growth and kill plant parts. A honeydew substance attracts mold.

Recommended controls: Organic: Hose off mild infestations. For more serious problems, apply insecticidal soap. Parasitic wasps provide some control. Horticultural oil can be used on some plants.

Nematodes

Symptoms: Invisible to the naked eye, these wormlike creatures live in the soil and attack plants, causing stunting of roots (as shown at left), swollen roots, yellowing, dead plant parts, reduced growth, and fewer flowers.

Recommended controls: Chemical: Test for nematodes if you have a chronic problems year after year with plants that wilt, yellow, and slowly die, and you've eliminated all other possibilities. Contact your county extension service which can make recommendations about chemical control measures for nematodes.

Scales

Symptoms: Hard, roundish insects adhere to stems and leaf undersides. Clustered together, they create the appearance of scales.

Recommended controls: Organic: If a chronic problem, spray with dormant oil in very early spring. Chemical: Use a systemic insecticide, following package directions.

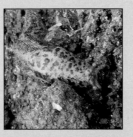

Slugs and snails

Symptoms: Chewed leaves, particularly those close to or touching the ground, and slime trails visible. Most active in shady or cool, moist areas or in cool, moist climates.

Recommended controls: Organic: Place short pieces of board or flat rocks around garden, where slugs and snails will take refuge during the day. Each morning, collect the pieces or rocks along with any clinging slugs or snails and dunk them into a pail of soapy water.

Pests continued on page 130

Maintenance

Edge garden beds with copper flashing to disrupt slug paths. Sprinkle wood ash heavily on soil of plants most bothered. Chemical: If problem is severe, use slug bait, following package directions.

Spider Mites
Symptoms: Tiny spiders, often forming fine webs on plant and sucking its juices, causing speckled, pale foliage. Worst during hot, dry weather.
Recommended controls: Organic: Keep plants well-watered. Hose off undersides of infested plants. If a chronic problem on shrubs each year, spray in early spring with dormant oil. Chemical: Choose a spray that specifies control of spider mites on the type of plant you want to spray.

Thrips
Symptoms: Tiny, darting black insects cause streaks and spots on flowers and young leaves. Common in roses, especially pale-colored ones.
Recommended controls: Organic: Apply insecticidal soap or pyrethrin. Chemical: Spray with a chemical specifying thrip control. If problem is chronic each year, use a systemic insecticide starting in spring.

Whitefly
Symptoms: Tiny white insects fly around when plant is brushed or moved.
Recommended controls: Organic: Apply horticultural oil, insectidal soap, rotenone, or pyrethrin. Repeat applications as label directs.

Bacterial wilt
Symptoms: Plants repeatedly wilt and recover, but finally wilt permanently and leaves turn yellow and brown. Can kill plants. Infected stems ooze slime if cut. Especially common in mums, delphiniums, nasturtiums, petunias, dahlias, and zinnias.
Recommended controls: Remove and destroy infected plants so the bacteria does not spread. Dip all tools used on infected plants in rubbing alcohol. Wash hands well with soap and water after handling the plants to prevent the spread to other plants.

Black spot
Symptoms: A fungal disease that causes tiny black spots on leaves. Yellow and orange rings usually develop around the dark spots. Leaves yellow and drop. Common on roses. Unusual in arid West where dry conditions inhibit fungal growth.
Recommended controls: Organic: Water in early morning and avoid overhead watering. Mulch to prevent mud splashing onto plants. Give plants as much sun as practical. Chemical: Spray with a fungicide, following timing and repeat spray directions.

Blight
Symptoms: Various fungal diseases of flowers, leaves, or stems. Results in sudden wilting and browning. Worst in humid, moist weather.
Recommended controls: Organic: Water in early morning and avoid overhead watering. Mulch to prevent mud splashing onto plants. Give plants as much sun as practical. Chemical: Spray with a fungicide, following timing and repeat spray directions.

Maintenance

Fusarium wilt
Symptoms: Yellowing, stunted plants wilt and die. If cut open, infected stems have dark streaks.
Recommended controls: Organic: Avoid planting the same plants in the same place each year. Mulch well to prevent mud splashing onto plants. Give plants as much sun as practical. Chemical: No available chemical treats fusarium wilt.

Gray mold (Botrytis blight)
Symptoms: Yellow or orange spots turn into masses of fuzzy gray mold which then turns into a slimy rot. Happens during damp weather or in moist climates.
Recommended controls: Organic: Never plant moldy plants or bulbs. Space plants as recommended on label to ensure good circulation. Remove fading flowers (deadhead) promptly. Give plants as much sun as practical. Chemical: In severe cases, apply an organic or chemical fungicide as package directs.

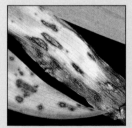

Leaf spot
Symptoms: Spots on leaves look water soaked or are brick red with yellow rings and black spots. Common during rainy or humid weather.
Recommended controls: Organic: Rotate plantings yearly. Mulch well to avoid splashing water or mud on plants. Space plants to ensure good circulation. Avoid handling wet plants, or disease may spread. Provide adequate sun. Chemical: In severe cases, apply sprays specifying leaf spot control.

Powdery mildew
Symptoms: Powdery white or gray areas show up on leaf surface. Leaves shrivel, dry, and drop.
Recommended controls: Organic: Mulch well to avoid splashing water or mud onto plants. Space plants as recommended on label to ensure good circulation. Give plants as much sun as practical. Chemical: Can also use a commercial fungicide.

Rust
Symptoms: Bright red, orange, or yellow lesions occur on undersides and tops of leaves and stems. Weakens and stunts plants in severe cases.
Recommended controls: Organic: Avoid overhead watering. Mulch well to avoid splashing water or mud on plants. Space plants as recommended on label to ensure good circulation. Give plants as much sun as practical. Avoid handling wet plants, or disease may spread. Chemical: In severe cases, spray with a product specifying rust control.

Verticillium wilt
Symptoms: Lower leaves turn pale green, then yellow, then brown and drop. Branches wilt. In severe cases, plants die. Cut into an infected branch to check for dark streaks.
Recommended controls: Organic: Destroy infected plants to prevent spread of disease. Trim off infected branches of shrubs or trees. Chemical: No chemical control available.

Work Smarter!

Using Disease and Pest Controls Wisely

Pest controls in the forms of sprays and powders are useful in your garden, but they're not a cure-all. Even organic controls can kill some beneficial insects, including butterflies, ladybugs, bees, praying mantises, and lacewings. Remember, more is not better—follow package directions carefully and use all controls in moderation.

Keeping Out Animals

Gardening means working with nature. And whether we want it or not, nature also provides some critters that like to munch, knock down, or burrow in our gardens. The good news is that, to some degree, you can minimize the damage.

■ Deer

Often called rats with antlers, deer can wipe out hundreds of dollars of plants in a single night.

Unfortunately, the only means to keep deer away is to fence them out. Even the best repellents reduce deer feeding by just half, according to research. Deer fencing is not cheap. Because deer are such high jumpers, the fencing needs to be at least 8 feet high, or as high as 12 feet in areas with large deer populations.

Electric fence is the most cost-effective option for larger properties. It needs to be about 5 feet high with the first wire 10 inches from the ground and four spaced wires about 12 inches apart.

Though deer can jump very high, their jumps aren't long. Take advantage of this with two 4-foot-high wire mesh fences spaced about 4 feet apart. Deer don't like tight spaces, so they'll avoid crossing the fence.

If you decide to use repellents, choose commercial formulations that repel deer with their putrid scents. Home remedies such as bars of soap, human hair, and hot-pepper sprays are the least effective. All repellents need to be reapplied or replenished every 10 days or so.

Another strategy is to plant flowers that deer do not like. Good choices include roses, tulips, lilies, azaleas, daylilies, rhododendrons, and hostas (see chart on page 133).

■ Moles, Voles, Mice, and Other Burrowing Animals

It's nearly impossible to prevent moles, mice, voles (meadow mice), and other burrowing animals from pestering your garden. You can slow them down with a wire barrier.

For moles, voles, and mice, install hardware cloth 2 feet deep around garden beds and lawns. For gophers, the hardware cloth will have to extend above ground by 2 feet for a total height of 4 feet.

Erect these barriers when there is no active burrowing in the bed, or you'll just be sealing in the pests.

Also, remove piles of brush

Fencing is the single most effective way to keep out unwanted wildlife.

and debris where these animals might nest. And never mulch more than 2 or 3 inches thick.

To protect bulbs, add gravel to the planting hole. It provides drainage for the bulbs and is believed to discourage the moles. You can also make wire cages from hardware cloth to bury underground and plant bulbs and other plants in. The cage should be topless and buried so the sides just barely protrude from the ground.

■ Squirrels
Squirrels love burrowing and digging, especially around newly planted bulbs.

Protect bulbs by planting them in groups, laying a piece of chicken wire over the top of the bulbs, then covering it. The flowers will grow through the wire and it will be difficult for the squirrels to get to them.

If squirrels are digging in other areas, especially around new plantings, lay a piece of chicken wire over the top of these, crumpling the sides slightly to make a rough cage. Remove when the plants become established and the loose soil has firmed, discouraging squirrels from digging.

■ Rabbits
The best way to keep out rabbits is to fence them out. Use wire mesh with mesh of less than 1 inch. The fence must be 2 feet high and buried 3 inches beneath the soil to prevent burrowing.

Rabbits love tender young annuals. Protect small plantings by making a chicken-wire cage several inches high and tucking it over the young plants, burying the edges 3 inches beneath the soil. When the plants are several inches high and less desirable to rabbits, remove the wire.

Wildlife-Resistant Plants

Note: No plant is immune to wildlife, but some are far less attractive to animals than others.

Name	Zones	Page
Deer-Resistant Plants		
Ageratum	2–11	160
Ageratum houstonianum		
Astilbe	3–8	165
Astilbe spp.		
Azure Monkshood	3–7	159
Aconitum carmichaelii		
Columbine	3–10	162
Aguilegia spp.		
Coreopsis	3–9	176
Coreopsis spp.		
Forsythia	4–8	230
Forsythia spp.		
Foxglove	4–9	179
Digitalis purpurea		
Grape hyacinth	3–8	223
Muscari spp.		
Irises, all types	3–10	191
Iris spp.		
Lamb's-ears	4–8	212
Stachys byzantina		
Lilac	2–8	235
Syringa spp.		
Mockorange	4–8	233
Philadelphus spp.		
Narcissus/daffodil	3–11	223
Narcissus spp.		
Peony	2–8	202
Paeonia spp.		
Purple coneflower	3–9	180
Echinacea purpurea		
Smokebush	5–8	229
Cotinus coggygria		
Spirea	3–9	234
Spiraea spp.		
Wax begonia	2–11	166
Begonia × semperflorens-cultorum		
Wisteria	5–9	241
Wisteria spp.		
Yarrow	3–9	159
Achillea spp.		
Rabbit-Resistant Plants		
Ageratum	2–11	160
Ageratum houstonianum		
Amethyst flower	2–11	168
Browallia		
Astilbe	3–8	165
Astilbe spp.		
Bee balm	4–8	200
Monarda didyma		
Blanket flower	2–11	184
Gaillardia spp.		
Bleeding heart	2–9	179
Dicentra spp.		
Butterfly bush	5–10	227
Buddleia spp.		
Candytuft	3–10	190
Iberis spp.		
Cardinal flower	2–9	196
Lobelia spp.		
Clematis	4–9	238
Clematis spp.		
Columbine	3–10	162
Aguilegia spp.		

Name	Zones	Page
Coreopsis	3–9	176
Coreopsis spp.		
Creeping phlox	2–8	206
Phlox stolonifera		
Daylily	3–10	189
Hemerocallis spp.		
Four-o-clock	2–11	199
Mirabilis jalapa		
Foxglove	4–9	179
Digitalis purpurea		
Fumewort	4–8	176
Corydalis spp.		
Geranium	2–11	203
Pelargonium spp.		
Globe thistle	3–8	180
Echinops spp.		
Goatsbeard	3–7	164
Aruncus dioicus		
Hardy geranium	4–8	185
Geranium spp.		
Hollyhock	3–11	160
Alcea rosea		
Hyacinth	3–11	222
Hyacinthus orientalis		
Hydrangea	4–9	231
Hydrangea spp.		
Lady's mantle	3–8	161
Alchemilla spp.		
Lavender	5–10	192
Lavandula spp.		
Lily-of-the-valley	3–7	175
Convallaria majalis		
Narcissus/daffodil	3–11	223
Narcissus spp.		
Peony	2–8	202
Paeonia spp.		
Perennial mum	4–9	173
Chrysanthemum spp.		
Perennial blue salvia	4–8	210
Salvia × superba		
Potentilla	2–7	233
Potentilla		
Queen-of-the-prairie	3–8	183
Filipendula rubra		
Red-hot poker	5–9	191
Kniphofia uvaria		
Russian sage	5–7	204
Perovskia atriplicifolia		
Sedum	3–11	211
Sedum spp.		
Shasta daisy	4–9	193
Leucanthemum × superbum		
Siberian iris	3–10	191
Iris sibirica		
Spiny bear's breeches	5–10	159
Acanthus spinosus		
Trumpet vine	4–9	237
Campsis radicans		
Veronica	3–8	214
Veronica spp.		
Vinca, periwinkle	2–11	170
Catharanthus roseus		
Virginia bluebells	3–8	199
Mertensia virginica		
Wax begonia	2–11	166
Begonia × semperflorens-cultorum		

Dividing Perennials

Dividing perennials keeps them healthy and vigorous; it also gives you more plants to put around your garden or to share with friends and family.

Dividing plants is not difficult. Most gardeners fear giving their plants what seems to be harsh treatment, but perennials are tough and will survive with good aftercare.

If possible, divide plants on a cool, overcast day on which rain is forecast. Gentle, moist weather helps prevent heat stress on the tender new divisions.

Different plants require slightly different approaches, but basically, you dig the plant, break it into sections, and replant.

Plants with shallow, fibrous roots are easy to pull apart with your hands. Others, such as Siberian irises and daylilies, have tough roots that need to be sliced into sections with a spade or even hacked into

pieces with a hand ax. Plants with very large root sections or spreading root sections such as peonies can be multiplied by slicing off a section of the roots rather than digging up the whole plant.

Depending on the size of the plant, you'll get anywhere from two or three new plants to a dozen. The new divisions can then be planted. Cut the foliage back by two-thirds or to just a few inches high. Prepare the soil where any of the divisions will be planted, working in ample compost or other organic matter (see page 63).

Water the divisions well and keep them well watered for at least the next four weeks. Apply a 2-inch layer of mulch around the plants to protect them from extremes of heat and cold and to conserve moisture.

Hostas (Hosta spp., page 190) are one of those wonderful plants that don't demand regular division, but if you want, you can divide them every few years for more plants.

CLOSER LOOK

Signs a Perennial Needs Dividing

Most perennials need dividing every three to four years. These clues indicate it's time:
• In the center of the crown at the base of the plant, there's no new growth and the plant may be forming a ring.
• Flowering is reduced.
• The plant has been doing well for a year or two but is now floppy when it flowers.
• Some plants need dividing far more often than others. Peonies are happy with no division for 10 years or more while others, such as sedum 'Autumn Joy' need dividing as often as every other year. As a rule, the faster the plant grows, the more often it needs dividing.

When to Divide?

• Divide spring-blooming plants immediately after flowering.
• Divide summer- and fall-blooming plants in early spring when they have 2 to 4 inches of top growth.
• In the South and Southwest, divide all but fall bloomers in the fall. They love the cooler, wetter weather of autumn.
• Give your perennials at least four weeks to establish themselves before either 90°F (32°C) or above or freezing temperatures arrive.

German bearded irises (Iris, page 191) grow from rhizomes that divide easily.

Dividing Perennials

Flowers with fibrous roots.
These shallow, often loosely knotted roots can be dug up with a spade. They often will break apart as they're dug, or they can easily be broken apart with your hands. If not, a little prod with a trowel or a spade usually will do the trick.

Flowers with large root balls.
Dig up the entire root. If the roots won't break apart with a spade, use a small hand ax to cut them apart. This works best if you lay the root ball on its side and cut from the sides inward, rather than from the top downward.

Flowers with tough roots.
If a plant's root ball is large but fairly easy to cut through, divide it by slicing off portions of the plant from its outside edges rather than digging up the entire plant.

Flowers with Fibrous Roots

Name	Zones	Page	Name	Zones	Page
Bee balm *Monarda didyma*	4–8	200	Moss phlox *Phlox subulata*	2–9	206
Bellflower *Campanula* spp.	3–8	170	Penstemon *Penstemon* spp.	3–9	204
Blanket flower *Gaillardia* spp.	2–11	184	Perennial lobelia *Lobelia* spp.	2–9	196
Candytuft *Iberis* spp.	3–10	190	Perennial blue salvia *Salvia* × *superba*	4–8	210
Catmint *Nepeta* spp.	4–9	201	Perennial sunflower *Helianthus* spp.	4–9	187
Coral bell *Heuchera*	3–8	189	Periwinkle, myrtle *Vinca minor*	4–7	241
Coreopsis *Coreopsis* spp.	3–9	176	Purple coneflower *Echinacea purpurea*	3–9	180
Creeping phlox *Phlox stolonifera*	2–8	206	Russian sage *Perovskia atriplicifolia*	5–7	204
Creeping thyme *Thymus* spp.	5–9	240	Shasta daisy *Leucanthemum* × *superbum*	4–9	193
Evening primrose *Oenothera* spp.	3–8	202	Snow-in-summer *Cerastium tomentosum*	2–9	172
Hardy geranium *Geranium* spp.	4–8	185	Statice *Limonium* spp.	2–11	194
Hosta *Hosta* spp.	3–9	190	Virginia bluebells *Mertensia virginica*	3–8	199
Lamb's-ears *Stachys byzantina*	4–8	212	Yarrow *Achillea* spp.	3–9	159

Plants with Large, Tough Root Balls

Name	Zones	Page
Daylily *Hemerocallis* spp.	3–10	189
Peony *Paeonia* spp.	2–8	202
Siberian iris *Iris sibirica*	3–9	191
Many ornamental grasses		

Spread the Joy

When dividing plants be sure to share one or two with friends or neighbors. It's a great way for them to fill their garden with memories of fellow gardeners.

Digging and Storing Summer Bulbs

In cold-winter regions, most summer-blooming bulbs must be dug up and stored indoors if you want to keep them year after year. (See the chart on the opposite page.) Of course, you can always replant fresh bulbs each year, but it's far less expensive to save them.

Tender (that is, not winter hardy) bulbs should be dug in the fall after frost has nipped the leaves (see page 13 for average first frost dates). Dig before the leaves die back completely so that you can find the bulbs.

Dig bulbs with a garden fork or spade, taking care not to damage any bulbs. Brush off the soil and allow the bulbs to dry. Then store them indoors.

Storing bulbs requires care. Even experienced gardeners lose a few bulbs each year when they rot or shrivel. Minimize your losses by following the few basic steps on this page.

STUFF YOU'LL NEED

✔ Spade or spading fork
✔ Soft brush
✔ Hand-pruning shears
✔ Newspapers
✔ Cardboard boxes
✔ Sawdust or packing material

What to Expect
You won't get 100 percent success during storage. Expect to lose at least a few summer-blooming bulbs each year.

1 **Dig bulbs after frost has blackened the foliage.** Dig carefully to avoid injuring the bulbs. Cut off the top part of the foliage for easier handling.

2 **Cut off all leaves and stems.** Shake off the soil, using a soft brush if necessary.

3 **Spread bulbs on newspapers to dry.** Keep careful track of the types of the bulbs, and let them dry for several days in a sheltered, breezy spot such as a covered porch or garage. (The newspapers keep your floors cleaner and add a little circulation underneath the bulbs.)

4 **Store bulbs in a cardboard box or paper bag.** Don't use plastic because it promotes mold. Fill the box or bag with slightly damp sawdust or other packing material and label. Store in a cool to moderate 35 to 75°F (7 to 23°C) room. Check every month or so to remove any shriveled, moldy bulbs.

Maintenance

Spring-Blooming Bulbs vs. Summer-Blooming Bulbs

Some bulbs bloom in the spring and are hardy (can survive the winter). They include tulips, daffodils, hyacinths, and crocuses. Others bloom in the summer and only a few of these are hardy. The notable exception is Asiatic, Oriental, and many other lilies, which bloom in the summer, yet also last through the winter and even multiply over the years.

• **Experiment with storage methods.** Some gardeners prefer wooden boxes, cardboard boxes, or paper bags (the container needs to breathe, so avoid plastic). Others prefer to store the bulbs in slightly damp sawdust, or sphagnum peat moss.

• **Store bulbs at the right temperature.** Bulbs such as tuberous begonias, dahlias, cannas, and gladiolas like cool temperatures, 35 to 55°F (2 to 13°C). Others, such as tuberoses and caladiums, like warmer conditions, 60 to 75°F (16 to 24°C). Cool spots include unheated garages, attics, and basements or crawl spaces. Warm spots include closets, underneath beds, or heated basements and attics. Place a thermometer in the spot so that you can check the temperature throughout storage to be sure.

• **Check on bulbs at least once a month.** Check temperature and move the bulbs if it is too warm or too cool. Examine bulbs for rot or softness and throw out bad bulbs. Moisten the packing material as needed to keep slightly moist.

Summer-Blooming Bulbs to Dig

Bulb	Dig and Store in These Zones	Page	Bulb	Dig and Store in These Zones	Page
Agapanthus *Agapanthus*	6 and colder	217	Dahlia *Dahlia*	7 and colder	220
Caladium *Caladium bicolor*	9 and colder	218	Freesia *Freesia* spp.	8 and colder	220
Calla lily *Zantedeschia aethiopica*	7 and colder	225	Gladiolus *Gladiolus* hybrids	6 and colder	221
Canna *Canna* hybrids	6 and colder	218	Peacock orchid *Gladiolus callinathus*	6 and colder	222
Crocosmia *Crocosmia × crocosmiiflora*	5 and colder	219	Ranunculus *Ranunculus asiaticus*	7 and colder	224

In colder climates most summer-blooming bulbs such as Gladiolus (Gladiolus hybrids, page 221) need to be dug and stored.

Maintenance

Saving Time

You can create a beautiful garden if you have unlimited time. But in truth, no one has unlimited time. Those who tend wonderful gardens do so with smart time management. Here's how:

• **Research your plant and landscape decisions.** Take a few minutes to read up on your next garden project. You'll make better choices that will save you from redoing the project later.

• **Block out time for gardening.** Some gardeners like to do a 10-minute weed and deadhead session before work each morning, for example. Others make Saturday mornings their time for puttering in the garden.

• **Get organized.** Devote a corner of the garage or a shed to gardening supplies and keep them in good working order. You'll save hours of wandering around, trying to find the right tool. In the garden, put all the smaller tools and supplies you need often into one basket or organizer so it's always handy.

• **Look at your garden every day.** Take just a minute or two every day to walk through your yard. Not only is it pleasant, it will give you a jump on small problems before they become big ones.

• **Keep a garden journal or notebook.** Centralize all those magazine articles, seed packets, and notes to yourself in one location.

• **Plant in large groups.** As a rule, planting a large group of the same type of flowers is more efficient. You spend the same amount of time preparing the site and getting out tools and supplies. Groupings tend to make for more efficient watering, weeding, and pruning.

• **Group plants according to their needs.** Put all acid-loving plants, for example, in the same area so you can acidify the soil more efficiently. Put all moisture-loving plants in another area so you can water more efficiently.

• **Mulch!** Mulching saves water, suppresses weed, and prevents many soil-borne diseases.

• **Avoid exotics.** Go for low-maintenance plants that don't require staking, spraying, excessive feeding, protection, or digging up each fall.

• **Experiment with flowering shrubs.** Excellent timesavers, they require little more than a bit of pruning once a year, if at all, and yet give you abundant flowers and scent.

Keep a Home and Garden Center List

Right next to your grocery list, keep a list of what you need at the home and garden center. That way, you'll always have on hand exactly what you need to get the job done quickly.

Organizing your smaller garden supplies into a handy caddy saves time.

Maintenance

Saving Money

Money alone does not a good garden make. But it helps. Stretch your garden dollar with smart shopping and frugal landscaping. Here's how:

• **Visit your home and garden center often.** Garden centers offer different plants and supplies throughout the year. If you stop by often, you'll get the best stuff at the best price at the best time.

• **Buy just one.** If you like an expensive perennial, buy one and grow it for two to three years; then divide it (see page 135). If the perennial is very large, you can often take it home and divide it into three or four plants that will reach the same mature size.

• **Know your light.** This is fundamental to making the right plant choices and will prevent the loss of a lot of expensive plants. (See page 74.)

• **Learn to propagate your own plants.** Starting plants from seed (page 79) or from cuttings is not hard and can save you hundreds of dollars, even if you have to invest in a little start-up equipment such as a good grow light.

Ask your garden center staff questions. They'll give you sound advice, and it won't cost you a penny!

BUYER'S GUIDE

Buy Small

Smaller plants, especially perennials, trees, and shrubs, cost less than their larger counterparts, but often grow rapidly.

In fact, in studies, smaller plants caught up to larger plants within a year or two.

• **Share plants.** Give your friends, family, and neighbors divisions of your favorite plants. They're likely to return the favor.

• **Split costs.** Get together with your sister-in-law and rent a leaf shredder for the day and both use it, sharing the cost. Or tell your neighbors you'll buy a weed trimmer and they can use it whenever they want if they buy a power hedge trimmer and you can use it whenever you want.

• **Grow plants that do double duty.** A cherry tree, for example, has gorgeous flowers in the spring and delicious fruit in the summer. A hedge of lilacs creates privacy and provides an armload of flowers. You get twice the pleasure for the same amount of work.

Homer's Hindsight

Invest In Your Soil

I'd heard that old saying about putting a $5 plant into a $15 hole, but got in a hurry when I was planting my perennial bed and didn't improve the soil like they say on page 62. Boy, am I sorry. A year later, my plants are struggling—some have died—and it's hard to go back and improve the soil.

Chapter 5
Specialized Flower Gardening

E ach garden is unique, with conditions of light, soil, moisture, heat, cold, and wind that make it like no other garden. There can even be different microclimates within a single garden.

This chapter explores some of the more specialized aspects of flower gardening. Shade gardening, for instance, is a special challenge to many gardeners. You will learn about rock gardens, wildflower gardens, woodland gardens, and cutting gardens as well as the pleasures of forcing bulbs for winter bloom and arranging flowers for indoors.

The distinctive shape of ornamental onions (Allium spp., page 217) make them a candidate for inclusion in a cutting garden.

Shade Gardens

The basic outlines of a shade garden can be defined by existing trees, plants, and structures.

■ Shade Garden Design

Don't fight the site or the light. Work with your climate and site by choosing plants that will thrive in existing conditions. Trees help create a naturalistic woodland style with winding paths and benches. Loose-growing shrubs blend easily into the casual landscape.

Take advantage of vertical spaces (walls or buildings) by incorporating climbing vines, window boxes and latticework.

■ Understanding Shade

All shade is not created equal. Accurate determinations of sun and shade levels only come by observations over time. Noting changing levels of light and shade over the course of several seasons will tell you what's happening in your garden. Most gardeners overestimate how much sun they are actually getting. (See page 74 for more information.)

Keep in mind the following:
• Large, light areas such as gravel driveways or concrete sidewalks reflect light and increase exposure to the sun.
• The north side of a house is nearly always in part shade.
• Some trees create dense shade, while others allow sunlight to filter through.
• In the South and the Southwest, plants thrive with more shade than they do in other parts of the country because the sun is more intense. So the wax begonias that need light shade in Maine do fine in deeper shade in Alabama.

■ Shade Garden Issues

• Roots of some trees, such as, silver maple and pine rob surrounding plants of moisture. Choose plants that thrive in dry shade (see chart).
• Plant around shallow roots. If you have to cut tree roots, get advice on how much you can remove without damaging the tree.
• The weight of raised beds any higher than a few inches around the base of a tree can damage it.
• In areas with oaks or walnut trees, the soil may be acidic. Choose plants that thrive in acid soils and shade, such as azaleas, hollies, hydrangeas, and rhododendrons.
• You can create more sun by cutting off lower limbs, allowing more light.

Flowers for Shade

KEY

☀ partial shade	💧 wet conditions
● full shade	∬∬ dry conditions

Name	Requirements	Page
Annuals/Perennials		
Agapanthus *Agapanthus*	☀ ● ∬∬	217
Amethyst flower *Browallia*	☀ 💧	168
Astilbe *Astilbe* spp.	☀ ∬∬ 💧	165
Azure monkshood *Aconitum carmichaelii*	☀	159
Bee balm *Monarda didyma*	☀ ∬∬	200
Bleeding heart *Dicentra* spp.	☀ ●	179
Blue lilyturf *Liriope muscari*	☀ ● ∬∬	195

Name	Requirements	Page
Bugbane *Cimicifuga*	☀ 💧	174
Cardinal flower *Lobelia* spp.	☀ 💧	196
Chinese forget-me-not *Cynoglossum amabile*	☀	177
Christmas rose *Helleborus* spp.	☀ ●	188
Columbine *Aquilegia* spp.	☀ ∬∬	162
Common foxglove perennial and biennial *Digitalis purpurea*	☀ ∬∬	179
Coral bell *Heuchera*	☀ ∬∬	189
Creeping phlox *Phlox stolonifera*	☀ ●	206
Cupflower *Nierembergia*	☀	201
Daylily *Hemerocallis* spp.	☀ ● ∬∬	189
Flowering tobacco *Nicotiana* spp.	☀	201
Forget-me-not *Myosotis sylvatica*	☀ 💧	200
Fuchsia *Fuchsia* spp.	☀	183

Annuals/Perennials (cont.)

Name	Requirements	Page
Fumewort — *Corydalis* spp.	☼ ● 💧	176
Garden phlox — *Phlox* spp.	☼	206
Goatsbeard — *Aruncus dioicus*	☼ ● 💧	164
Hardy geranium — *Geranium* spp.	☼ 〰	185
Hosta — *Hosta* spp.	☼ ●	190
Impatiens — *Impatiens* spp.	☼ ●	190
Lady's-mantle — *Alchemilla* spp.	☼ 〰	161
Lenten rose — *Helleborus* spp.	☼ ● 〰	188
Leopard plant — *Ligularia* spp.	☼	194
Lungwort — *Pulmonaria* spp.	☼ 〰	208
Monkey flower — *Mimulus hybridus*	☼ ● 〰	199
Obedient plant — *Physostegia virginiana*	☼	207
Pink turtlehead — *Chelone lyonii*	☼ 💧	173
Primrose — *Primula* spp.	☼	208
Queen-of-the-prairie — *Filipendula rubra*	☼	183
Salvia, annual red — *Salvia splendens*	☼	209
Sedum — *Sedum* spp.	☼	211
Sweet woodruff — *Galium odoratum*	☼ ● 〰	184
Vinca — *Catharanthus roseus*	☼ 〰	170
Violets — *Viola* spp.	☼ 〰	215
Virginia bluebells — *Mertensia virginica*	☼ ●	199
Wax begonia — *Begonia* × *semperflorens-cultorum*	☼ ●	166
Wishbone flower — *Torenia fournieri*	☼	213

Bulbs

Name	Requirements	Page
Caladium — *Caladium bicolor*	☼ ●	218
Crocus — *Crocus* spp.	☼ 〰	219
Daffodil — *Narcissus* spp.	☼ 〰	223
Freesia — *Freesia* spp.	☼ 〰	220
Hardy cyclamen — *Cyclamen hederifolium*	☼	220
Snowdrop — *Galanthus nivalis*	☼	221
Tuberous begonias — *Begonia tuberhybrida*	☼	218
Trillium — *Trillium* spp.	☼ 〰	224
Windflower — *Anemone* spp.	☼	217

Vines and Groundcovers

Name	Requirements	Page
Bittersweet — *Celastrus scandens*	☼	237
Black-eyed Susan vine — *Thunbergia alata*	☼	240
Carolina jasmine — *Gelsemium sempervirens*	☼	238
Clematis — *Clematis* spp.	☼	238
Creeping thyme — *Thymus* spp.	☼ 〰	240
Goldenstar — *Chrysogonum virginianum*	☼ ●	173
Lily-of-the-valley — *Convallaria majalis*	☼ ● 〰	175
Mandevilla — *Mandevilla* spp.	☼	240
Periwinkle — *Vinca minor*	☼ ● 〰	241
Star jasmine — *Trachelospermum* spp.	☼	241
Trumpet vine — *Campsis radicans*	☼ 💧	237

Shrubs

Name	Requirements	Page
Azalea — *Rhododendron* spp.	☼ ● 💧	233
Butterfly bush — *Buddleia* spp.	☼	227
Camellia — *Camellia* spp.	☼ 💧	228
Daphne — *Daphne* spp.	☼	229
Gardenia — *Gardenia augusta*	☼ 💧	230
Hibiscus — *Hibiscus* spp.	☼ 💧	231
Hydrangea — *Hydrangea* spp.	☼ 💧	231
Japanese rose — *Kerria japonica*	☼ 💧	232
Mockorange — *Philadelphus* spp.	☼	233
Purple beautyberry — *Callicarpa* spp.	☼	227
Rhododendron — *Rhododendron* spp.	☼ ● 💧	233
Summersweet — *Clethra alnifolia*	☼	228
Viburnum — *Viburnum*	☼	235
Weigela — *Weigela florida*	☼	235
Winterberry — *Ilex verticillata*	☼ 💧	232
Witch alder — *Fothergilla* spp.	☼	230
Witch hazel — *Hamamelis* spp.	☼ 💧	231

Caladium (Caladium, page 218)

Rock Gardens

A rock garden can be as elaborate as dozens of giant boulders embedded in a hillside or as simple as a small arrangement of modest-sized rocks in a favored spot in your backyard.

A serious rock garden incorporates precise layers of gravel and grit with careful selection of stones and knowledgeable position of plants around those stones. But even beginners can get in on the fun with smaller, less complicated versions. After all, rock gardens are simply an elegant way to incorporate beautiful stones into your yard, creating the ideal climate for those plants that thrive with excellent drainage.

■ Planning a Rock Garden

Find a site in your garden where a rock garden would look natural. You don't want to pile up rocks in a heap on a flat lawn—a definite design mistake. Slopes are the ideal location, especially south-facing slopes. However, if you have a flat site, you can also create a raised bed of stone or work in rock-garden plants between flat paver stones laid flush into the soil.

For inspiration, check out naturally occurring stone formations in your area. Notice how the rocks are positioned, what size they are, how they fit into the terrain, and how plants grow on the formations. Replicate that look on a smaller scale in your own rock garden.

Whenever possible, use local stone. Not only will it look more natural in your part of the country, it's also likely to create better growing conditions for plants native to your area,

making a lower-maintenance garden. Use the same stone throughout your garden or the result will be a hodgepodge.

Tufa is considered the stone of choice among rock-garden aficionados, but it's expensive and local only in a few tropical areas. Sandstone and limestone are good to work with because they weather well and are porous enough to retain moisture. Irregularly shaped stones make the most interesting rock gardens. Rounded boulders and river rocks tend to lack the character of craggier stones, making them less desirable in a rock garden.

■ Building and Planting a Rock Garden

If you plan on nurturing several alpine plants, which demand perfect drainage and precise microclimates, or if you're creating a flat rock garden, put a drainage layer behind or underneath your rock garden. Dig out a 6-inch layer and fill it with broken bricks, stones, sand, gravel, and other similar, loose material.

Top with the stones, arranging them carefully to achieve a natural look. Many stones look best if buried by one- to two-thirds. Wear heavy leather gloves and sturdy shoes or boots while working with stone.

Very large stones require the help of a friend or two. Extremely large stones are best left to the professionals. (Ask the home and garden center or landscaping company from which you purchased the stones if they will position all or some of the stones for you for a fee.)

Backfill with topsoil. If you have poor-quality soil, purchase top-quality topsoil or compost. For the top 6 inches or so of the rock garden, mix your own special rock-garden soil, consisting of one part topsoil,

one part compost, and one part grit or stone chippings. This soil mixture assures the perfect combination of fertile soil and excellent drainage.

When planting, consider the position of the plant in relationship to the stones. Plants that sprawl or drape, such as creeping phlox or creeping thyme, look best if given some stone to flow over. Plants that like shade or cooler conditions will do better on the north side of a large stone, while plants that like it warmer and sunnier will thrive on the south side. Rocks, too, act like heating mats. They absorb heat during the day and release it during the evening, a plus for heat-loving plants.

Add interest to rock gardens with an occasional vertical element, such as an upright evergreen. Most rock garden plants are low, so breaking the profile up a little makes for a more dynamic garden.

Homer's Hindsight

Go Natural

I spent a lot of time (and muscle) getting large boulders for my rock garden in place. Only thing is, I just set the round boulders right on the surface. It wasn't until I got the thing planted that I realized how odd those boulders looked, just sitting on top of the ground as though martians had dropped them down. I ended up burying them halfway to get a natural look, something I should have figured on in the first place.

A rock garden is a creative way to tame a difficult slope.

Scotch heather (Calluna vulgaris, page 169) is a lovely plant for rock gardens.

Good Rock Garden Plants

Name	Zones	Page
Agapanthus (short types) *Agapanthus* spp.	2–11	217
Basket-of-gold *Aurinia saxatilis*	3–7	166
Bellflower *Campanula* spp.	3–8	170
Bleeding heart *Dicentra* spp.	2–9	179
Broom *Cytisus* spp.	6–10	229
Candytuft *Iberis* spp.	3–10	190
Columbine *Aquilegia* spp.	3–10	162
Cranesbill *Geranium* spp.	4–8	185
Creeping phlox *Phlox stolonifera*	2–8	206
Creeping thyme *Thymus* spp.	5–9	240
Crocus *Crocus* spp.	5–7	219
Daffodil *Narcissus* spp.	3–11	223
False rockcress *Aubretia deltoidea*	4–8	165
Grape hyacinth *Muscari* spp.	3–8	223
Moss phlox *Phlox subulata*	2–9	206

Name	Zones	Page
Moss rose *Portulaca*	2–11	207
Ornamental onion *Allium* spp.	4–10	217
Scotch heather *Calluna vulgaris*	3–11	169
Sedum *Sedum* spp.	3–11	211
Snowdrop *Galanthus nivalis*	3–7	221
Spring and winter heath *Erica* spp.	5–7	181
Squill *Scilla*	2–8	224
Sweet william *Dianthus* spp.	2–11	178
Thrift *Armeria*	4–8	163
Tulip *Tulipa* spp.	3–11	225
Yarrow *Achillea* spp.	3–9	159

Yarrow (Achillea spp. page 159)

Gardening For Wildlife

Attracting wildlife to your garden isn't hard. In fact, you're likely to attract birds, butterflies, and hummingbirds just by planting a garden.

You can greatly increase their numbers by doing a few basic things:

• **Provide shelter.** Trees are the best shelter there is. Plant just a tree or two, and the birds will start flocking. In more limited spaces, shelter can be provided by large shrubs and large vines. Both provide good spots for nesting and fleeing from predators. Birdhouses are a nice touch, too, and they add a decorative element. (Clean them out in late winter or early spring to encourage returning birds.)

• **Provide water.** Water attracts birds and other animals. Even a basic birdbath will do. The favorite water, however, is in a low basin or pool where water falls or bubbles up from a fountain. The splashing sound attracts many types of wildlife. Birds love to bathe in this, and butterflies will drink from moist spots along the edge.

• **Provide food.** Many flowers naturally provide good food (such as berries) for wildlife, especially if you let the flowers go to seed—a real bird treat.

A bird feeder will attract even more birds. A flat-tray bird feeder filled with a general blend of seed will attract the widest variety of birds. To attract specific types of birds, check with your local seed and bird feeder supplier.

Goldfinches, for example, love nyser seed delivered from a tube feeder.

• **Go for color.** As a rule, birds, butterflies, and hummingbirds are most attracted to clear reds and brilliant pinks. Red zinnias, for example, will attract more butterflies than white ones. And magenta morning glories will attract more hummingbirds than blue ones.

• **Use chemicals sparingly, especially insecticides.** Many chemicals create conditions that discourage wildlife. And many insecticides—even organic ones—kill helpful insects as well as harmful ones.

• **Be messy.** When it comes to gardening for wildlife, you need to be more casual about maintenance. Birds love to feast on the seed heads created by flowers left to ripen on the stem. They adore tall grass and thrive in tall, unpruned shrubs.

This hummingbird moth is drawn to tubular-shaped flowers with sweet nectar, such as this bellflower (Campanula spp., page 170).

A birdbath is a fast and easy way to attract more birds to your garden.

Flowers That Attract Butterflies

Annuals/Perennials

Name	Zones	Page
Ageratum *Ageratum houstonianum*	2–11	160
Aster *Aster* spp.	4–8	165
Bachelor's button *Centaurea cyanus*	3–10	171
Basket-of-gold *Aurinia saxatilis*	3–7	166
Bee balm *Monarda didyma*	4–8	200
Black-eyed Susan *Rudbeckia* spp.	3–10	209
Blanket flower *Gaillardia* spp.	2–11	184
Blue daisy *Felicia amelloides*	7–11	183
Blue false indigo *Baptisia australis*	3–9	166
Butterfly weed *Asclepias tuberosa*	4–10	164
Candytuft *Iberis* spp.	3–10	190
Coreopsis *Coreopsis* spp.	3–9	176
Cosmos *Cosmos* spp.	2–11	176
Creeping thyme *Thymus* spp.	5–9	240
Gayfeather *Liatris spicata*	3–9	193
Globe thistle *Echinops* spp.	3–8	180
Goldenrod *Solidago* hybrids	3–9	211
Heliotrope *Heliotropium arborescens*	2–11	188
Hollyhock *Alcea rosea*	3–11	160
Hyssop *Agastache* spp.	2–11	160
Joe-Pye weed *Eupatorium* spp.	3–9	182
Lantana *Lantana camara*	2–11	192
Larkspur *Consolida ambigua*	2–11	175
Marigold *Tagetes* spp.	2–11	212
Mexican sunflower *Tithonia rotundifolia*	2–11	213
Morning glory *Ipomoea* spp.	2–11	239
Petunia *Petunia* spp.	2–11	205
Phlox *Phlox* spp.	2–11	205–206
Pinks (China pinks) *Dianthus chinensis*	2–11	178
Primrose *Primula* spp.	3–10	208
Purple coneflower *Echinacea purpurea*	3–9	180

Name	Zones	Page
Scabiosa *Scabiosa caucasica*	3–7	210
Sedum *Sedum* spp.	3–11	211
Snapdragon *Antirrhinum majus*	2–11	162
Strawflower *Helichrysum bracteatum*	2–11	187
Sunflower *Helianthus* spp.	4–9	187
Sweet alyssum *Lobularia maritima*	2–11	196
Sweet william *Dianthus* spp.	2–11	178
Verbena, especially *Verbena bonarensis* *Verbena* spp.	2–11	214
Violet *Viola* spp.	2–11	215
Wisteria *Wisteria* spp.	5–9	241
Yarrow *Achillea* spp.	3–9	159
Zinnia *Zinnia* spp.	2–11	215

Bulbs

Name	Zones	Page
Dahlia *Dahlia*	2–11	220
Lily *Lilium* spp.	3–9	222
Ornamental onion *Allium* spp.	4–10	217

Shrubs

Name	Zones	Page
Azalea *Rhododendron* spp.	3–9	233
Butterfly bush *Buddleia* spp.	5–10	227
Rhododendron *Rhododendron* spp.	3–9	233
Viburnum *Viburnum* spp.	2–9	235

Flowers That Attract Hummingbirds

Annuals/Perennials

Name	Zones	Page
Annual phlox *Phlox drummondii*	2–11	205
Annual red salvia *Salvia splendens*	2–11	209
Bee balm *Monarda didyma*	4–8	200
Flowering tobacco *Nicotiana* spp.	2–11	201
Fuchsia *Fuchsia* spp.	2–11	183
Geranium *Pelargonium* spp.	2–11	203
Honeysuckle *Lonicera* spp.	3–9	239
Lantana *Lantana camara*	2–11	192
Larkspur *Consolida ambigua*	2–11	175

Name	Zones	Page
Morning glory *Ipomoea* spp.	2–11	239
Penstemon *Penstemon* spp.	3–9	204
Perennial lobelia *Lobelia* spp.	2–9	196
Petunia *Petunia* spp.	2–11	205
Snapdragon *Antirrhinum majus*	2–11	162
Trumpet vine *Campsis radicans*	4–9	237

Bulbs

Name	Zones	Page
Canna *Canna* hybrids	2–11	218
Dahlia *Dahlia*	2–11	220
Gladiolus *Gladiolus* hybrids	2–11	221

Shrubs

Name	Zones	Page
Butterfly bush *Buddleia* spp.	5–10	227
Flowering quince *Chaenomeles speciosa*	4–9	228
Honeysuckle *Lonicera* spp.	3–9	239
Rose of sharon *Hibiscus* spp.	5–11	231
Weigela *Weigela florida*	4–9	235

Flowers That Attract Songbirds

Annuals/Perennials

Name	Zones	Page
Aster *Aster* spp.	4–8	165
Bittersweet *Celastrus scandens*	3–8	237
California poppy *Eschscholzia californica*	2–11	181
Coreopsis *Coreopsis* spp.	3–9	176
Cosmos *Cosmos* spp.	2–11	176
Goldenrod *Solidago* hybrids	3–9	211
Honeysuckle *Lonicera* spp.	3–9	239
Marigold *Tagetes* spp.	2–11	212
Purple coneflower *Echinacea purpurea*	3–9	180
Scabiosa *Scabiosa caucasica*	3–7	210
Trumpet vine *Campsis radicans*	4–9	237
Zinnia *Zinnia* spp.	2–11	215

Wildflower Gardens

Wildflower gardens are increasingly popular—and for good reason. Once established they require little work and tend to attract birds and butterflies. Gardeners also are learning to appreciate their casual, easy-going look and are finding ways to incorporate them into their backyard.

■ Designing a Wildflower Garden

If you have an open, sunny area, it's an ideal spot for a meadow-like wildflower garden—a happy jumble of colorful, loosely organized wildflowers. However, there are many wildflowers that like the shade, too, so don't rule out a shady site for a wildflower garden.

The overall design of a garden with wildflowers can be nothing but many flowers growing together in no real pattern. You can also incorporate wildflowers into even the tidiest of flower beds, but you'll need to choose carefully for neat growth habit that looks at home in a more cultivated setting.

Remember, too, that not all wildflowers are annuals or perennials. Many native flowers are shrubs, easy-to-incorporate natives for your garden.

■ Choosing Seeds

Wildflower mixes vary widely. Some are a mix of perennial and annuals; others are one or the other. (Perennials take time to establish but are long-lived. Annuals create fast color but are gone in a year unless they reseed.) Other mixes are tailored to certain regions or growing conditions. Read labels carefully and remember that you get what you pay for. The best wildflower mixes are not cheap.

■ Planting and Caring for Wildflowers

There's a myth that starting a wildflower garden is nothing more than sprinkling some seeds, watering them, and watching them grow. In fact, wildflower gardens need preparation and care the first year or two. It's in subsequent years that they become nearly maintenance free.

To start a wildflower garden from seed, first remove existing vegetation and weeds; then work the soil to create a seedbed. Spread the seed and water well. Keep the area moist and weed by hand. The second year, it's still important to keep the area weeded. That fall or next spring, mow dead foliage.

After that, your wildflower garden will need minimal maintenance, other than a little annual weeding and mowing.

Even a small strip of land between the yard and street can become a miniature meadow.

Bee balm (Monarda didyma, *page 200*) is a freely spreading North American native that's excellent for wildflower gardens.

Wildflower Terms to Know

Wildflower: A flower that grows with little or no human intervention. Some wildflowers are the true "species" wildflowers that haven't been hybridized for neater growth habit and bigger or more varied flowers. Hybrids of wildflowers may or may not have more disease resistance than their less well-bred cousins.

Native plant: A plant or flower that grew before the arrival of European settlers. Some plants are native to just one part of North America but have since been imported to other states or provinces.

Naturalized plants: Plants or flowers that have multiplied freely in the wild, either by accident or on purpose. Many daylilies, for example, "escaped" from gardens decades ago and now grow in abandon in fields and ditches everywhere. And people love to naturalize bulbs; that is, plant them in wooded or other semiwild areas to multiply on their own.

Wildflowers by Region

Region and name	Page
Arid West and Southwest	
California poppy	181
Eschscholzia californica	
Larkspur	175
Consolida ambigua	
Shasta daisy	193
Leucanthemum × superbum	
Florida	
Honeysuckle	239
Lonicera spp.	
Sea lavender	194
Limonium latifolium	
Summersweet	228
Clethra alnifolia	
Trumpet vine	237
Campsis radicans	
Mountainous West	
Blue flax	195
Linum perenne	
Columbine	162
Aquilegia spp.	
Evening primrose	202
Oenothera spp.	
Larkspur	175
Consolida ambigua	
Penstemon	204
Penstemon spp.	
Northeast/Midwest/Plains	
Aster	165
Aster spp.	
Bee balm	200
Monarda didyma	
Black-eyed Susan	209
Rudbeckia spp.	
Blanket flower	184
Gaillardia spp.	
Butterfly weed	164
Asclepias tuberosa	
Coreopsis	176
Coreopsis spp.	
Flanders poppy	203
Papaver rhoeas	
Lupine	197
Lupinus hybrids	
Purple coneflower	180
Echinacea purpurea	
Yarrow	159
Achillea spp.	
Southeast	
African daisy	163
Arctotis	
Annual phlox	205
Phlox drummondii	
Cardinal flower	196
Lobelia spp.	
Cosmos	176
Cosmos spp.	
Evening primrose	202
Oenothera spp.	
Virginia bluebells	199
Mertensia virginica	

Region and name	Page
Texas/Oklahoma	
Bachelor's button	171
Centaurea cyanus	
Gayfeather	193
Liatris spicata	
Ox-eye daisy	188
Heliopsis helianthoides	
Texas bluebonnet	197
Lupinus texensis	
Toadflax	194
Linaria spp.	
West/Pacific Northwest	
African daisy	163
Arctotis	
California poppy	181
Eschscholzia californica	
Shasta daisy	193
Leucanthemum × superbum	

Other Options*

*Availability varies. Check with your local garden center.

Arid West and Southwest
Baby blue-eyes
  Nemophila menziesii
Mexican hat
  Ratibida columnaris

Florida
Mountain laurel
  Kalmia latifolia
Native azaleas
  Rhododendron spp.
Swamp mallow (or rose mallow)
  Hibiscus moscheutos

Mountainous West
Catchfly
  Lychnis alpina
Wallflower
  Erysimum spp.

Northeast/Midwest/Plains
Dames rocket
  Hesperis matronalis

Southeast
Moss verbena
  Verbena tenuisecta

Texas/Oklahoma
Texas paintbrush
  Castilleja coccinea

West/Pacific Northwest
Bird's eyes
  Gilia tricolor
California bluebell
  Phacelia campanularia
Five spot
  Nemophila maculata
Tidy tips
  Layia platyglossa
Wallflower
  Erysimum spp.

Woodland Gardens

■ Designing a Woodland Garden

To design a woodland garden, let mature trees be your guide. Dig out small, weedy trash trees less than 4 inches in diameter. Then step back and see where a path suggests itself. Lay fieldstones along the path as stepping stones or put down a 3-inch layer of wood-chip or pine-needle mulch. The path will be more weed free and permanent if you lay down black landscape fabric first.

Once the path is laid out, design and install the planting areas, then create focal points with benches, sundials, birdbaths, or gazing balls. Just remember to keep the accessories simple.

■ Planting a Woodland Garden

The soil of many woodland gardens is riddled with tree roots. The best strategy for dealing with shallow roots is to plant between them. If you're doing extensive planting, you may need to remove some roots, but proceed carefully because you can damage the tree. Never cut roots closer than 1–2 yards from the base of the tree and never cut a root thicker than 1 inch.

CLOSER LOOK

Coping with Dry Shade

Most woodland plants love moist, rich soil. However, some trees with shallow roots are water robbers, sucking the moisture out of the soil. In these conditions use plants that are both shade and drought tolerant.

Moonlight Gardens

Datura (Brugmansia)

Moonlight gardens are a great solution for those who can enjoy their gardens only after a long day's work. However, moonlight gardens are so beautiful that you may want to create one even if you can hang out in your landscape any time you want.

• **Choose plants with white flowers.** White flowers glow in dim light. Other light colors, such as pale yellows and grays, also show up well.

• **Go for fragrant plants.** Because you won't be able to see some visual subtleties in a night garden, treat another sense—smell.

• **Bring in sound.** Bring pleasure to yet another sense—hearing. A small fountain or bubbler will let you hear the beauty of your garden any time of day or night.

• **Make it glow.** Landscape lighting allows you to see your garden well past sundown. Use small downlights scattered among flower beds. Or try a few uplights to play up an especially beautiful tree or other landscape feature.

Plants for Moonlight Gardens

Name	Zones	Page
Clematis, sweet autumn *Clematis terniflora*	4–9	238
Columbine, fragrant *Aquilegia fragrans*	3–10	162
Datura *Brugmansia*	3–11	168
Evening primrose *Oenothera*	3–8	202
Flowering tobacco *Nicotiana sylvestris*	2–11	201
Four-o-clock *Mirabilis jalapa*	2–11	199
Honeysuckle *Lonicera japonica*	5–9	239
Hosta *Hosta plantaginea*	3–9	190
Jasmine *Jasminum*	6–9	239
Mockorange *Philadelphus coronarius*	4–7	233
Pinks *Dianthus* spp.	2–11	178
Stock, evening *Matthiola incana*	3–11	198

Bulbs for Indoor Beauty

Forcing bulbs by planting them in a pot, wrapping them in plastic, chilling them for several weeks, and then setting them in a sunny window to bloom will guarantee fresh flowers all winter long. In fall, buy spring-blooming bulbs recommended for forcing.

Most of them will need a chilling period at 40 to 55°F (4.5 to 7°C) for several weeks. (See "Closer Look", right.) Stagger planting times for a steady supply of blooms.

It's easiest to chill the bulbs, pot and all, in the fridge (many gardeners have a separate one for this purpose); but an unheated garage, cold frame, or uninsulated crawlspace will work as well.

CLOSER LOOK

How Long to Bloom?

Different bulbs need different treatments to bloom.
Amaryllis: No chilling; bloom 4–10 weeks after planting.
Paper-whites: No chilling; bloom 3–5 weeks after planting.
Daffodils: Chill 15–17 weeks; bloom 2–3 weeks after chilling is complete.
Hyacinths: Chill prepared bulbs 10–12 weeks; unprepared 11–14. Bloom 2–3 weeks after.
Tulips: Chill 14–20 weeks; bloom 2–3 weeks after.
Crocuses: Chill 15 weeks; bloom 2–3 weeks after.
Grape hyacinths: Chill 13–15 weeks; bloom 2-3 weeks after.

Forcing Daffodils

1 Plant the bulbs in the fall. Place pointed side up as close together as possible. Barely cover their tops with soil. Water well. Put the pot in a plastic bag in the fridge or other cold spot. Keep moist.

2 Remove from the cold when shoots are an inch or so high. Put the pot in the sunniest spot available, such as a south-facing window. Keep watered.

STUFF YOU'LL NEED

✔ Daffodil bulbs
✔ Potting soil
✔ Pot with drainage

What to Expect
The plant should bloom in 2 to 3 weeks as long as the soil is kept moist but not soggy.

Top Bulbs for Forcing

Tulips:
'Golden Melody'
'Christmas Marvel'

Daffodils:
'Tete-a-Tete'
'Thalia'
'February Gold'

Hyacinths:
'Carnegie'
'Delft Blue'
'Pink Pearl'

Specialized Flower Gardening

Flowers for Cutting

■ *Choosing Good Cut Flowers*

Nearly any flower, twig, berry, or leaf can be brought indoors and put in a vase. However, some flowers are easier to work with. Those flowers have the following characteristics:

• Last a long time in the vase, anywhere from a week to three weeks.

• Have sturdy, slender stems that make them easy to arrange.

• Have petals that are firmly attached and don't fall off easily.

• Don't have sticky saps that make them difficult to handle or that foul the water.

• Stay open for several days. Flowers such as morning glories and daylilies close each day.

• Have a pleasant or neutral fragrance. Some plants have strong scents that are fine outdoors but unpleasant indoors. Others, such as marigolds and catmint, have scents people don't care for.

■ *Growing Flowers for Cutting*

If you have room, a cutting garden set aside just for flowers to take indoors is wonderful.

However, when space is more limited, it still works well to harvest lots of flowers from your regular beds and borders. In fact, cutting them makes your garden prettier because it encourages more flower production.

Another way to grow flowers for cutting is to plant them in rows in your vegetable garden. This is especially practical with fast-growing annuals planted from seed, such as zinnias and cosmos.

This vegetable garden has flowers for cutting planted throughout.

Top Flowers for Cutting

Name	Zones	Page	Name	Zones	Page
Annual sunflower *Helianthus annuus*	2–11	187	Larkspur *Consolida ambigua*	2–11	175
Aster *Aster* spp.	4–8	165	Lavender *Lavandula* spp.	5–10	192
Astilbe *Astilbe* spp.	3–8	165	Lilac *Syringa* spp.	2–8	235
Baby's breath *Gypsophila paniculata*	3–9	186	Lily *Lilium* spp.	3–9	222
Black-eyed Susan *Rudbeckia* spp.	3–10	209	Lily-of-the-valley *Convallaria majalis*	3–7	175
Celosia *Celosia* spp.	2–11	170	Lisianthus *Eustoma*	2–11	182
Cosmos *Cosmos* spp.	2–11	176	Peony *Paeonia* spp.	2–8	202
Daffodil *Narcissus* spp.	3–11	223	Perennial mum *Chrysanthemum* spp.	4–9	173
Dahlia *Dahlia*	2–11	220	Roses *Rosa* spp.	2–11	86–95
Delphinium *Delphinium elatum*	2–7	178	Scabiosa *Scabiosa caucasica*	3–7	210
Freesia *Freesia* spp.	2–11	220	Shasta daisy *Leucanthemum × superbum*	4–9	193
Gayfeather *Liatris spicata*	3–9	193	Snapdragon *Antirrhinum majus*	2–11	162
Gerbera daisy *Gerbera*	3–10	185	Sweet pea *Lathyrus odoratus*	2–11	192
Gladiolus *Gladiolus* hybrids	2–11	221	Tulip *Tulipa* spp.	3–11	225
Goldenrod *Solidago* hybrids	3–9	211	Yarrow *Achillea* spp.	3–9	159
Iris, all types *Iris* spp.	3–10	191	Zinnia *Zinnia* spp.	2–11	215

Flowers for Drying

During the late fall and winter, bouquets and wreaths of dried flowers cheer a gardener's soul. Dried flowers have become so popular, in fact, that many gardeners keep them around all year.

Drying flowers is easy. The simplest way is to let them air-dry. Just hang them upside down in a warm, dry place for a few weeks until they're ready to use.

Another way to dry flowers is to use silica gel. Resembling coarse salt, silica gel is used to cover flowers in an airtight container. After a few weeks, the gel draws all the moisture from the flowers, leaving a perfectly dried flower.

Air drying is the simplest, least expensive way to dry flowers. Silica gel is useful in drying delicate flowers with large flower heads that would otherwise shrivel excessively. Also, silica gel (available at crafts stores) better preserves the color of most flowers.

Not all flowers dry easily. For best success, use only those

Old-fashioned drying upside down works with many late-summer flowers.

flowers recommended for drying. (See "Top Flowers for Drying.") Cut the flowers in mid- to late morning after all the dew has dried but before flowers wilt in the heat of the day. Choose only unblemished, well-formed flowers.

Once your flowers are dried, arrange them by putting them loosely in a vase. Or use a block of dry floral foam, tucked into a vase or basket, for a more elaborate arrangement. Many foam forms are now available in wreath shapes for easy wreath-making.

Silica gel, which looks like coarse salt, is an excellent way to dry most flowers.

Top Flowers for Drying

Name	Zones	Page
Baby's breath *Gypsophila paniculata*	3–9	186
Celosia *Celosia* spp.	2–11	170
Globe amaranth *Gomphrena globosa*	2–11	186
Hydrangea *Hydrangea* spp.	4–9	231
Lavender *Lavandula* spp.	5–10	192
Love-in-a-mist *Nigella damascena*	2–11	202
Money plant *Lunaria annua*	4–8	196
Oriental poppy seed heads *Papaver orientale*	2–7	203
Roses *Rosa* spp.	2–11	86–95
Salvia 'Victoria Blue' *Salvia farinacea*	2–11	209
Sedum 'Autumn Joy' *Sedum* spp.	3–10	211
Statice *Limonium* spp.	2–11	194
Strawflower *Helichrysum bracteatum*	2–11	187
Yarrow *Achillea* spp.	3–9	159

Arranging Flowers

People who are able to toss a few flowers into a container and create a beautiful arrangement of flowers aren't magicians. They just know a few floral tricks and how to use those inexpensive little gadgets and materials that help turn a bunch of flowers into a professional-looking arrangement.

■ *Arranging Aids*

Floral foam is one of the most commonly used materials. Green floral foam, often sold under the brand name Oasis, is usually water absorbent and used for fresh flowers, while brown foam, sometimes sold under the name Sahara, actually repels water and is used for dried flowers.

Frogs are anchors made of a grid of wire, a glass circle with staggered holes, or a plastic base covered with little needles. Flower stems are pushed into the frog to hold them in place.

Floral tape or even crushed wire can be fashioned to create an anchor for flowers near the top of the container.

Floral wire is good to wind around flopping stems to direct them in the way you want.

Whatever technique you use, the flowers you select should look good together. Go for coordinating colors and contrasting shapes and textures.

Ideally, cut the flowers early in the day, after the dew dries. Choose the most perfect blossoms available and, when possible, those that are not quite fully open. Put them in a pitcher or a bucket of tepid water up to their necks and let them "condition" this way for several hours. This allows them to soak up as much water as possible and stay fresh days longer.

When it comes time to arrange the flowers, strip them of any leaves that will be below water in the vase. Leaves look unattractive in clear containers and foul the water after a day or two.

Recut the ends. With roses, recut the ends under water in a bowl to improve their ability to absorb water.

Add a commercial floral preservative to the water to keep flowers fresher longer or add a dash of lemon juice and a pinch of sugar to the water.

Once flowers are arranged, keep them in a cool spot away from direct light. Change water every other day. After two or three days, if practical, recut the ends of the flowers to help them absorb more water.

Tips for Arranging Flowers

A container within a container. You can use a wider variety of containers such as baskets or delicate metals and ceramics, if you first slip in a plastic container.

A chicken-wire frog. Crumpled chicken wire is a great way to make sure flowers are held in place in large or very wide-mouthed containers.

Floral tape. Make a neat grid with floral tape to hold flowers in place at the top of various vases, where other devices would be too obvious.

Arranging Flowers

STUFF YOU'LL NEED

✔ Container
✔ Floral foam
✔ Scissors
✔ Assorted flowers and foliage
✔ Floral preservative
   (optional)

What to Expect

Your arrangement should last three to six days as long as you change the water daily.

Floral wire

Floral tape

Floral foam

Floral frog

There are many different ways to create a beautiful arrangement. Here's one method to get you started.

1 **Add bits of foliage first** to cover the floral foam (which must be soaked in water first). Strip off lower leaves to make a clean end for inserting into the foam. Be sure to insert some foliage horizontally so it drapes over the edge of the container.

2 **Add "focal point" flowers next.** These are the large flowers that will dominate the arrangement and make a bold statement. You can have more than one type of focal point flower.

3 **Next add tall, spiky flowers.** These are the flowers that will add height and drama to the arrangement. Add them just to the top or space them evenly around the arrangement.

4 **Finish with fluffy filler flowers.** These flowers soften and fill out the arrangement. Tuck them in wherever the arrangement seems sparse.

Chapter 6
Flower Encyclopedia

F lowers are a little like people. They grow healthy, thrive, and bloom only when their specific needs are met. Some demand full sun, while others would burn up with the same light. Most flowers do best in rich, moist, fertile soil, but some are natives of dry regions and thrive under dry and difficult conditions and would drown in conditions that others love. Many plants thrive in hot, humid subtropical regions and blacken with a touch of frost, while others need winter's cold to grow and bloom properly.

This Flower Encyclopedia will help you decide exactly what your plants need and will also give you ideas on what will—and won't—thrive in your climate. It gives specifics on sun, soil, size, planting, and care. It's organized in alphabetical order according to plants' botanical names with a sublisting for common names.

The aptly named love-lies-bleeding (Amaranthus caudatus, page 161) thrives in dry conditions.

Annuals and Perennials

An annual thrives and blooms for one year and then dies. A perennial comes back each year. And a biennial develops foliage one year, blooms the next, and then dies. Some plants will behave as either an annual or a perennial depending on your climate zone and growing conditions. A mealycup sage, for example, may be an annual in Zone 6 in Ohio, where it dies out each winter. However, in Zone 8 in North Carolina, mild winters allow it to come back each year as a perennial.

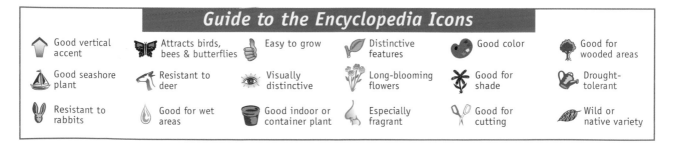

Guide to the Encyclopedia Icons

Good vertical accent	Attracts birds, bees & butterflies	Easy to grow
Good seashore plant	Resistant to deer	Visually distinctive
Resistant to rabbits	Good for wet areas	Good indoor or container plant

Distinctive features	Good color	Good for wooded areas
Long-blooming flowers	Good for shade	Drought-tolerant
Especially fragrant	Good for cutting	Wild or native variety

Acanthus spinosus

perennial

spiny bear's breeches

Light Needs:

Full sun to part shade

Mature Height: 3'–4'

Mature Width: 2'–3'

Zones: 5–10

Features:

Gorgeous flower spikes

Drought-tolerant

Rabbit-resistant

Blooms early summer.

Needs: Does best in average to sandy soil. Drought-tolerant; it needs to be planted where roots won't be overly wet in winter. Choose a site where this vigorous spreader will have room to expand; can be invasive.

Plant seedlings in spring or fall, keeping well watered for the first few months. Fertilize lightly if at all. Divide in spring. Handle mature plants with leather gloves because plant parts are sharp.

Slugs and snails are sometimes a problem.

Choices: This plant is available with mauve or white flowers.

Achillea spp.

perennial

yarrow

Light Needs:

Full sun

Mature Height: 2'–5'

Mature Width: 2'–3'

Zones: 3–9

Features:

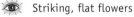

Striking, flat flowers

Drought-tolerant

Excellent for cutting and drying

Blooms late summer.

Needs: Thrives in average to sandy soil; gets leggy if soil is too rich, wet, or heavy. It likes dry conditions and otherwise can be prone to fungal diseases.

Plant established plants in spring or fall. Mulch to prevent weeds. Fertilize lightly if at all. This plant needs to be divided every 2–3 years. Common yarrow can sometimes be invasive. It is prone to fungal diseases in wet or humid climates.

Choices: This plant comes in yellows, creams, reds, pinks, and apricots.

Fern-leaf yarrow (*Achillea filipendulina*) and common yarrows (*Achillea millefolium*) do well in Zones 3–9; 'Moonshine' is hardy in Zones 3–8.

Aconitum carmichaelii

perennial

azure monkshood

Light Needs:

Full sun to light shade, especially afternoon shade

Mature Height: 2'–3'

Mature Width: 2'–3'

Zones: 3–7

Features:

Thrives in shade

Provides hard-to-find fall color

Flowers are a lovely blue

Blooms late summer to early fall.

Needs: Likes well-drained, humus-rich, moist soil, so add compost. Water moderately unless plant is in full sun. Then water more often.

Plant established plants in spring or fall. Mulch to conserve moisture. Fertilize occasionally, every 6 weeks, or work in a slow-release fertilizer in spring.

This plant dislikes dividing or transplanting. Stake if plant becomes floppy.

It is prone to crown rot or mildew.

Choices: Monkshood is available with blue to violet flowers; also some varieties, such as 'Bicolor', are available with blue-and-white flowers.

Annuals and Perennials

Agastache spp.

hyssop

Light Needs:

Full sun to part shade

Mature Height: 1½'–5'

Mature Width: 1'–3'

Zones: 2–11

Features:

Good container plant

Attracts butterflies

Good for cutting

Blooms midsummer to autumn.

Needs: Thrives in average, well-drained soil and only moderate water. This plant dislikes wet conditions; most types are drought-tolerant.

Most species last through the winter only in Zones 6 and warmer. In other areas, grow as an annual.

Plant in spring in Zones 2–5; in spring or fall in Zones 6–11. Fertilize lightly. Divide in spring as needed.

Hyssop is prone to mildew, rust, downy mildew, and some other fungal leaf diseases.

Choices: It comes in orange, apricot, red, purple, pink, blue, and white.

'Firebird' has copper-orange flowers; 'Tutti Fruitti' is a good substitute for the beautiful but invasive purple loosestrife.

Ageratum houstonianum

ageratum, flossflower

Light Needs:

Full sun to part shade

Mature Height: 6"–30"

Mature Width: 6"–20"

Zones: 2–11

Features:

Good container plant

Lovely blue color for front of border

Tall varieties good for cutting

Blooms early summer to frost.

Needs: Full sun in cooler parts of country; partial shade where summers are hot. Rich, well-drained soil with plenty of water.

Plant seedlings in spring after all danger of frost has passed. Mulch to conserve moisture. Fertilize regularly, every 4 weeks, or work in a slow-release fertilizer at planting time. Trim spent blooms regularly. In Zones 8–11 replant if desired in late summer for fall bloom. This plant often reseeds in warm, moist climates.

Choices: It comes in pinks, whites, purples, and blues.

Dwarf varieties, such as 'Hawaii', grow just 6 inches tall, while 'Blue Mink' grows 12 inches, and 'Blue Horizon' grows 30 inches.

Alcea rosea

hollyhock

Light Needs:

Full sun Zones 3–8; light shade Zones 9–11

Mature Height: 1'–12'

Mature Width: 1'–2'

Zones: 3–11

Features:

Excellent vertical accent

Easy to grow

Rabbit-resistant

Blooms in spring in warm climates; midsummer in cool climates.

Needs: Rich, well-drained soil with moderate water. Depending on the region and the hollyhock type, this plant may behave as an annual, biennial, or perennial. Read package directions carefully.

In Zones 3–8 start seeds of any hollyhock indoors 2–4 weeks before last average frost date or sow directly outdoors after frost. In Zones 9–11 plant seedlings in fall or late winter for spring bloom. If planting established plants, plant outdoors after all danger of frost has passed. Mulch to prevent disease. Work a 9-month, slow-release fertilizer into the soil each spring. Stake for best appearance.

Alchemilla spp.

lady's mantle

Light Needs:

Full sun to part shade

Mature Height: *1'–2'*

Mature Width: *12"–18"*

Zones: *3–8*

Features:

Pretty lime-green flowers

Beautiful jewel-like dew on leaves each morning

Good edging plant

Grown primarily for foliage; blooms in early summer.

Needs: Full sun in Zones 3–6 and Pacific Northwest; otherwise partial shade. This plant likes rich, well-drained soil that remains moist but will tolerate drier soil with more shade. It needs moderate moisture.

Plant established plants in spring or fall. Work a 9-month, slow-release fertilizer into the soil surface each spring. Mulch to conserve moisture. Trim spent blooms to promote second bloom and prevent reseeding (it will readily resow in most climates). Cut back plant by half if foliage gets ratty, to promote fresh growth. This plant is susceptible to fungal diseases, especially in the South.

Alstroemeria spp.

peruvian lily, inca lily

Light Needs:

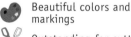

Full sun to part shade

Mature Height: *2'–4'*

Mature Width: *6"–10"*

Zones: *6–10*

Features:

Beautiful colors and markings

Outstanding for cutting

Blooms late spring to midsummer.

Needs: Full sun Zones 6–7 and Pacific Northwest; otherwise part shade. Needs very well-drained, acidic to neutral soil with plentiful water.

Plant rhizomes 6–8 inches deep in early spring in all zones or in fall in Zones 8–10. It benefits from an annual spring application of compost or a slow-release fertilizer. In Zone 7 *alstroemeria* may survive winter with a 3-inch layer of mulch. In Zone 6 you can dig and store the bulbs for winter (see page 136), but the plants often don't survive. Attractive to deer and rodents.

Choices: The flowers come in bicolors and beautifully mottled patterns of yellows, oranges, apricots, creams, reds, purples, and whites.

Amaranthus caudatus

amaranth, love-lies-bleeding

Light Needs:

Full sun to part shade

Mature Height: *1'–6'*

Mature Width: *1'–4'*

Zones: *2–11*

Features:

Fabulous dripping flowers

Striking in arrangements

Blooms early summer through frost.

Needs: Full sun Zones 6–7 and Pacific Northwest; partial shade Zones 8–11. This plant likes rich, well-drained soil and ample moisture but will rot if kept too moist.

Plant established seedlings outdoors in spring after all danger of frost has passed. Mulch to help keep soil moist. This plant benefits from an application of compost or slow-release fertilizer when flowering starts. Stake taller varieties.

It is susceptible to aphids, spider mites, and aster yellows virus.

Choices: Though usually grown for its dripping red flowers, upright as well as green and golden flower variations of this plant are available, as are variations in foliage color, including deep purple-red.

Annuals and Perennials

Anchusa spp.

bugloss, alkanet

Light Needs:

Full sun

Mature Height: *3'–5'*

Mature Width: *2'–3'*

Zones: *3–11*

Features:

One of the purest blues found in the garden

Blooms summer through fall.

Needs: Loose but not too rich soil. This plant becomes floppy if soil is too fertile, so don't fertilize. It likes somewhat dry soil and will rot if too wet in winter.

Plant both perennial and annual bugloss in spring; perennial types can also be planted in fall.

Stake because this plant tends to be floppy. Cut for arrangements or deadhead often to promote further bloom.

In areas where it's well adapted, this plant spreads rapidly and can even become invasive.

Choices: *Anchusa azurea* is a perennial; *Anchusa capensis* (also called summer forget-me-not) is grown as an annual.

Antirrhinum majus

snapdragon

Light Needs:

Full sun to part shade

Mature Height: *7"–3'*

Mature Width: *6"–3'*

Zones: *2–11*

Features:

 Easy to grow

Excellent cut flower

Blooms in winter, spring, or fall.

Needs: Grow as an annual in Zones 2–8; as an annual or perennial in Zones 9–11. Full sun in Zones 2–9 and Pacific Northwest; light shade in Zones 9–11. Rich to average well-drained soil; moderate water.

In Zones 2–8 plant established seedlings in spring for summer and fall color. In Zones 9–11, plant in fall or late winter for winter through spring color.

Fertilize regularly, every 4 weeks, during flowering or work in a 9-month, slow-release fertilizer at planting time.

Stake taller types. Deadhead for best production, but flowering usually slows or stops altogether when temperatures hit the high 80s°F (over 30°C). Cut back by two-thirds if plants get leggy.

Aquilegia spp.

columbine

Light Needs:

Full sun to part shade

Mature Height: *2'–3'*

Mature Width: *1'–2'*

Zones: *3–10*

Features:

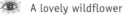 A lovely wildflower

Good for shade or woodland gardens

 Rabbit-resistant

Blooms late spring to early summer.

Needs: Full sun to part shade in areas where temperatures seldom hit 100°F (38°C); only part shade in warmer climates. Rich, loose, well-drained soil. This plant will rot in soil that is too wet, especially during the winter. Prefers moderate moisture, but will survive some dryness.

Plant established seedlings in spring or fall. Fertilize occasionally, every 6 weeks, or apply a 9-month, slow-release fertilizer in spring. If plants get shabby in late summer, cut back by half or more.

Mulch well over winter. Plants usually live just 3 or 4 years and therefore need no division. However, they often reseed. Space different-colored varieties at least 50 feet apart to prevent new plants from crossbreeding.

Annuals and Perennials

Arabis caucasica (Arabis albida)

wall rockcress

Light Needs:

Full sun

Mature Height: 10"–18"

Mature Width: 12"–18"

Zones: 4–7

Features:

🌿 Good rock garden plant

🌿 Ideal companion for spring-blooming bulbs

Blooms early to midspring.

Needs: Poor, loose, very well-drained soil; moderate moisture.

Plant established plants in spring or fall. Mulch is helpful to keep soil cool. Avoid fertilizing. Cut back stems after flowering to keep plants tidy.

Divide every 2–3 years. In the right climate, diseases are seldom a problem. Hot, humid, or wet climates encourage root or crown rot.

Choices: Flowers come in whites, pinks, and purples.

Arabis caucasica variegata has white flowers with white-edged leaves. *Arabis procurrens* tolerates light shade.

Arctotis

african daisy

Light Needs:

Full sun

Mature Height: 6"–24"

Mature Width: 6"–18"

Zones: 2–11

Features:

🎨 Provides color during cool weather

Blooms winter or spring.

Needs: Extremely well-drained, loose, and preferably gravelly soil. This plant needs even but not excessive watering.

In Zones 2–6 plant established seedlings in early spring. In Zones 7–11 plant in late fall or early winter. Mulch to conserve moisture. Fertilize lightly, if at all. Plants reseed in climates where well adapted, but seedlings tend to revert to orange.

This plant does best in the winter and early spring in the Southwest; it thrives in areas with extended cool weather and moderate but not excessive moisture. It doesn't tolerate heat or humidity well.

Choices: Although some are technically perennials, African daisies do best when grown as annuals. This plant is sometimes sold as *Dimorphotheca* and *Osteospermum.*

Armeria

thrift, sea thrift

Light Needs:

Full sun to part shade

Mature Height: 6"–12"

Mature Width: 6"–12"

Zones: 4–8

Features:

⛵ Tolerates drought and salt spray

🌸 Long-blooming perennial

Blooms midspring through early summer.

Needs: Full sun in Zones 4–5; light shade in Zones 6–8. Well-drained, sandy soil and moderate moisture.

Plant established plants in spring or fall. Mulch to keep soil moist. Fertilize infrequently, if at all. Keep spent flowers trimmed for longest bloom time.

Divide every few years in spring or autumn.

Choices: Flowers come in pinks and whites. 'Pride of Dusseldorf' is nearly red; 'Alba' is white.

Artemisia spp.

artemisia, wormwood

Light Needs:

Full sun

Mature Height: *6"–3'*

Mature Width: *2'–3'*

Zones: *3–11*

Features:

Beautiful silver foliage

Drought-tolerant

Grown for foliage; all-season flowers are tiny.

Needs: Sandy, quick-draining soil. This plant is drought-tolerant.

Plant established plants in spring, summer, or fall; in Zones 9–11 plant also in winter. Mulch to prevent disease. Avoid fertilizing. Plants get floppy in certain conditions and will look more attractive when cut back by about half in midsummer. Divide every year or two to keep in bounds if invasiveness is a problem. Also pull out unwanted sprouts and runners.

Root rot or fungal diseases are a problem in wet or very humid areas.

Choices: 'Silver Mound' forms mounds, doesn't flop, and isn't aggressive. 'Silver Brocade' and 'Boughton Silver' are low and creeping. 'Silver King' and 'Silver Queen' can be invasive.

Aruncus dioicus

goatsbeard

Light Needs:

Part to full shade

Mature Height: *1'–3'*

Mature Width: *1'–5'*

Zones: *3–7*

Features:

Large, striking plant

Thrives in shade

Good for wet areas

Blooms in summer.

Needs: Will tolerate full sun in Zones 3–4 but needs shade in Zones 5–7. It needs rich, moist, deep soil high in organic matter. Always keep soil moist.

Plant established plants in spring or fall, working compost into the soil. Mulch to conserve moisture. Fertilize occasionally, every 6 weeks, or work in a 9-month, slow-release fertilizer each spring.

Division is usually not necessary but can be done in spring with difficulty. The roots are large and hard to cut.

It is troubled by few pests or diseases, but leaf edges will turn brown with insufficient water.

Choices: Flowers are creamy white. 'Kneiffii' is a popular cultivar.

Asclepias tuberosa

butterfly weed, butterfly milkweed

Light Needs:

Full sun

Mature Height: *2'–4'*

Mature Width: *10"–2'*

Zones: *4–10*

Features:

Attracts butterflies

Drought-tolerant

North American native

Blooms midsummer.

Needs: Average to poor soil with good drainage. This plant likes sandy soil and is fairly drought-tolerant.

Plant established plants in spring. Mulch to prevent disease. Avoid fertilizing. Cut flowers freely for arrangements and deadhead because cutting often sparks a second bloom.

Don't bother dividing because this plant has a long, brittle taproot, and it often doesn't survive either division or transplanting. It's slow to emerge each spring, so mark it in fall and be careful not to damage or hoe it out while doing early weeding.

It is somewhat susceptible to aphids and powdery mildew.

Aster spp.

aster, michaelmas daisy

Light Needs:

Full sun to part shade

Mature Height: *1'–5'*

Mature Width: *1'–3'*

Zones: *4–8*

Features:

Blooms in the fall

Excellent for cutting

Blooms late summer through fall.

Needs: Best in full sun but will tolerate light shade. This plant needs rich, well-drained but moist soil and does best where fall is cool and moist.

Plant established plants in spring or fall. Pinch taller varieties back by half in early summer to prevent flopping, though they may still need staking. Fertilize lightly, if at all. Mulch well after cutting back in fall to prevent dying out during the winter.

Mildew and fungal diseases are a chronic problem, so avoid watering overhead and choose disease-resistant cultivars.

Choices: New England aster *(Aster novae-angliae)* is hardy in Zones 4–8. Michaelmas daisy, also called New York aster *(Aster novi-belgii)*, is hardy in Zones 4–8. Frikart's aster *(Aster × frikartii)* is hardy in Zones 5–8.

Astilbe spp.

astilbe, false spirea

Light Needs:

Part to full shade

Mature Height: *1'–4'*

Mature Width: *10"–3'*

Zones: *3–8*

Features:

Excellent perennial color for shade

Thrives in wet conditions

Rabbit-resistant

Blooms mid- to late summer.

Needs: Needs shade, more in the south and less in the north. Astilbe requires rich, constantly moist but well-drained, deep rich soil.

Plant established plants in spring or fall, working in compost. Fertilize regularly, every 4 weeks, for best health and flowering. Mulch to conserve moisture. After plant blooms, cut off fading flower stalks. Keep well watered. Leaves will scorch and shrivel if soil dries.

Divide every 3–4 years in spring or fall. This plant is susceptible to crown rot in wet soil in winter. Japanese beetles and spider mites can also be problems.

Choices: Flowers come in rich reds, pinks, lilacs, salmons, creams, and whites.

Aubretia deltoidea

false rockcress

Light Needs:

Full sun

Mature Height: *6"–8"*

Mature Width: *18"–24"*

Zones: *4–8*

Features:

Excellent rock garden plant

Good companion for spring bulbs

Blooms in midspring.

Needs: Must have excellent drainage; plant only in rock gardens, slopes, along walls, or in other places where it will never have wet feet. Rockcress needs only moderate moisture.

Plant established plants in spring. Work plenty of sand or grit into the soil in all but the sandiest areas. Mulch to conserve moisture. Fertilize lightly if at all because it's not a heavy feeder. Cut back by one- to two-thirds after blooming to keep it neat and compact. Rockcress is a short-lived perennial, usually dying out after a few years. Be prepared to replace it as needed or to take cuttings every year or so.

This plant is prone to root rot if not well-drained and is also susceptible to aphids, nematodes, and flea beetles.

basket-of-gold, gold dust alyssum

Light Needs:

Full sun

Mature Height: *8"–12"*

Mature Width: *12"–14"*

Zones: *3–7*

Features:

🌿 Excellent rock garden plant

🌿 Good companion for bulbs

💧 Drought-tolerant

Blooms midspring.

Needs: Loose, well-drained soil; must have excellent drainage. This plant is drought-tolerant once mature.

Plant in spring or fall in loose, well-drained soil, adding sand or grit if the soil has much clay. Fertilize lightly if at all because it will become floppy if the soil is too rich. Mulch to conserve moisture. After it blooms cut back by one- to two-thirds to keep the plant neat and to encourage possible reblooming. It dislikes transplanting but can usually be transplanted with success in the fall. This plant is prone to aphids.

Choices: Basket-of-gold is known for its brilliant yellow color. 'Citrina' bears pale lemon yellow flowers while 'Sunny Border Apricot' has apricot flowers.

---

blue false indigo

Light Needs:

Full sun to part shade

Mature Height: *3'–6'*

Mature Width: *3'–5'*

Zones: *3–9*

Features:

🎨 Beautiful blue spires

🦋 Attracts butterflies

💧 Somewhat drought-tolerant

Blooms in early summer.

Needs: Full sun in Zones 3–6 and Pacific Northwest; light shade in hot summer in Zones 7–9. Prefers rich, well-drained soil but tolerates many different soils. It needs moderate to light moisture and is fairly drought-tolerant once mature.

Plant established plants in spring or fall and avoid moving because it has a deep taproot that resists transplanting. Mulch to conserve moisture in all but the wettest climates. This plant benefits from light fertilizing, especially an application of an inch or two of compost in spring. It is usually pest and disease free. Stake lightly to prevent flopping.

Choices: Blue false indigo is renowned for its blue flowers; a white variety, *Baptisia alba,* is also available.

---

wax begonia, bedding begonia

Light Needs:

Tolerates full sun; prefers light to full shade

Mature Height: *6"–12"*

Mature Width: *6"–12"*

Zones: *2–11*

Features:

👍 Easy to grow

❋ Thrives in shade

🌱 Long-blooming annual

Blooms spring to frost.

Needs: Full sun to light shade in Zones 2–4; light to deep shade in Zones 6–11. Bronze-leaved types tolerate more sun. Rich, well-drained soil and moderate moisture.

Plant established seedlings in spring or any time after danger of frost has passed. Mulch to conserve moisture and prevent disease. Fertilize regularly for best bloom and health. Water moderately, but don't overwater, or roots will rot.

Pinch or brush off spent blooms. Usually pest and disease free; but spider mites, leaf rot, and whiteflies can sometimes be a problem.

Choices: Wax begonia has flowers in pinks, whites, reds, and peaches. Leaves are bright green, bronze, or mottled.

Annuals and Perennials

Bellis perennis

english daisy

Light Needs:

Full sun to part shade

Mature Height: *6"–18"*

Mature Width: *5"–12"*

Zones: *4–10*

Features:

Welcome spring color

Good companion for bulbs

Blooms midspring as a perennial; in late winter as an annual.

Needs: Full sun in cool, moist climates but more shade in drier, warmer climates. This plant needs ample moisture and rich soil that never dries out, especially in full sun.

Grow as a perennial by planting established seedlings in spring or fall in Zones 4–7. In warm, humid Zones 8–10, plant in fall as an annual for spring bloom and then tear out when summer heat hits. Deadhead regularly because the plant reseeds prolifically and becomes a lawn weed in some climates.

Apply a winter mulch in Zones 6 and colder. English daisy is prone to powdery mildew.

Choices: Flowers come in pinks, reds, or whites. Some varieties bear single flowers, while others look more like tiny pompons.

Boltonia asteroides

boltonia

Light Needs:

Full sun to part shade

Mature Height: *3'–7'*

Mature Width: *3'–4'*

Zones: *4–9*

Features:

Blooms in autumn

Native wildflower

Good cut flower

Blooms in fall.

Needs: Prefers full sun but will tolerate very light shade. It needs rich, moist, but well-drained soil and moderate water the first year. It is drought-tolerant when mature.

Plant established plants in spring. Mulch to prevent disease. Fertilize lightly. Stake in very rich soil or in shade.

Divide plant every 3-4 years. It is fairly pest and disease free.

Choices: Boltonia flowers come in pinks and blues.

'Snowbank' is a popular white variety, growing 4 feet tall. 'Pink Beauty' has pale lilac-pink flowers and grows 3–4 feet.

Brachycome iberidifolia

swan river daisy

Light Needs:

Full sun

Mature Height: *8"–18"*

Mature Width: *8"–18"*

Zones: *2–11*

Features:

Excellent container and window box plant

Provides welcome early spring color

Blooms late winter or early spring.

Needs: Rich, well-drained soil. It needs moderate water but is somewhat drought-tolerant once established.

In Zones 2–8 plant established seedlings 3–4 weeks before last frost date. In Zones 9–11 plant in late fall or early winter for winter or early spring color. Mulch to conserve moisture and prevent weeds. Fertilize lightly, if at all. Shear by a few inches occasionally (every few weeks or so) to deadhead and promote further blooms. It will reseed in favorable climates. Plants fade when weather gets hot. In cooler regions cut back to just a few inches for more blooms. This plant is sometimes prone to botrytis, aphids, and slugs.

Annuals and Perennials

Brassica oleracea — annual

flowering cabbage, kale

Light Needs:

Full sun

Mature Height: *12"–18"*
Mature Width: *15"–20"*

Zones: *2–11*

Features:

Exotic color for fall

Spectacular foliage

Showy in fall or winter.

Needs: Average, well-drained soil. Moderate water.

Plant established plants in fall. Fertilize at planting time. Mulch to conserve moisture.

This plant look good well past first frost in all zones and will hold its color through winter in Zones 8–11. Tear out in spring or as soon as plants become unattractive.

It is prone to cabbageworms, slugs, cutworms, and clubroot.

Choices: Deep green outer leaves set off showy inner leaves of red, cream, and pink. 'Peacock' is extremely colorful and feathery.

Browallia — warm-season annual

amethyst flower, sapphire flower

Light Needs:

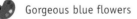

Full sun to part shade

Mature Height: *12"–18"*
Mature Width: *10"–14"*

Zones: *2–11*

Features:

Gorgeous blue flowers

Good color for shade

Rabbit-resistant

Blooms late spring through fall.

Needs: Full sun in Zones 2–5; light shade in Zones 6–11. Rich, well-drained soil. Ample water.

Plant established seedlings in spring, working in compost. Mulch to retain moisture. For best health and flowering, fertilize regularly, every 4 weeks, or work in a 9-month, slow-release fertilizer at planting time. It may not bloom where summers are very cool or very short. In mild winter areas, it may survive the winter. If this happens, just cut back plants to a few inches in spring and fertilize to spur new growth. In warm climates this plant may also reseed.

It is prone to aphids and whiteflies.

Choices: This plant has flowers in purples and blues.

Brugmansia — annual, perennial, or shrub

datura, angel's trumpet

Light Needs:

Full sun to part shade

Mature Height: *3'–10'*
Mature Width: *3'–7'*

Zones: *3–11*

Features:

Huge, exotic flowers

Fragrant at night

Good for wet areas

Blooms summer through late fall.

Needs: Grow as a perennial or shrub where temperatures don't go below 45°F (7°C). Elsewhere grow as an annual. Full sun in most areas; part shade in hot summer regions, Zones 7–11. Site should also be protected from wind, which damages the oversized flowers. Water often; never allow plant to dry out.

Plant established plants in spring in rich, well-drained soil. If growing as an annual, fertilize frequently, every 2–4 weeks, with liquid fertilizer to fuel this plant's very rapid growth.

In Zones 4–8 if the plant is in a pot, bring it indoors in fall before the first frost and place in a sunny spot to overwinter, if desired. It is susceptible to aphids and whiteflies.

Calendula

pot marigold

Light Needs:

Full sun

Mature Height: *1'–2'*

Mature Width: *10"–14"*

Zones: *2–11*

Features:

 Easy to grow

Great for cottage gardens

Brilliant yellow flowers

Blooms spring through summer.

Needs: Poor to rich well-drained soil. Moderate water.

In Zones 2–7 plant established seedlings in garden in early spring, no earlier than 2–3 weeks before last frost date. In Zones 8–11 plant in fall for winter and spring bloom. Fertilize regularly, every 4 weeks, or work a 9-month, slow-release fertilizer into the soil at planting time. Trim spent blooms for best flowering.

This plant is prone to powdery mildew, leaf spot, cabbage loopers, and aphids.

Choices: Flowers are mainly brilliant oranges and yellows, but apricots and creams are also available.

Callistephus chinensis

china aster

Light Needs:

Full sun to part shade

Mature Height: *6"–36"*

Mature Width: *6"–12"*

Zones: *2–11*

Features:

Excellent for cutting

Provides autumn color

Blooms in late summer to early fall.

Needs: Rich, well-drained soil. Moderate water.

Plant established seedlings in spring after all danger of frost has passed. Feed regularly, every 4 weeks, or work in a 9-month, slow-release fertilizer. Mulch to conserve moisture. If continuous bloom is desired, replant every few weeks. Stake tall varieties.

This plant is prone to a number of diseases and pests, including aster yellows virus, septoria leaf spot, aphids, mealybugs, rust, wilt diseases, and gray mold. Avoid replanting in the same area to minimize these problems.

Choices: Flowers come in nearly every color. 'Ostrich Plume' is wilt-resistant; 'Florette Champagne' has unusual pink quilled petals.

Calluna vulgaris

scotch heather

Light Needs:

Full sun

Mature Height: *4"–2'*

Mature Width: *6"–4'*

Zones: *3–11*

Features

 Good groundcover

Excellent cut flower

Bloom time varies widely.

Needs: Full sun best, especially on the east side of a building or hedge for protection from winter sun and wind. Well-drained or sandy soil, rich in organic matter but low in nutrients, is ideal. Acidic soil and moderate moisture are preferable.

Plant established plants in spring. Keep moderately moist. Too much water will cause root rot. Don't fertilize. In Zones 7–8 in winter protect with boughs of pine or other cut evergreens until spring. This plant is usually pest free.

Choices: Flowers come in pinks, lavenders, whites, and creams. Many cultivars have striking gold foliage.

See also *Erica* on page 181.

Campanula spp.

bellflower

Light Needs:

Full sun to part shade

Mature Height: 6"–4'

Mature Width: 6"–3'

Zones: 3–8

Features:

Long-blooming

Beautiful, bell-shaped flowers

Tall types excellent for cutting

Blooms midsummer through fall.

Needs: Full sun in Zones 3–4; part shade in Zones 5–8. Rich, moisture-retentive, but extremely well-drained soil. Moderate to ample moisture.

Plant established seedlings in spring or fall. Mulch to keep soil cool and moist. It should never be allowed to dry out. Fertilize lightly. Trim spent blooms regularly. Divide most *campanulas* every three or so years, with the exception of milky bellflower (*Campanula lactiflora*), which doesn't like transplanting.

Most are perennials, but Canterbury bells (*Campanula medium*) is a biennial. It must be planted in the garden in spring or fall the first year in order to bloom the second year.

Choices: Heights vary widely by species.

'Campanula persicifolia'

Catharanthus roseus

vinca, periwinkle

Light Needs:

Full sun to part shade

Mature Height: 4"–14"

Mature Width: 4"–2'

Zones: 2–11

Features:

Very easy to grow

Long-blooming

Tolerates heat

Blooms summer through fall.

Needs: Rich, well-drained soil; full sun; light shade, especially in Zones 6–11; moderate water. It is somewhat drought-tolerant.

Grow as an annual in Zones 2–8; as a perennial in Zones 9–11. Plant established seedlings in spring after all danger of frost has passed. Mulch. Fertilize regularly. Cut plants back by about one-fourth to one-third in late summer to encourage new, fresh growth and flowering.

Choices: Flowers come in pinks, whites, and purples. 'Cooler' series is good for Zones 3–4; 'Carpet' is just 4 inches tall and 24 inches wide, making it excellent for baskets, window boxes, and rock gardens.

Celosia spp.

celosia, cockscomb

Light Needs:

Full sun

Mature Height: 4"–3'

Mature Width: 4"–18"

Zones: 2–11

Features:

Easy to grow

Excellent for cutting or drying

Brilliant colors

Blooms spring through fall.

Needs: Rich, well-drained soil. Moderate moisture.

Plant established seedlings in spring after all danger of frost has passed. Mulch to conserve water and prevent disease. Fertilize regularly, every 4 weeks, or work in a 9-month, slow-release fertilizer at planting time. Trim fading blooms to encourage further flowering. Cockscomb is generally trouble-free, but spider mites can be a problem as can root rot.

Choices: Flowers come in oranges, peach, gold, pink, red, and maroon. Dwarf cultivars just 4 inches high are available. 'Century' is a popular plumed type; 'Apricot Beauty' is an especially lovely plumed type. 'Toreador' and 'Fireglow' are two crested types.

Annuals and Perennials

Centaurea cineraria (Senecio cineraria)
annual or perennial

dusty miller

Light Needs:

Full sun

Mature Height: 6"–24"
Mature Width: 6"–18"
Zones: 2–11

Features:

 Silvery leaves

Drought-tolerant

Easy to grow

Grown for foliage.

Needs: Average, well-drained soil. If soil is acid, add lime. Moderate to light moisture; most types are heat- and drought-tolerant once established.

Plant established seedlings in spring after danger of frost has passed. Fertilize rarely, if at all. When watering avoid getting leaves wet. Dusty miller produces small white or yellow flowers; trim them off to preserve foliage effect.

Annual in Zones 2–5; perennial in Zones 6–11. It is most attractive if pulled out at the end of the growing season.

Aphids are sometimes a problem.

Choices: 'Silver Dust' and 'Silver Lace' are both beautifully lacy. 'Cirrus' has more solid, rounded foliage.

Centaurea cyanus
cool-season annual

annual cornflower, bachelor's button

Light Needs:

Full sun

Mature Height: 18"–24"
Mature Width: 18"–24"
Zones: 3–10

Features:

 Attracts butterflies

Good wildflower

Excellent cut flower

Blooms late spring or midsummer.

Needs: Average, well-drained soil. If soil is acid, add lime. Moderate to light moisture.

Plant from seed directly in soil for best results. In Zones 5–8 sow seeds outdoors 2 weeks before spring's last frost date. In Zones 9–10 plant seeds outdoors in fall for spring bloom. Plant just deep enough to cover and keep soil moist. When plants are about 1 inch tall, thin to 8 inches apart.

If planting established seedlings, do so outdoors after last frost date. Keep seeds and young plants evenly moist; they are somewhat drought-tolerant once established. Trim spent blooms to prevent excessive reseeding, but plant will still reseed freely. Fertilize lightly, if at all.

Centaurea montana
perennial

perennial cornflower, mountain bluet

Light Needs:

Full sun

Mature Height: 18"–24"
Mature Width: 18"–24"
Zones: 3–8

Features:

 Beautiful blue color

Good wildflower

Blooms late spring through midsummer.

Needs: Average to sandy, poor soil; must have excellent drainage. Moderate moisture.

Plant established plants in spring. Mulch to conserve moisture. Fertilize lightly if at all. Trim spent blooms to prevent excessive reseeding. In late summer cut plant back to just a few inches to promote fall bloom. Stake to prevent floppiness.

This plant may spread aggressively where well suited to conditions and often will spread and form a large colony. Divide every 3–4 years as desired.

It is susceptible to slugs and snails.

Choices: Renowned for its startlingly deep blue color, this plant is also available in white and pink varieties.

Annuals and Perennials

Centhranthus ruber
perennial

red valerian, jupiter's beard

Light Needs:

Full sun

Mature Height: *2'–3'*

Mature Width: *1'–2'*

Zones: *4–8*

Features:

Ideal for rocky areas, poor soil

Attracts butterflies

Blooms late spring through early summer.

Needs: Poor, average to alkaline soil, with excellent drainage; it will not thrive if soil is too rich. This plant needs even moisture at first, but then is drought-tolerant.

Plant established plants in spring. Do not fertilize. Keep spent blooms trimmed to minimize reseeding; this plant can become a slightly problematic (but beautiful) weed if left alone. However, it is a short-lived plant, lasting only 3–5 years, so allow at least a few to reseed.

It is trouble free if well suited to the site.

Choices: Flowers come in coral pink, white, and deep rose-red.

Cerastium tomentosum
perennial

snow-in-summer

Light Needs:

Full sun

Mature Height: *3"–6"*

Mature Width: *12"–2'*

Zones: *2–9*

Features:

Eye-catching silver foliage with white flowers

Drought-tolerant

Good flowering groundcover

Blooms late spring or early summer.

Needs: Average to poor, sandy, well-drained soil. Moderate water. It is drought-tolerant and dies out in hot, humid areas.

Plant seedlings in spring in Zones 2–5; spring or fall in Zones 6–7. Cut back to foliage after flowering. Fertilize little if at all. It can become invasive in sites where it's well suited and where soil is fertile.

Usually pest and disease free, this plant may develop root rot in damper sites.

Choices: It has white flowers only. 'Yo Yo' is less invasive than other cultivars.

Ceratostigma plumbaginoides
perennial

plumbago

Light Needs:

Full sun to part shade

Mature Height: *8"–12"*

Mature Width: *1'–2'*

Zones: *5–9*

Features:

Rich blue flowers

Excellent groundcover

Good companion with spring-blooming bulbs

Blooms late summer through fall.

Needs: Full sun in Zones 5–6; light shade in Zones 7–9. Average, well-drained soil, moderate moisture.

Plant seedlings in spring. Fertilize lightly. Mulch in winter in Zone 5. In late winter or very early spring, cut back woody stems to stimulate new growth.

This plant is prone to root rot in wet conditions and powdery mildew.

Choices: It has blue flowers only.

Chelone lyonii

pink turtlehead

Light Needs:

Full sun to part shade

Mature Height: *2'–4'*

Mature Width: *1'–2'*

Zones: *3–8*

Features:

💧 Good for wet spots

🍃 Native plant

Blooms late summer.

Needs: Full sun if conditions are wet; partial shade in drier conditions. Rich, preferably acid soil. Ample moisture; never allow soil to dry out. This plant loves boggy conditions.

Plant established plants in spring. Pinch tips of plants in early summer for bushier plants with more flowers. Fertilize for best flowering. Stake if site is too shady.

It is pest and disease free as long as conditions are right.

Choices: Flowers come in pink or white. *Chelone glabra* has pinkish-white flowers, grows 4 feet, and is hardy in Zones 5–9. *Chelone obliqua* has deep pink or white flowers, grows up to 3 feet, and is hardy in Zones 3–9.

Chrysanthemum spp. (Dendranthema)

perennial mum

Light Needs:

Full sun

Mature Height: *1'–3'*

Mature Width: *8"–3'*

Zones: *4–9*

Features:

🎨 Beautiful color for fall

✂ Excellent cut flower

🐰 Rabbit-resistant

Blooms in fall.

Needs: Rich, well-drained soil, preferably slightly acid. Ample moisture.

Plant established plants in spring. Fertilize regularly. Mulch to keep roots cool and moist. Pinch tips every 2 weeks to promote bushiness and better flowering, stopping mid-July in Zones 4–6 and mid- to late August in Zones 7–9. The shallow roots of mums die out easily in winter, so mulch well in fall, especially in Zones 4–6. Wait to cut back foliage until early spring. This plant is usually problem free, though prone to problems if too wet.

Choices: Perennial mums may be labeled with the botanical name *Dendranthema*, but both are the same flower.

Chrysogonum virginianum

goldenstar, green-and-gold

Light Needs:

Full sun to full shade

Mature Height: *6"–10"*

Mature Width: *1'–2'*

Zones: *5–9*

Features:

👁 Beautiful, unusual flowering groundcover

🍃 Native to North America

Blooms spring through fall.

Needs: Full sun to part shade in Zones 5–6; partial to full shade in Zones 7–9. Rich, well-drained, moist soil. Ample moisture, especially in full sun.

Plant in spring or fall. Plant in groups of 10 or more for best effect. Fertilize occasionally. Divide in spring or fall every 3 or so years as needed. This plant often reseeds, but not problematically.

It is prone to mildew if it does not get enough sun.

Choices: Flowers are bright yellow, 'Allen Bush' is especially long-blooming.

Cimicifuga

perennial

bugbane

Light Needs:

Full sun to part shade

Mature Height: *3'–6'*
Mature Width: *2'–3'*
Zones: *3–8*

Features:

* Good shade flower

 Ideal choice for wet spots

Blooms late summer to late fall.

Needs: Part shade best; will tolerate full sun if constantly moist. Rich, deep, moist, preferably acid soil. Ample moisture.

Plant established plants in spring. Mulch to retain moisture. Keep well watered, or leaves will brown and plants will be stunted. Fertilize occasionally. It seldom needs division, perhaps every several years.

Diseases and pests are seldom a problem as long as conditions are good.

Choices: Flowers are white. 'The Pearl' is a popular cultivar. *Cimicifuga racemosa* may grow to 6 feet and may need staking. 'Atropurpurea' has dark purple foliage.

Clarkia amoena

cool-season annual

godetia

Light Needs:

Full sun to part shade

Mature Height: *8"–30"*
Mature Width: *4"–12"*
Zones: *2–11*

Features:

* Beautiful cut flower

* Welcome spring color

Blooms in spring.

Needs: Full sun in Zones 2–5; partial shade in Zones 6–11. Poor, well-drained soil. Moderate moisture.

In Zones 2–7 plant seeds directly in soil in midspring, as early as 2 weeks before last frost date and no later than the last frost date itself. In Zones 9–11 plant seeds in fall for early spring color. When plants are about 1 inch high, thin to 4 inches to 1 foot apart, depending on how bushy the plants will get (check the seed packet). Godetia looks and blooms best when thickly planted. When plants are 2 inches high, pinch by half to promote bushier, less floppy plants.

Push a few twiggy branches into the ground among the planting to help support the flowers. Do not fertilize.

Cleome hassleriana

warm-season annual

spider flower

Light Needs:

Full sun to part shade

Mature Height: *3'–6'*
Mature Width: *3"–1'*
Zones: *2–11*

Features:

* Beautiful, airy effect

* Excellent cut flower

* Easy to grow

Blooms mid- to late summer through frost.

Needs: Full sun in Zones 2–5; full sun to part shade in Zones 6–11. Rich, moist soil. Ample water.

Plant seedlings in spring after all danger of frost has passed. Fertilize sparingly to prevent from getting too tall. Stake when 1 foot, being careful around the small thorns.

This plant often reseeds, sometimes problematically so. It is usually pest and disease free but is susceptible to rust, aphids, and leaf spot.

Choices: Flowers are pinks, whites, roses, or lavender. 'Queen' is a popular variety.

Consolida ambigua

larkspur

Light Needs:

Full sun to part shade

Mature Height: 9"–3'
Mature Width: 1"–10"

Zones: 2–11

Features:

🚤 Good seaside plant

🧄 Intensely fragrant

🌳 Good woodland plant

Blooms in early spring, spring, or early summer, depending on planting time.

Needs: Full sun in Zones 2–7; light shade in Zones 8–11. Plenty of moisture.

In Zones 2–8 plant seeds directly in soil outdoors in early to midspring. In Zones 9–11 plant in fall for winter or very early spring bloom. Thin seeds according to package directions. This plant looks best in large stands of 20 or more plants. Stake tall varieties.

Fertilize occasionally. Keep well watered but avoid wetting leaves. When plants are done blooming, tear them out and shake them upside down to scatter seeds, assuring reseeders next spring. Weed carefully the following spring to avoid disturbing tiny larkspur seedlings.

Convallaria majalis

lily-of-the-valley

Light Needs:

Full sun to full shade

Mature Height: 6"–10"
Mature Width: 2"–4"

Zones: 3–7

Features:

🧄 Wonderfully fragrant

🍃 Fast-spreading groundcover

✳ Thrives in shade

Blooms midspring.

Needs: Will take full sun in Zones 3–5 and the Pacific Northwest but needs at least part shade in Zones 6–7. Average to poor, well-drained, acid to neutral soil with plenty of moisture. Leaves will brown prematurely if conditions are too dry.

Plant in fall or spring, working plenty of compost into the soil.

Prone to leaf rot and stem rot if conditions are too wet.

Choices: Flowers are almost always white, but 'Rosea' is light pink; 'Plena' is double-flowered white.

Convolvulus tricolor

dwarf morning glory

Light Needs:

Full sun

Mature Height: 12"–16"
Mature Width: 9"–1'

Zones: 2–11

Features:

🪴 Good container plant

👍 Easy to grow

Blooms in mid- through late summer.

Needs: Average, well-drained soil. Moderate moisture.

After all danger of frost has passed in spring, soak seeds overnight and then plant directly in the soil outdoors. Do not transplant. Fertilize lightly. It thrives with little attention. Keep evenly moist. Deadhead regularly for most bloom. Although it's a perennial in Zones 9–11 and sometimes even as far north as Zone 7, it's best to pull up plants in the fall and replant in the spring for fresh, attractive flowers.

Choices: 'Royal Ensign', a beautiful blue, is popular, but now there are red and rose-colored varieties as well.

Do not plant *Convolvulus arvensis* (bindweed), which is highly invasive.

Coreopsis spp.
perennial

coreopsis, tickseed

Light Needs:

Full sun to part shade

Mature Height: 2'–3'
Mature Width: 3"–1'

Zones: 3–9

Features:

Long-blooming

Easy

Native wildflower

Blooms late spring through fall.
Needs: Average to sandy, well-drained soil; doesn't need to be particularly fertile. Moderate water for pink coreopsis (*Coreopsis rosea*), but others are fairly drought-tolerant.

Plant seedlings in spring or fall. It is important to shear off spent blooms to keep plant blooming for long periods. Fertilize occasionally.

Taller types may sprawl; in spring push a ring-type support into the soil when plants are several inches high if sprawling becomes a problem.

Plants may last only a few years, so divide every 3 or so years to assure an ongoing supply.

It is bothered by few pests with the exception of rabbits.

Corydalis spp.
perennial

fumewort

Light Needs:

Full sun to part shade

Mature Height: 10"–16"
Mature Width: 8"–10"

Zones: 4–8

Features:

Thrives in shade

Deer- and rabbit-resistant

Blooms spring to frost.
Needs: Average to fertile, well-drained soil. Especially likes gravelly soil. It will tolerate alkaline soil and light drought but does best with ample moisture.

Plant tubers 3 inches deep in fall or plant established seedlings in spring. It needs no deadheading.

Fertilize occasionally; divide in fall every 2–3 years as needed.

Plants may die back after blooming. Mark the spot to prevent digging up; plants should come back next year. They spread vigorously in ideal conditions.

Fumewort is usually pest free and is not attractive to deer and rabbits.

Choices: Renowned for its yellow species; blue and pink species are also beautiful.

Cosmos spp.
warm-season annual

cosmos

Light Needs:

Full sun

Mature Height: 1'–6'
Mature Width: 10"–3'

Zones: 2–11

Features:

Very easy to grow

Excellent wildflower

Wonderful for cutting

Blooms midsummer to frost.
Needs: Poor to average, well-drained soil. Moderate moisture, but it tolerates some drought.

Plant seedlings outdoors after all danger of frost has passed. You can also plant from seed directly in soil at that time, but it will take longer to bloom. Pinch plants' tops when they're a few inches tall to encourage bushier growth. Avoid fertilizing. Water regularly as needed. Stake as needed. Trim spent blooms or regularly cut for bouquets to promote longer bloom time. It is usually pest and disease free.

Choices: *Cosmos bipinnatus* grows in Zones 3–10; *Cosmos sulphureus* in Zones 2–11. Heights vary radically; check label.

Annuals and Perennials

Crambe cordifolia

crambe, colewort

Light Needs:

Full sun

Mature Height: *4'–6'*

Mature Width: *2'–4'*

Zones: *5–9*

Features:

 Spectacular perennial

Blooms early summer.

Needs: Average to rich, well-drained soil; neutral to alkaline. Ample moisture, never allow to dry out.

Plant established plants in spring or fall. Fertilize occasionally, every 4 weeks, or work in a 9-month, slow-release fertilizer each spring.

Stake the tall, flowering stalk to prevent flopping. Trim off fading stalk to prevent reseeding. Doesn't need dividing.

This plant is very susceptible to caterpillars and aphids. It may need a regular pesticide program if problems are chronic.

Choices: Blooms are white. *Crambe maritima* (sea kale) grows just 2 feet tall and tolerates the sand and salt found in seaside conditions.

Cuphea spp.

mexican heather

Light Needs:

Full sun to part shade

Mature Height: *12"–30"*

Mature Width: *1'–3'*

Zones: *2–11*

Features:

Excellent container plant

Some types have exotic-looking flowers

Blooms summer through fall.

Needs: Grow as an annual in Zones 2–9; as a perennial in Zones 10–11. Full sun in Zones 2–7; part shade in Zones 8–11. Needs very rich, moist, well-drained soil; never allow to dry out.

Plant seedlings in spring after all danger of frost has passed. Pinch tips at planting time for bushier growth. Fertilize regularly, especially if growing as an annual.

If growing as a perennial, cut back heavily each spring to prompt fresh growth.

This plant is prone to whitefly, aphids, and powdery mildew.

Choices: Flower colors are pinks, purples, whites, and reds. *Cuphea hyssopifolia* is known as Mexican, Florida, or false heather. *Cuphea ignea* is known as cigar plant.

'Cuphea hyssopifolia'

Cynoglossum amabile

chinese forget-me-not

Light Needs:

Full sun to part shade

Mature Height: *18"–2'*

Mature Width: *12"–18"*

Zones: *2–9*

Features:

 Gorgeous blue flowers

Good for naturalistic plantings

Blooms late spring or early summer.

Needs: Average to rich, well-drained soil. Plenty of moisture.

Sow from seed directly onto soil, or plant as seedlings. Plant in very early spring as soon as soil can be worked in Zones 2–7; in fall in Zones 8–9.

Avoid fertilizing. Trim spent blooms to promote more flowering. Pull out plants when they have finished blooming in summer. This plant usually reseeds freely, coming back year after year.

It is prone to mildew, especially if not well watered.

Choices: It is renowned for its electric blue, but white and pink cultivars are available. 'Firmament' is especially stocky and less prone to flopping.

Annuals and Perennials

Delphinium elatum

delphinium

Light Needs:

Full sun

Mature Height: *3'-7'*

Mature Width: *1'-3'*

Zones: *2-7*

Features:

Dramatically beautiful

Good for cutting

Blooms early summer.

Needs: Demands very rich, fertile, deep, moist soil and moderate, never extremely hot, conditions. Keep evenly moist; never allow to dry out.

Grow as an annual in Zones 2–7; will grow as a perennial in Zones 6–7 where summers are cool. Plant established plants in spring and fertilize regularly. Mulch to keep soil cool and moist. Staking is a must; stake when plants are about 1½ feet high. Trim spent blooms to promote longer flowering.

This plant is prone to mildew, slugs, and snails. A regular pesticide program should be considered.

Choices: Pacific hybrids grow to 7 feet; white 'Connecticut Yankee' grows just 2–3 feet and is more heat-resistant.

Dianthus spp.

pinks, sweet william

Light Needs:

Full sun to part shade

Mature Height: *4"-2'*

Mature Width: *6"-30"*

Zones: *2-11*

Features:

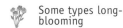 Some types long-blooming

Some types intensely fragrant

Tall types make good cut flowers

Blooms in spring.

Needs: Full sun to light shade in Zones 3–6; light shade appreciated in Zones 7–9. Average to rich, well-drained, slightly alkaline soil. Moderate moisture.

For annual cool-season color, plant annual China pinks in late fall or very early spring in Zones 8–11 or early spring in Zones 3–7. Plant perennial types in spring.

Choices: China pink *(Dianthus chinensis)* is a scented annual. Sweet William *(Dianthus barbatus)* can be grown as a perennial or an annual. Maiden pink *(Dianthus deltoides)* is a perennial that blooms up to 2 months. Cottage pink *(Dianthus plumarius)* and Cheddar pink *(Dianthus gratianopolitanus)* are two very fragrant perennial types.

'Dianthus chinenis'

Diascia spp.

twinspur

Light Needs:

Full sun to part shade

Mature Height: *10"-12"*

Mature Width: *1'-2'*

Zones: *2-11*

Features:

Unusual annual

Good rock-garden plant

Good container plant

Blooms late winter or early spring.

Needs: Full sun in Zones 2–6; part shade in Zones 7–11. Average, well-drained soil. Somewhat drought-tolerant, it will die out if soil is heavy and wet. In Zones 2–7 treat as an annual that thrives in the cool conditions of early spring. In Zones 9–11 grow as a perennial.

Either way, plant seedlings in early spring after danger of frost has passed. When blooms begin to fade, shear back the plant by about one-quarter to rejuvenate. In Zones 2–7 tear out the plant when all blooming stops.

This plant may spread vigorously. Divide every 2–3 years in autumn.

Choices: *Diascia barberae* is an annual. Perennial species include *Diascia cordata, Diascia* 'Ruby Field', and *Diascia vigilis*.

Annuals and Perennials

Dicentra spp.

bleeding heart

Light Needs:

Full sun to full shade

Mature Height: *9"–4'*
Mature Width: *9"–3'*

Zones: *2–9*

Features:

- Charming heart-shaped flowers
- Shade-loving woodland flower
- Pretty cut flower

Blooms early spring or early spring through frost.

Needs: Full sun to light shade in Zones 2–5; light to full shade in Zones 5–9. Rich, well-drained soil with plenty of compost. Keep constantly moist, especially in full sun. Plant established plants in fall or spring. Mulch. Trim spent blooms.

Choices: *Dicentra eximia,* also called everblooming or fringed bleeding heart, blooms with the daffodils and, in Zones 2–5, continues lightly until frost. Its ferny foliage stays pretty all season long in Zones 3–9. *Dicentra spectabilis,* called common or old-fashioned bleeding heart, makes a spectacular show in early spring but goes dormant by midsummer. Hostas nearby can cover bare spots in Zones 2–9.

Digitalis purpurea

common foxglove

Light Needs:

Full sun to part shade

Mature Height: *18"–5'*
Mature Width: *10"–2'*

Zones: *4–9*

Features:

- Excellent vertical accent
- Wonderful for cottage gardens
- Rabbit-resistant

Blooms late spring or early summer.

Needs: Full sun in Zones 4–7; partial shade in Zones 8–9. Rich, well-drained soil. Some types tolerate little water, but moderate to ample moisture is ideal.

Plant established seedlings of any type of common foxglove in spring. For biennial types you can plant seeds directly in soil in midsummer and keep moist. In warm Zones 7–9, you can plant established seedlings in fall for bloom the following spring. Plant in groups of 10 or more for best effect and easiest care.

Stake as needed. Mulch. This plant may reseed.

Choices: Depending on climate and the type, foxglove can be grown as an annual, biennial (see page 46), or a perennial. Read label carefully.

Dimorphotheca spp.

african cape daisy, cape marigold

Light Needs:

Full sun

Mature Height: *4"–16"*
Mature Width: *6"–14"*

Zones: *2–11*

Features:

 Good for naturalistic and wildflower gardens

Blooms late winter, spring, or summer.

Needs: Average to poor, loose, well-drained soil. Light to moderate moisture.

Plant seeds directly in soil in early spring. In Zones 9–11 plant seeds this way in late fall or early winter also.

Avoid fertilizing. Trim spent blooms regularly to promote longest flowering time. Discard plants after blooming has ceased.

Choices: Flowers are white, oranges, yellows, creams, or apricot. 'Glistening White' is purest white.

Echinacea purpurea

purple coneflower

Light Needs:

Full sun

Mature Height: 2'–4'

Mature Width: 2'–3'

Zones: 3–9

Features:

Attracts butterflies and finches

Good wildflower

Drought-tolerant

Blooms midsummer.

Needs: Average to poor, well-drained soil. Moderate moisture but tolerates drought well.

Plant established plants in spring or autumn. Avoid fertilizing. If soil is rich or moist, may need staking. Deadhead for longer bloom or leave flower heads standing to attract birds and butterflies.

This plant spreads easily in most conditions. Divide every 3–4 years.

It usually is pest and disease free, but caterpillars and Japanese beetle are sometimes a problem.

Choices: Flowers are pinks, whites, and reds. 'White Swan' is an unusual white cultivar; 'Crimson Star' is a red type. 'Magnus' is a particularly choice pink type.

Echinops spp.

globe thistle

Light Needs:

Full sun

Mature Height: 2'–4'

Mature Width: 2'–3'

Zones: 3–8

Features:

Attracts bees, butterflies, and moths

Unusual blue ball-like flowers

Drought-tolerant

Blooms mid- or late summer.

Needs: Average to poor, well-drained soil. Best with moderate water but will tolerate drought when mature.

Plant established seedlings in spring or autumn. Avoid fertilizing; if soil is too rich, staking will be needed. Deadhead after bloom is finished. Divide plants in spring or fall every 3–4 years as needed. This plant is usually pest free.

Choices: Flowers are striking steely blues and purples. 'Taplow Blue' is one of the most popular cultivars.

Eremurus

foxtail lily, desert candle

Light Needs:

Full sun

Mature Height: 2'–10'

Mature Width: 2'–4'

Zones: 5–8

Features:

Dramatic vertical accent

Outstanding cut flower

Deer-resistant

Blooms late spring or early summer.

Needs: Rich, very well-drained (sandy is good) soil. Moderate moisture while growing; tolerates drought once dormant in late summer and fall.

Plant rhizomes in fall; plant established plants in spring. Fertilize during bloom time. Handle roots carefully; they're brittle and tend to rot if damaged. Stake taller types. Foliage dies down after blooming; mark spot to avoid injuring the roots. It is susceptible to slugs and snails.

Choices: Plants come in whites, pinks, yellows, and oranges. Read label carefully to choose desired height. *Eremurus stenophyllus* grows just 2–3 feet. *Eremurus robustus* may reach 10 feet.

Erica spp.

spring and winter heath

Light Needs:

Full sun to part shade

Mature Height: *8"–10"*

Mature Width: *6"–18"*

Zones: *5–7*

Features:

 Long bloom and interest

Excellent cut flower

Bloom time varies widely.

Needs: Full sun best, especially the east side of a building or hedge for protection from winter sun and wind. Well-drained or sandy soil, rich in organic matter but low in nutrients, is ideal. Prefers acidic soil.

Plant established plants in spring. Keep moderately moist, but too much water causes root rot. Don't fertilize. In Zones 7–8 in winter, protect smaller heathers with boughs of pine or other cut evergreens until spring.

Plants are usually pest free.

Choices: Colors are pinks, lavenders, whites, and creams. Many cultivars have striking gold foliage.

Eryngium spp.

sea holly

Light Needs:

Full sun

Mature Height: *18"–3'*

Mature Width: *2'–3'*

Zones: *2–9*

Features:

Excellent cut and dried flower

Good for seaside locations

Drought-tolerant

Blooms midsummer to frost.

Needs: Poor, dry, sandy soil; thrives on drought and seashore conditions.

Plant established plants in spring. Once mature, dislikes transplanting. Avoid fertilizing; plants may flop in soil that is too rich. If necessary, stake. It is prone to root rot in wet sites, especially if wet over the winter. Sooty mold is a problem in humid conditions.

Choices: Silvery blues or whites. The amethyst sea holly, *Eryngium amethystinum,* is the most cold-hardy, thriving in Zones 2–8.

Eschscholzia californica

california poppy

Light Needs:

Full sun

Mature Height: *8"–2'*

Mature Width: *2"–4"*

Zones: *2–11*

Features:

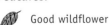 Good wildflower

Drought-tolerant

Blooms spring or summer.

Needs: Sandy, poor, neutral soil; doesn't like acid soil. Moderate moisture at first; becomes drought-tolerant once established.

Plant seeds directly in soil in early spring for early summer bloom; in Zones 7–11 also sow in fall for spring bloom. Don't fertilize; rich soil may prevent bloom.

Tear out plants after bloom time has passed. This plant often self-seeds. It is usually pest free.

Choices: Flowers are oranges, yellows, creams, whites. Now some reds, pinks, and violets are also available.

Most cultivars are single flowers, but 'Ballerina' and 'Mission Bells' are semi-double and double.

Eupatorium purpureum or *fistulosum*

perennial

Joe-Pye weed

Light Needs:

Full sun

Mature Height: *4'–7'*
Mature Width: *3'–4'*
Zones: *3–9*

Features:

Native plant; good wildflower

Attracts butterflies

Good for wet spots

Blooms late summer or early fall.
Needs: Average to rich, moist soil. Tolerates wet soil; needs ample moisture.
Plant established plants in spring. Fertilize occasionally. Mulch to conserve moisture. Pinch back in midsummer, if desired, to control height, but flowers will be smaller. This plant seldom needs division.
It is usually pest free.
Choices: Flowers are reddish-purple or white. 'Atropurpureum' has striking deep purple stems. *Eupatorium fistulosum* is very attractive to butterflies.

Euphorbia polychroma (Euphorbia epithymoides)

perennial

cushion spurge

Light Needs:

Full sun to part shade

Mature Height: *12"–18"*
Mature Width: *12"–18"*
Zones: *4–8*

Features:

Easy to grow

Long bloom time and interest

Somewhat drought-tolerant

Blooms early spring.
Needs: Full sun in Zones 4–6 and Pacific Northwest; part shade in Zones 7–8. Average to sandy, well-drained soil; moderate moisture but will tolerate drought; can be invasive in moist soils.
Plant established plants in spring or fall. Mulch to conserve moisture. Fertilize occasionally. Usually there is no need to trim spent blooms. Divide only when plants become floppy after a few years.
It is usually pest free.
Choices: Yellow flowers only.

Eustoma (Eustoma grandiflora)

warm-season annual

lisianthus

Light Needs:

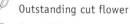

Full to part shade

Mature Height: *6"–2'*
Mature Width: *6"–10"*
Zones: *2–11*

Features:

Outstanding cut flower

Beautiful colors, including blue

Blooms mid- to late summer.
Needs: Average, well-drained soil; ample moisture.
Plant established seedlings in spring after all danger of frost has passed. Pinch off tops at planting time to encourage bushier growth and more flowers. Mulch to conserve moisture. Fertilize regularly, every 4 weeks, or work in a 9-month, slow-release fertilizer at planting time. Trim spent blooms to encourage further flowering.
This plant is usually pest free.
Choices: Flowers are pinks, whites, and blues. Dwarf types grow just 6 inches tall; taller types are excellent for cutting. 'Flamenco' is especially heat-tolerant.

Annuals and Perennials

Felicia amelloides

annual

blue daisy, blue marguerite

Light Needs:

Full sun

Mature Height: *1'–3'*

Mature Width: *2'–5'*

Zones: *7–11*

Features:

 Gorgeous blue flowers

Good for naturalistic gardens

Good cut flower

Blooms very early spring to midspring.

Needs: Rich, well-drained soil. Drought-tolerant, but flowers better with moderate water.

Plant in early spring in Zones 7–8; in fall in Zones 9–11. Pinch, deadhead, and cut back by about one-quarter frequently to keep plant neat looking and flowering abundantly. This will also prevent it from spreading too much. Fertilize every 4–6 weeks or work in a 9-month, slow-release fertilizer in spring. It will usually overwinter in Zones 9–11 but gets shabby after a year or two. Best to grow as an annual. It is usually pest free.

Choices: Flowers come in shades of blue. 'Astrid Thomas' is a dwarf type and stays open at night. 'Midnight' is a lovely dark blue.

Filipendula rubra

perennial

queen-of-the-prairie

Light Needs:

Full sun to part shade

Mature Height: *6'–8'*

Mature Width: *3'–4'*

Zones: *3–8*

Features:

Striking vertical accent

Good plant for wet spots

Rabbit-resistant

Blooms early to midsummer.

Needs: Prefers light shade but will tolerate full sun with plenty of moisture; keep soil moist to wet.

Plant established plants in spring. Mulch to keep soil moist. Fertilize occasionally, every 4–6 weeks, or work in a 9-month, slow-release fertilizer each spring. Trim off spent flowers. This plant rarely needs staking. Divide tough roots in spring as needed.

Spider mites and mildew are a problem if plant isn't adequately watered.

Choices: Flowers come in pink or white.

Fuchsia spp.

annual, perennial or shrub

fuchsia, lady's eardrops

Light Needs:

Tolerates full sun; prefers part to full shade

Mature Height: *1'–12'*

Mature Width: *2'–12'*

Zones: *2–11*

Features:

Beautiful for hanging baskets and containers

Attracts hummingbirds

Blooms spring through frost.

Needs: Grown as an annual in Zones 2–7; as a woody perennial or small to large shrub in Zones 8–11. Average, neutral to acidic, well-drained soil. Needs moderate to ample moisture. Never allow to dry out.

Plant established plants in spring. Use potting soil if plants are grown in a container. Pinch tips of small plants at planting time for better bushiness. Mulch to conserve moisture. Fertilize with a liquid fertilizer every 2–3 weeks. Pinch off spent blooms to promote more flowering. This plant is prone to mites, spider mites, whiteflies, and aphids.

Choices: The elaborate flowers come in pinks, purples, reds, and white. Often the same flowers may have two colors.

Annuals and Perennials

Annuals and Perennials   183

Gaillardia spp.

blanket flower

Light Needs:

Full sun

Mature Height: *10"–3'*
Mature Width: *10"–2'*

Zones: *2–11*

Features:

 Good for seaside gardens

Heat- and drought-tolerant

Long-blooming

Blooms mid- to late summer.

Needs: Fertile to average, sandy, well-drained soil; tolerates seashore conditions. Allow to dry between waterings; heat- and drought-tolerant.

Plant in spring; perennial type can also be planted in fall. Fertilize lightly, if at all; trim spent blooms and plant will likely bloom until early autumn or even frost.

This plant is prone to powdery mildew and leaf hoppers. It is also prone to crown rot in wet conditions.

Choices: Flowers are usually bicolored in autumn colors—reds, golds, yellow, burgundy, and cream.

Gaillardia pulchella is the annual blanket flower and can be grown in Zones 2–11; *Gaillardia × grandiflora* is the perennial type and can be grown in Zones 2–10.

Galium odoratum (Asperula odorata)

sweet woodruff

Light Needs:

Part to full shade

Mature Height: *6"–8"*
Mature Width: *8"–10"*

Zones: *4–8*

Features:

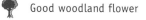 Good woodland flower

Delightfully fragrant

Thrives in shade

Blooms early spring.

Needs: Rich soil high in organic matter; spreads less rapidly in poor or clay soil. Needs plentiful moisture; never allow to dry out.

Plant established plants in spring. Fertilize occasionally, every 4–6 weeks. It is best to spread 1 inch of compost around plants each fall.

This plant spreads rapidly in good conditions and can become invasive in lawns. Use edging near lawn areas to prevent this. Trim spent flower heads, if needed, to further control spreading. Evergreen in warmer climates.

Usually pest free, it is prone to crown and root rot in poorly drained sites.

Choices: Flowers are white only.

Gaura lindheimeri

white gaura

Light Needs:

Full sun to part shade

Mature Height: *3'–7'*
Mature Width: *2'–3'*

Zones: *5–9*

Features:

Drought-tolerant

Native plant

 Long-blooming

Blooms late spring through frost.

Needs: Full sun; tolerates light shade in Zones 7–9. Sandy, well-drained soil; will tolerate some clay. Drought-tolerant, but moderate moisture is best.

Plant established plants in spring. Trim spent blooms to prolong flowering. Cut back in midsummer to control size and to encourage further flowering. If soil is too moist and rich, plants may sprawl; stake as needed.

This plant has a deep taproot; division is seldom needed. Where well suited to existing conditions, it self-seeds to the point of being slightly invasive. It is prone to leaf spot, rust, and mildews.

Choices: 'Whirling Butterfly' gets just 3–4 feet high and reseeds seldom.

Gazania rigens

gazania, treasure flower

Light Needs:

Full sun to part shade

Mature Height: *6"–1'*

Mature Width: *6"–10"*

Zones: *2–11*

Features:

 Thrives in heat and drought

Long-blooming

Good seaside flower

Blooms summer through frost or even all year in warmer climates.

Needs: Grow as an annual in Zones 2–7; as a perennial in Zones 8–11. Full sun in Zones 2–8; will tolerate some shade in Zones 9–11. Average to poor, sandy, well-drained soil. Tolerates drought and heat well.

Plant established plants in spring after all danger of frost has passed. Fertilize lightly if at all. Keep spent blooms trimmed to promote longest blooming; it will bloom year round in warm-winter climates.

In wet climates this plant is prone to crown rot.

Choices: Flowers come in yellows, reds, and bronzes. 'Chansonette' is compact and early flowering.

Geranium spp.

hardy geranium, cranesbill

Light Needs:

Full sun to part shade

Mature Height: *1'–2'*

Mature Width: *1'–2'*

Zones: *4–8*

Features:

Easy to grow

 Long-blooming perennial

Blooms summer through fall.

Needs: Full sun in Zones 4–6; part shade in Zones 7–8. Average to rich, well-drained soil; tolerates somewhat dry conditions but does best with moderate moisture.

Plant seedlings in spring or fall. Mulch. Fertilize occasionally, every 4–6 weeks, or work in a 9-month, slow-release fertilizer each spring. After the first flowering, shear back by as much as half once or twice during the growing season to keep growth compact and to encourage better blooming. This plant spreads rapidly; divide every 2–4 years as needed. It is usually pest free.

Choices: Flowers come in pinks, blues, whites, and purples. 'Johnson's Blue' is an especially lovely clear blue; 'Wargrave Pink' blooms all summer and fall.

Gerbera

gerbera or transvaal daisy

Light Needs:

Full sun to part shade

Mature Height: *8"–2'*

Mature Width: *6"–20"*

Zones: *3–10*

Features:

Excellent cut flower

Blooms midsummer through fall.

Needs: Grow as a cool-season annual in Zones 3–6; as a perennial in Zones 7–10. Full sun in Zones 3–6; part shade in hot summer in Zones 7–10. Rich, well-drained, preferably sandy soil. Moderate, even moisture.

Plant established plants in early spring in Zones 3–6; in spring or fall in Zones 8–10. Fertilize occasionally, every 6 weeks, or work in a 9-month, slow-release fertilizer in spring. Trim spent blooms regularly to promote flowering.

It is prone to gray mold, aphids, whitefly, thrip, and leaf miner.

Choices: Flowers come in reds, yellows, peaches, pinks, and cream. 'Rainbow' is especially easy to grow. 'California Giants' hits 2 feet, while 'Skipper' is a compact 8 inches tall.

Annuals and Perennials

Gomphrena globosa

globe amaranth

Light Needs:

Full sun

Mature Height: *8"–2'*

Mature Width: *10"–20"*

Zones: *2–11*

Features:

 Excellent cut or dried flower

Drought-tolerant

Easy to grow

Blooms midsummer through fall.

Needs: Average to poor or sandy, well-drained soil. Does best with moderate water, but tolerates drought.

Plant seedlings in spring after all danger of frost has passed. Fertilize regularly, every 4 weeks, or work in a 9-month, slow-release fertilizer at planting time. Taller varieties may flop; stake as needed.

Aphids and spider mites are sometimes a problem.

Choices: Flowers are pinks, whites, purples, reds, and oranges. 'Strawberry Fields' is a popular red type; 'Lavender Lady' is an elegant lavender. 'Buddy' grows just 8 inches tall.

Gypsophila paniculata

baby's breath

Light Needs:

Full sun

Mature Height: *18"–30"*

Mature Width: *2'–4'*

Zones: *3–9*

Features:

Outstanding cut flower

Lovely cloudlike effect

Drought-tolerant

Blooms early to midsummer.

Needs: Average to poor, well-drained soil. Thrives in alkaline soil; perishes if too acid. Does best if kept evenly moist, but will tolerate drought once mature. Dislikes extreme humidity.

Plant seedlings in spring. Staking is usually needed to support top-heavy stems. Fertilize sparingly if at all. Cut back immediately after first bloom to encourage a second, late-summer bloom.

This plant is usually pest free.

Choices: Flowers come in whites or pinks. 'Bristol Fairy' is a popular white type. 'Compacta Plena' grows just 18 inches tall.

Helenium autumnale

sneezeweed, Helen's flower

Light Needs:

Full sun

Mature Height: *3'–5'*

Mature Width: *2'–4'*

Zones: *3–8*

Features:

Great autumn bloomer

 Native flower; good for wildflower plantings

Blooms late summer through early autumn.

Needs: Average, not fertile, moist to wet soil. Does best if kept evenly moist, but will tolerate drought once mature.

Plant seedlings in spring. Fertilize rarely, if ever; overfertilizing makes these plants flop. Pinch back by about one-third in late spring to assure bushier, more sturdy plants. Stake as needed with taller types. Trim spent blooms for longest flowering.

Divide every 2–3 years as needed. This plant is susceptible to rust, powdery mildew, and leaf spot.

Choices: Flowers come in yellows, golds, reds, and burgundy.

Annuals and Perennials

Helianthus annuus

annual sunflower

Light Needs:

Full sun

Mature Height: *2'–12'*
Mature Width: *1'–3'*
Zones: *2–11*

Features:

 Wonderful cut flower

Easy to grow; great for kids

Simple to start from seed

Blooms midsummer, late summer, or early autumn.

Needs: Average to poor, well-drained soil; moderate moisture.

Plant seeds in spring directly in soil, or plant seedlings after all danger of frost has passed. Thin or transplant newly emerged seedlings to recommended spacing. Mulch. Fertilize lightly, if at all. Stake taller types. For a continuing supply of sunflowers, plant every 2 weeks until midsummer. This plant is prone to verticillium wilt, powdery mildew, and wilt.

Choices: Flowers come in yellows, golds, oranges, burgundy, and creams. 'Italian White' is an elegant cream; 'Valentine' is very long blooming; 'Sunspot' grows just 2–3 feet tall; 'Soraya' needs no staking.

Helianthus spp.

perennial sunflower, false sunflower

Light Needs:

Full sun

Mature Height: *4'–8'*
Mature Width: *3'–4'*
Zones: *4–9*

Features:

Welcome late-season color

Native plant; good wildflower

Blooms late summer or early to late fall.

Needs: Rich, moist to well-drained soil. Adequate to ample moisture.

Plant established plants in spring. Mulch to conserve moisture and prevent weeds. Fertilize occasionally, every 6 weeks, or work a 9-month, slow-release fertilizer into the soil each spring. Trim spent flowers for longest bloom. Divide every 2–4 years as needed. This plant is prone to mildew, rust, and leaf spot.

Choices: Flowers come in yellows and golds. *Helianthus × multiflorus* thrives in Zones 4–8; 'Lodden Gold' is especially nice; in the South choose swamp sunflower—*Helianthus angustifolius*.

Helichrysum bracteatum

strawflower

Light Needs:

Full sun

Mature Height: *1'–4'*
Mature Width: *6"–10"*
Zones: *2–11*

Features:

 Outstanding dried flower; good cut flower

Easy to grow

Blooms mid- through late summer.

Needs: Average to sandy, well-drained, alkaline soil. Light moisture; drought-tolerant.

Plant seedlings in spring after all danger of frost has passed. Fertilize little, if at all. This plant self-sows where conditions are favorable.

It is prone to aster yellows virus and aphids.

Choices: Flowers come in yellows, oranges, pinks, reds, white, bronzes, and purples.

'Bright Bikini Mix' is one of the most popular varieties, as are some of the pastel mixes.

false sunflower, ox-eye daisy

Light Needs:

Full sun

Mature Height: *3'-6'*
Mature Height: *1'-2'*

Zones: *4-9*

Features:

Welcome late-season color

Native plant; good wildflower

Good cut flower

Blooms late summer.

Needs: Rich, moist to well-drained soil. Adequate to ample moisture.

Plant established plants in spring. Fertilize occasionally, every 6 weeks, or work in a 9-month, slow-release fertilizer each spring. Trim spent flowers for longest bloom.

Divide every 2–4 years to maintain vigorous, healthy plants.

This plant is prone to powdery mildew and rust.

Choices: Flowers come in yellows and golds.

heliotrope, cherry-pie plant

Light Needs:

Full sun

Mature Height: *14"-3'*
Mature Width: *1'-2'*

Zones: *2-11*

Features:

Excellent for containers

Delightfully fragrant

Good flower for bouquets

Blooms spring through frost.

Needs: Annual in Zones 2–10; perennial in Zones 10–11. Full sun, though appreciates some afternoon shade in hot summer areas in Zones 7–11. Rich to average, well-drained soil. Keep evenly moist, though thrives with occasional slightly dry periods.

Plant seedlings in spring after all danger of frost has passed. Apply a 1–2 inch layer of mulch to prevent disease. Fertilize regularly, every 4 weeks. Trim spent blooms to encourage more flowering. In Zone 10 mulch in fall to protect from winter cold and assure regrowth in spring. Or dig up right before the first autumn frost and bring indoors. It will last several months as a fragrant houseplant.

lenten rose, christmas rose

Light Needs:

Part to full shade

Mature Height: *14"-18"*
Mature Width: *18"-2'*

Zones: *3-9*

Features:

Blooms even in snow

Wonderful woodland flower

Good for shade

Blooms mid- or late winter. Often evergreen.

Needs: Very rich, well-drained soil with ample moisture.

Plant established plants in spring, working in compost. Once it is blooming, trim winter-worn foliage to better show off flowers. It spreads rapidly in good conditions, so there is usually little need to divide.

This plant is usually pest and disease free in suitable climates.

Choices: Flowers are white or soft pinks. Lenten rose *(Helleborus orientalis)* is hardy in Zones 4–9 and blooms in late winter. Christmas rose *(Helleborus niger)* blooms mid- to late winter, depending on the climate, and is hardy in Zones 3–8.

Annuals and Perennials

Hemerocallis spp.

daylily

Light Needs:

Full sun to full shade

Mature Height: *10"–4'*

Mature Width: *8"–2'*

Zones: *3–10*

Features:

 Among the easiest of plants to grow

Many long-blooming types

Some fragrant types

Blooms midsummer, late summer, and early autumn.

Needs: Full sun. Tolerates shade but flowers less. Rich, well-drained soil, but thrives in many different soils. Best with moderate to ample moisture but will also tolerate drought.

Plant established plants in spring or fall. Group in clusters of 6 or more for best effect. Fertilize occasionally, about every 6 weeks, or work in a 9-month, slow-release fertilizer. Pinch off any spent flowers daily and trim off spent flower stalks to promote further bloom. Divide every 3–4 years as needed. Some types spread easily. This plant is usually pest free.

Choices: Avoid the orange "ditch lily," *Hemerocallis fulva*, which is invasive.

Heuchera

coral bells

Light Needs:

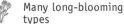

Full sun to part shade

Mature Height: *8"–1'*

Mature Width: *6"–10"*

Zones: *3–8*

Features:

Excellent cut flowers

Pretty edging plant

Long-bloomer

Blooms early to late spring.

Needs: Full sun to very light shade in Zones 3–5; partial shade in Zones 6–8. Rich, well-drained soil; likes slightly alkaline conditions. Moderate moisture; will tolerate slight drought.

Plant established plants in spring or fall. Mulch. Fertilize occasionally, perhaps every 6 weeks, or work in a 9-month, slow-release fertilizer each spring. Trim off spent flower stalks to encourage longer blooming. Divide plants every 3–4 years as needed. They are usually pest and disease free.

Choices: Flowers come in pinks, reds, and whites. While most coral bells have green leaves, the purple-leaved types are striking and add contrast in flower beds.

Hibiscus spp.

hibiscus, rose mallow

Light Needs:

Full sun to part shade

Mature Height: *1'–8'*

Mature Width: *1'–4'*

Zones: *2–11*

Features:

Big, showy flowers

Good choice for wet spots

Shade lover

Bloom times vary.

Needs: Full sun in Zones 2–5; partial shade in hot summer areas in Zones 6–11. Rich, well-drained, but moist soil; needs ample water; thrives in wet, hot conditions.

Plant established plants in spring after all danger of frost has passed. Mulch. Fertilize occasionally, every 6 weeks, or work in a 9-month, slow-release fertilizer each spring. Stake tallest types. Perennial types are slow to emerge from the soil in spring; be careful not to hoe or pull out.

Choices: *Hibiscus sabdariffa* is an annual. Rose or swamp mallow (*Hibiscus moscheutos*) will act as an annual or a perennial depending on the climate (check the label to be sure).

Hosta spp.

hosta, plantain lily

Light Needs:

Part to full shade

Mature Height: *6"–3'*

Mature Width: *8"–4'*

Zones: *3–9*

Features:

Popular shade-lover

Easy to grow

Some fragrant types

Blooms mid- or late summer.

Needs: Rich, well-drained soil; moderate to plentiful moisture, though some tolerate dry soil.

Plant established plants in spring or fall. Fertilize occasionally, every 6 weeks, or work in a slow-release fertilizer in spring. Trim spent flower stalks.

These plants are very prone to slugs and snails, though those with thicker, more leathery leaves are less susceptible. See page 129 for tips on controlling.

Choices: Foliage comes in all shades of green and white with lovely variations.

There are hundreds of varieties. *Hosta plantaginea* is very fragrant. 'Sum and Substance' grows 3 feet wide, is fairly slug resistant, and tolerates light sun.

Iberis spp.

candytuft

Light Needs:

Full sun to part shade

Mature Height: *6"–10"*

Mature Width: *8"–18"*

Zones: *3–10*

Features:

Lovely flowering groundcover

Good companion for bulbs

Excellent for rock gardens and walls

Blooms in early spring.

Needs: Average, well-drained, neutral to alkaline soil. Moderate moisture.

Plant established plants in spring or fall. It looks best in groups of eight or more. Mulch. Fertilize lightly in spring with a slow-release fertilizer. After flowering is over, cut back by one-third to one-half. Perennial types seldom need division, but divide if desired. Every few years, after flowering, cut back perennial candytuft especially hard—by one-half to two-thirds—to assure compact growth.

Choices: In Zones 3–9 grow evergreen candytuft (*Iberis sempervirens*) as a perennial. In Zones 9–10 grow either evergreen candytuft or globe candytuft (*Iberis umbellata*) as a cool-season annual, planting in fall or late winter.

Impatiens spp.

impatiens, busy lizzy

Light Needs:

Part to full shade

Mature Height: *6"–3'*

Mature Width: *8"–2'*

Zones: *2–11*

Features:

Extremely easy to grow

Excellent for containers

Thrives in shade

Blooms spring through frost.

Needs: Light shade in Zones 2–5; deep shade in hot-summer areas in Zones 6–11; lots of moisture.

Plant in spring after all danger of frost has passed. Best in groups of a dozen or more. Fertilize occasionally, every 6 weeks, or work a slow-release fertilizer into the soil once or twice during the growing season. Mulch. In Zones 10–11 grow as a perennial but cut back hard—by two-thirds or more—in spring to promote fresh growth. It is usually pest and disease free.

Choices: Flowers come in nearly all colors. Common impatiens (*Impatiens wallerana*) is widely grown. Roselike, double-flowered impatiens and New Guinea impatiens are now available.

Annuals and Perennials

Iris spp.

iris: german bearded, siberian, dutch

Light Needs:

Full sun to part shade

Mature Height: *6"–3'*
Mature Width: *4"–2'*
Zones: *3–10*

Features:

Outstanding cut flower

Easy to grow

Blooms early to midsummer.

Needs: Growing conditions vary depending on type of iris. Read label carefully. German bearded iris *(Iris germanica)* does best in full sun and average, well-drained soil. It needs moderate moisture but is drought-tolerant once established in Zones 3–10. Siberian iris *(Iris sibirica)* prefers rich to average, well-drained soil with moderate moisture, but will tolerate both very wet and moderately dry conditions in Zones 3–9. It doesn't do well in the Southwest. This plant is very pest and disease resistant.

Dutch iris *(Iris xiphium)* is grown as an annual in Zones 3–7 but is perennial in Zones 8–10. It requires rich, well-drained soil and moderate water during growth. It is drought tolerant when dormant in summer.

'*Iris* × *germanica*'

Kniphofia uvaria

red-hot poker, torch lily

Light Needs:

Full sun

Mature Height: *3'–5'*
Mature Width: *3'–4'*
Zones: *5–9*

Features:

Drought-tolerant

Exotic-looking flowers

Rabbit-resistant

Bloom times vary from spring to fall.

Needs: Full sun in Zones 5–6; part shade in hot summer areas in Zones 7–9. Rich to average, well-drained soil; moderate moisture.

Fertilize rarely, if at all. Cut off spent flower spikes. Plant in spring or fall. Cut back plant by half after flowering if leaves become unsightly. In Zones 5–7 tie leaves over crown with twine in winter to help the plant shed water; the crown rots if it's wet too long. There is no need to divide, though small plants that form around the base of the plant can be transplanted for more plants.

Choices: Flowers come in reds, yellows, oranges, and creams. 'Little Maid', 'Citrina', and 'Royal Castle' are especially long bloomers.

Lamium maculatum

spotted dead nettle

Light Needs:

Full sun to part shade

Mature Height: *6"–1'*
Mature Width: *1'–2'*
Zones: *3–8*

Features:

Good choice for dry shade

Excellent flowering groundcover

Blooms midspring through summer.

Needs: Can handle full sun, especially in Zones 3–5, but prefers light shade. Average to rich, moist soil. Ample moisture best, especially in full sun, but will tolerate drought once established.

Plant established plants in spring or fall. Plant several together for best effect. This plant benefits from occasional fertilizing but seldom needs it because it tends to be slightly invasive, especially in moist conditions. However, bare spots may occur if a planting is too dry. Cut back by one-third or so after bloom time if plants become straggly. Divide in spring or fall as desired. Slugs, leaf spot, and root rot are sometimes a problem.

Choices: 'Beacon Silver' is one of the most popular varieties.

Annuals and Perennials

Lantana camara

warm-season annual or perennial

lantana

Light Needs:

Full sun

Mature Height: 1'–4'

Mature Width: 2'–5'

Zones: 2–11

Features:

Excellent for containers

Thrives in hot conditions

Blooms late spring to frost.

Needs: Warm-season annual in Zones 2–9; perennial in Zones 10–11. Average to rich, well-drained soil. Moderate water; will tolerate slightly dry conditions, but does far better with adequate moisture.

Plant established plants in spring. Mulch to conserve moisture. Fertilize in spring with a 9-month, slow-release fertilizer. If plant gets shabby, shape lightly to retain attractive shape.

It is prone to whiteflies, aphids, caterpillars, mealybugs, and mites.

Choices: Flowers come in white, orange, yellow, red, and lavender. 'Camara Mixed Hybrids' is a dwarf, growing just 18 inches tall.

Lathyrus odoratus

cool-season annual

sweet pea

Light Needs:

Full sun

Mature Height: 1'–8'

Mature Width: 1'–2'

Zones: 2–11

Features:

Good cottage garden flower

Some with outstanding fragrance

Some excellent for cutting

Blooms in winter, spring, or summer.

Needs: Full sun. Rich, well-drained soil. Ample moisture; plant must never dry out during growth.

Plant directly in the soil when the weather is cool and a light frost is still possible, perhaps 2–3 weeks before the last frost in late winter or early spring. In Zones 8–11 plant in late autumn or early winter. First soak seeds in warm water for 24 hours and then plant ½ inch deep. Provide support. Once plants have emerged, mulch to conserve moisture and keep soil cool. Fertilize regularly, every 2–4 weeks. Trim spent blooms or cut often for bouquets to encourage longer flowering. Plants die when temperatures get hot; discard.

Lavandula spp.

perennial

lavender

Light Needs:

Full sun

Mature Height: 1'–3'

Mature Width: 1'–3'

Zones: 5–10

Features:

Legendary fragrance

Drought-tolerant

Excellent dried flower

Blooms early summer.

Needs: Full sun. Poor, very well-drained, neutral to alkaline soil; dislikes rich or wet clay soils. Very drought-tolerant; dislikes too much water or humidity.

Plant in spring. If needed, work sand or grit into the soil to loosen and improve drainage. Do not fertilize. Water with care in areas with ample moisture. A gravel mulch is useful. Cut back foliage by half or more after first blooming to prompt fresh growth and more blooms. Mulch for winter protection in Zones 5–6. Fungal diseases may occur where too wet or humid.

Choices: 'Munstead' is the most hardy. 'Lavender Lady' blooms the first year from seed and can be treated as an annual. Useful in cold climates where it may die out. 'Hidcote' is a very deep purple.

tree mallow, annual mallow

Light Needs:

Full sun

Mature Height: *2'–4'*

Mature Width: *1'–2'*

Zones: *2–11*

Features:

Fast-growing vertical accent

Good cut flower

Blooms early summer to frost.

Needs: Full sun. Loose or sandy, somewhat rich, well-drained soil. Moderate moisture.

Plant in spring directly in soil after all danger of frost has passed; resents transplanting. Mulch to conserve moisture after seedlings have emerged. Feed occasionally, every 4 weeks. Stake taller types. Trim spent blooms to prolong flowering, which will last all summer in cooler climates.

Choices: Flowers come in pinks and whites. 'Mont Blanc' is white and just 2 feet tall; 'Loveliness' is deep pink and 4 feet tall.

shasta daisy

Light Needs:

Full sun to part shade

Mature Height: *6"–3'*

Mature Width: *6"–2'*

Zones: *4–9*

Features:

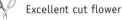

Excellent cut flower

Long-blooming perennial

Rabbit-resistant

Blooms early summer through frost.

Needs: Full sun in most regions; part shade in hot, dry regions of Zones 8–9. Rich, well-drained, neutral to alkaline soil. Moderate moisture.

Plant established plants in spring or fall. Mulch. Feed occasionally, every 6 weeks, or work a 9-month, slow-release fertilizer into the soil each spring. May need to stake. Keep spent flowers trimmed to ensure longer bloom. In Zones 4–5 protect in fall with more mulch. Plant dies out if winter soil is too wet.

Choices: Flowers come in whites or creamy yellow. 'Alaska' has large white flowers and grows to 20 inches tall; 'Lady' grows just 6–8 inches and blooms early; 'Polaris' grows to 36 inches. Some double and frilled types are also available.

gayfeather, blazing star

Light Needs:

Full sun

Mature Height: *30"–4'*

Mature Width: *8"–1'*

Zones: *3–9*

Features:

Excellent cut flower

Native prairie plant

Attracts butterflies and bees

Blooms mid- or late summer.

Needs: Full sun. Average to sandy, rich soil. Moderate moisture.

Plant established plants in spring. Mulch to conserve moisture. Fertilize occasionally, every 6 weeks or so, or work in a slow-release fertilizer each spring. Stake as needed. Trim spent blooms promptly to encourage second bloom.

Divide about every 4 years or so if needed. This plant is generally trouble free, though root knot nematodes can be a problem in the South.

Choices: Blooms come in pinks, purples, and whites. 'Kobold' grows just 2½ feet tall; Kansas gayfeather (*Liatris pycnostachya*) grows to 5 feet tall.

Annuals and Perennials

Ligularia spp.

ligularia, leopard plant

Light Needs:

Part shade

Mature Height: *3'–4'*

Mature Width: *3'–5'*

Zones: *5–8*

Features:

👁 Interesting foliage

👁 Dramatic spiky flowers

Blooms mid- to late summer.

Needs: Rather picky about light; afternoon shade preferred in Zone 5 and a must in hot summer regions of Zones 6–8. Rich, moist to wet soil. Ample moisture; never let dry out.

Plant established plants in spring, working in ample compost. Mulch to help conserve moisture. Feed occasionally, every 6 weeks, or apply a slow-release fertilizer each spring. Trim off spent flower spikes after blooming. Slugs can be a problem.

Choices: Flower spikes are bright yellow or orange. 'The Rocket' is the most popular cultivar, with deep green leaves and yellow flower spikes rising to 5 feet tall; 'Desdemona' has deep red spring leaves that turn green just on top.

Limonium spp.

statice, sea lavender

Light Needs:

Full sun to part shade

Mature Height: *1'–3'*

Mature Width: *6"–2'*

Zones: *2–11*

Features:

🌿 Outstanding dried flower

⛵ Good for seaside gardens

Blooms mid- to late summer.

Needs: Annual statice needs full sun; perennial will take some shade in Zones 8 and warmer. Sandy, well-drained soil. Somewhat drought-tolerant but does best with even, moderate moisture.

Plant established plants in spring after all danger of frost has passed. Fertilize occasionally, every 6 weeks, or work in a slow-release fertilizer each spring. Stake tall types. Needs no division; propagate by digging up the small side rosettes that form at the plant's base.

Choices: Annual statice (Zones 2–11) is ideal for drying. Perennials are sea lavender (*Limonium latifolium*—Zones 3–9—and *Limonium perezii*—Zones 8–11).

Linaria spp.

toadflax, baby snapdragon

Light Needs:

Full sun

Mature Height: *2'–3'*

Mature Width: *9"–1'*

Zones: *4–9*

Features:

🌿 Good choice for rock gardens

🌿 Intriguing snapdragon-like flowers

Bloom times vary from late winter to late summer.

Needs: Full sun. Light, well-drained, preferably sandy soil. Moderate moisture; perennial type is drought-tolerant once established.

For annual types, in Zones 4–7, sow seeds directly in garden in early spring as soon as snow thaws. In Zones 8–9, sow seeds for annual types in fall for late-winter bloom. Thin 6–12 inches between plants.

For perennial types, plant established plants in spring.

Mulch both types. Shear plants after first bloom to encourage a second bloom.

Choices: An annual, *Linaria maroccana* dies out when midsummer heat hits. A perennial, *Linaria purpurea* blooms all summer in many climates.

Annuals and Perennials

Linum perenne

blue flax

Light Needs:

Full sun to part shade

Mature Height: *12"–18"*

Mature Width: *10"–1'*

Zones: *4–9*

Features:

Lovely sky blue flowers

Drought-tolerant

Blooms late spring through summer.

Needs: Full sun to part shade. Average to sandy, well-drained soil. Moderate moisture. Drought-tolerant.

Plant established plants in spring. Avoid fertilizing. Mulch, if desired, to conserve moisture. However, mulch will retard this plant's light self-sowing. Cut back by one-half to two-thirds after flowering to prevent floppiness. This plant tends to die out after a few years but often will reseed itself, assuring an ongoing supply. Prone to damage by grasshoppers.

Choices: Flowers come in blues and whites. 'Saphyr' is a popular cultivar with sapphire-blue flowers on 8- to 10-inch plants. 'Diamond' has white flowers and grows to about the same height.

Liriope muscari

blue lilyturf, monkey grass

Light Needs:

Part to full shade

Mature Height: *12"–18"*

Mature Width: *18"–2'*

Zones: *6–9*

Features:

Thrives in shade

Drought-tolerant

Excellent edging plant

Blooms late summer.

Needs: Part to full shade. Rich to average, well-drained soil. Moderate moisture, but will tolerate drought.

Plant established plants in spring. Work in a slow-release fertilizer at planting time and again each spring. Mulch to conserve moisture. No need to divide, though clumps may be divided in spring for more plants. Cut back plants to a few inches in late winter to remove tattered leaves and prompt new growth.

These plants are susceptible to slugs and snails.

Choices: Flowers come in blues, purples, and whites.

'Majestic' grows 8–10 inches with dark blue flowers; 'Variegata' has green leaves with pretty white margins.

Lobelia erinus

edging lobelia, trailing lobelia

Light Needs:

Full sun to part shade

Mature Height: *3"–8"*

Mature Width: *6"–1'*

Zones: *2–11*

Features:

Comes in an intense blue

Some types excellent for edging

Trailing type ideal for containers

Blooms during cool weather.

Needs: Full sun in cooler regions in Zones 4–6, part shade in hot summer in Zones 7–11. Light, rich, well-drained soil. Moderate to ample moisture.

Plant established plants outdoors after all danger of frost has passed. Feed occasionally, every 4–6 weeks, or work in a slow-release fertilizer at planting time. Mulch to conserve moisture and keep soil cool. When temperatures regularly hit the high 80s°F (29-32°C), plants will stop blooming. Cut back by half to two-thirds when this happens; plants will rebloom in fall and continue until the first frost.

Choices: 'Riviera' and 'Blue Moon' form compact mounds. The 'Fountain' and 'Cascade' series have a cascading habit.

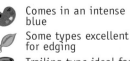

Annuals and Perennials

Lobelia spp.

perennial lobelia, cardinal flower

Light Needs:

Full sun to part shade

Mature Height: *2'–4'*

Mature Width: *1'–2'*

Zones: *2–9*

Features:

Thrives in wet spots

Attracts hummingbirds

Native wildflower

Blooms late summer or early autumn.
Needs: Full sun in Zones 2–5; shade, especially afternoon shade, in Zones 5 and warmer. Rich, moist, preferably boggy soil; ample moisture.

Plant established plants in spring or fall. Fertilize at planting time and each following spring with a slow-release fertilizer. Mulch. Trim spent blooms. It is a short-lived perennial, lasting just a few years. This plant may self-sow. If it doesn't self-seed, divide every other year to assure an ongoing supply. It is pest free.

Choices: Red cardinal flower *(Lobelia cardinalis)* attracts hummingbirds. It needs a wet site in Zones 2–9. Great blue lobelia *(Lobelia siphilitica)* tolerates dryer conditions in Zones 4–8.

Lobularia maritima

sweet alyssum

Light Needs:

Full sun to part shade

Mature Height: *3"–1'*

Mature Width: *8"–2'*

Zones: *2–11*

Features:

Good for containers

Lightly fragrant

Excellent rock-garden plant

Blooms during cool weather.
Needs: Full sun in Zones 2–5; tolerates light shade in Zones 6–11. Average to poor, well-drained soil. Moderate moisture.

Grow as an annual in Zones 2–9; as a perennial in Zones 10–11. Plant established seedlings in spring after all danger of frost has passed. Mulch. Fertilize lightly, every 4–6 weeks, or work in a slow-release fertilizer. This plant gets tall with sparse blooms when temperatures regularly hit high 80s°F (29-32°C); cut back by about half to rejuvenate and promote further bloom. It reseeds readily in good conditions, but colors of new plants will be muddy. Downy mildew and caterpillars are sometimes a problem.

Choices: Blooms come in white, purples, and roses.

Lunaria annua

money plant; honesty

Light Needs:

Full sun to part shade

Mature Height: *18"–3'*

Mature Width: *10"–18"*

Zones: *4–8*

Features:

Outstanding dried flower

Blooms in spring; seedpods in late summer.
Needs: This biennial prefers light shade but will tolerate full sun. Average to poor soil. Moderate water.

In Zones 4–7 plant seeds directly in soil ⅛-inch deep in spring a week or two before the last frost date. In Zone 8 sow seeds in autumn. Thin to 12 inches. Avoid fertilizing. If sowing in autumn, mulch to help plant survive winter. Flowers come in spring. Do not trim spent blooms. This plant produces seedpods in late summer. It often reseeds and can become slightly invasive in some areas. Usually free of diseases and pests.

Choices: Colors are white, purples, and pinks.

Lupinus hybrids

lupine

Light Needs:

Full sun to part shade

Mature Height: *2'–3'*
Mature Width: *1'–2'*

Zones: *4–9*

Features:

Striking vertical accent

Thrives in acidic soil

Blooms early summer.

Needs: Full sun; tolerates light shade. Rich, acidic, well-drained soil. Ample moisture.

In Zones 4–5 plant established plants in spring and grow as a perennial that will last just a few years. In Zones 6–9 plant in fall as a cool-season annual. Plant in groups of 6 or more for best effect. Fertilize occasionally, every 4–6 weeks, or work in a slow-release fertilizer at planting time. Mulch to keep soil cool and moist. Trim spent flower stalks to encourage a second bloom. This plant is susceptible to aphids, powdery mildew, slugs, and crown rot.

Choices: Nearly all colors are available. 'Russell Hybrids' are the most popular.

Lupinus texensis

texas bluebonnet

Light Needs:

Full sun to part shade

Mature Height: *10"–1'*
Mature Width: *10"–1'*

Zones: *2–11*

Features:

Native wildflower

Blooms spring or summer.

Needs: Full sun or light shade. Average to poor soil. Moderate water.

In Zones 2–6 sow seeds indoors 8–10 weeks before spring's last frost and plant seedlings outdoors after all danger of frost has passed. In Zones 7–11 sow seeds in fall.

If established plants are available, plant after all danger of frost has passed.

Plant or thin plants to 1 foot apart. They will not bloom well if crowded. Reseeds well in ideal conditions.

Choices: Flowers are blue or white.

Lysimachia spp.

gooseneck and yellow loosestrife

Light Needs:

Full sun to part shade

Mature Height: *2'–3'*
Mature Width: *1'–3'*

Zones: *3–8*

Features:

Grows in dry shade

Pretty cut flower

Blooms in summer.

Needs: Average to rich soil. Likes ample moisture but will tolerate somewhat dry conditions.

Plant established plants in spring or fall. Mulch to conserve moisture. No need to fertilize.

Choices: Gooseneck loosestrife (*Lysimachia clethroides*) has lovely white, arching spires 3 feet high. It likes ample moisture in sun but will tolerate dry shade. Can be very invasive; plant in a large pot buried in the soil or provide other barriers to counter invasive nature (in Zones 3–8). Yellow loosestrife (*Lysimachia punctata*) has brilliant yellow flowers blooming along 3-foot stems. This plant needs even moisture but will also tolerate somewhat dry conditions. It can also be somewhat invasive in Zones 4–8.

Lysimachia clethroides

Malva

hollyhock mallow, miniature mallow

Light Needs:

Full sun to part shade

Mature Height: *2'–4'*

Mature Width: *6"–2'*

Zones: *4–8*

Features:

Pretty vertical accent

Good for cutting

Long-blooming perennial

Blooms midsummer to late fall.

Needs: Full sun, but prefers light shade in hot summer areas in Zone 6 and warmer. Rich to average, well-drained soil. Drought-tolerant in cool-summer areas in Zones 4–5; moderate moisture in hot summer areas in Zones 6–8.

Plant established plants in spring. Fertilize occasionally or work in a slow-release fertilizer. It self-sows excessively; mulch and cut back in fall to control reseeding. Stake as needed. Each plant lasts only a few years but reseeds to assure an ongoing supply.

Choices: *Malva alcea* has lovely 2-inch white or pink flowers. *Malva sylvestris*, sometimes sold as *Malva zebrina* or Zebrina hollyhock, has eye-catching pale pink flowers veined with deep purple.

Matthiola incana

stock

Light Needs:

Full sun to part shade

Mature Height: *8"–3'*

Mature Width: *6"–1'*

Zones: *3–11*

Features:

Delightful, spicy fragrance

Excellent for cutting

Blooms late winter or early spring.

Needs: Full sun in Zones 3–6; otherwise full or part sun. Rich, well-drained soil. Moderate moisture.

In Zones 3–8 plant established plants outdoors in spring a few weeks before last frost date. In Zones 9–11 plant in late autumn for winter color. Mulch to keep soil cool and moist but do not overwater or roots will rot. Fertilize regularly, every 2–4 weeks, or work in a slow-release fertilizer. This plant stops blooming when warm weather hits.

Choices: Dwarf types grow 8–15 inches and tend to be more heat-tolerant, especially 'Midget'. Tall, columnar types are wonderful for cutting but need 5 months of temperatures below 65°F (18°C).

Melampodium paludosum

butter daisy

Light Needs:

Full sun

Mature Height: *10"–14"*

Mature Width: *10"–14"*

Zones: *2–11*

Features:

Withstands heat and humidity

Somewhat drought-tolerant

Blooms early summer to frost.

Needs: Full sun but will tolerate light shade, especially in hot summer areas. Average to poor soil. Drought-tolerant, but does far better with even moisture.

Plant established plants in spring after all danger of frost has passed. Avoid fertilizing, which will reduce blooms. There is no need to deadhead.

It is prone to slugs in moist conditions. Otherwise, aphids and red spider mites are sometimes a problem.

Choices: Flowers are yellow.

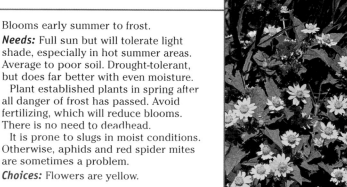

Annuals and Perennials

Mertensia virginica

virginia bluebells

Light Needs:

Full sun to full shade

Mature Height: *10"–2'*

Mature Width: *3"–10"*

Zones: *3–8*

Features:

 Native wildflower

Good woodland and shade flower

Rabbit-resistant

Blooms early spring.

Needs: Full sun to light shade in Zones 3–6 and Pacific Northwest; light to full shade in hot summer regions in Zones 7–8. Rich, moist, neutral to acidic soil. Ample moisture during spring bloom, then just moderate moisture.

Plant established plants outdoors in spring. Mulch to keep soil cool and moist. However, mulching inhibits any desired spreading, because plants self-seed well in ideal conditions. Fertilize by applying 1–2 inches of compost each spring.

Plants go dormant after blooming. Overplant with ferns to cover bare spots. No division is needed. To move plants, dig deeply to get at deep roots.

Choices: Flowers come in blues, pinks, purples, and white.

Mimulus hybridus

monkey flower

Light Needs:

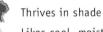

Tolerates full sun, prefers part to full shade

Mature Height: *6"–10"*

Mature Width: *8"–10"*

Zones: *2–11*

Features:

Thrives in shade

Likes cool, moist conditions

Blooms late spring to frost.

Needs: Full sun tolerated in Zones 2–5; otherwise part to full shade. Rich, well-drained soil. Ample moisture.

Plant established plants in spring after all danger of frost has passed. Mulch to keep soil cool and moist. Never allow plant to dry out. Fertilize regularly, every 2–4 weeks, or work in a slow-release fertilizer at planting time. Cut back after first bloom to promote further flowering.

Dry spells can halt flowering. If this happens, water lavishly to restore bloom. This plant can be grown as a perennial in Zones 9–11 but usually doesn't live for more than a few years. It is prone to aphids and whitefly.

Choices: Flowers are yellows, roses, reds, oranges, and bicolors.

Mirabilis jalapa

four-o-clock, marvel-of-peru

Light Needs:

Full sun; tolerates part shade

Mature Height: *1'–4'*

Mature Width: *1'–4'*

Zones: *2–11*

Features:

Old-fashioned cottage flower

Interesting bloom habit

Fragrant

Blooms midsummer to frost.

Needs: Annual in Zones 2–6; perennial in Zones 7–11. Prefers full sun; tolerates light shade. Average to rich, well-drained soil. Best with ample moisture but will tolerate drought.

Plant established plants in spring after all danger of frost has passed. This plant looks best in groups of a dozen or more. Mulch to keep soil moist and control weeds. Fertilize occasionally, every 4–6 weeks, or work in a slow-release fertilizer in spring. Deadheading not needed. In Zones 6–7, provide winter mulch to help plants survive the winter. In colder zones tuberous roots can be dug and stored. It is usually pest and disease free.

Choices: Flowers come in brilliant pinks, reds, yellows, and whites; often mottled.

Annuals and Perennials

Moluccella laevis

bells of ireland, shell flower

Light Needs:

Full sun

Mature Height: 2'–3'

Mature Width: 6"–8"

Zones: 2–11

Features:

↑ Good vertical accent

✂ Excellent for cutting, drying

Blooms in summer.

Needs: Full sun. Rich, loose, well-drained soil. Moderate moisture.

In Zones 2–6 sow seeds directly on soil surface in early spring, a few weeks before last frost date. In Zones 8–11 sow seeds in late autumn.

Fertilize occasionally, every 4–6 weeks, or work in a slow-release fertilizer at planting time. Mulch, if desired. Cut flowers at their peak for arrangements or drying. Few pests or diseases bother this plant.

Choices: It has green, flowerlike bells.

Monarda didyma

bee balm, bergamot

Light Needs:

Full sun to part shade

Mature Height: 2'–4'

Mature Width: 1'–3'

Zones: 4–8

Features:

🌿 Native prairie plant

🦋 Attracts butterflies and hummingbirds

🌿 Good wildflower

Blooms mid- to late summer.

Needs: Full sun in cool regions and Zones 4–6; part shade in hot, arid Zones 7–9. Rich, well-drained soil. Moderate to ample moisture.

Plant established plants in spring or fall. Feed occasionally, every 6 weeks, or work in a slow-release fertilizer at planting time. Trim spent blooms to prolong flowering. Mulch. This plant spreads easily and can be invasive. Divide every 2–4 years as needed. It is prone to mildew. Cut plants back to the ground after flowering to promote growth of fresh, disease-free foliage.

Choices: Mildew-resistant types include 'Gardenview Red', 'Marshall's Delight' (pink), 'Stone's Throw Pink', and 'Violet Queen'.

Myosotis sylvatica

forget-me-not

Light Needs:

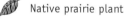

Full sun to part shade

Mature Height: 5"–1'

Mature Width: 4"–6"

Zones: 4–9

Features:

🌳 Excellent woodland flower

🌱 Thrives in shade

✂ Good cut flower

Blooms early spring.

Needs: Full sun to part shade in Zones 4–6; part shade in Zones 7–8. Rich to poor, well-drained soil that stays moist. Ample to moderate moisture.

In Zones 4–6 plant seeds by scattering seed directly on prepared soil 2–3 weeks before last frost date. In Zones 7–8 plant seeds in late autumn. In all zones plant established plants outdoors in late winter or early spring, a few weeks before last frost date. Avoid fertilizing. Do not deadhead; it prevents desirable reseeding. Mulch if desired to conserve moisture, but this will reduce reseeding.

Choices: Blue, but sometimes pink is available. It is sometimes sold incorrectly as *Myosotis alpestris*. 'Victoria' is a popular, intense blue. 'Victoria Rosea' is pink.

Nepeta spp.
catmint, catnip

Light Needs:

Full sun to part shade

Mature Height: 1'–3'

Mature Width: 8"–4'

Zones: 4–9

Features:

 Long-bloomer

 Easy to grow

Blooms early summer.

Needs: Full sun preferred but will tolerate light shade. Average to sandy, very well-drained soil; it tends to die out in clay or wet soils. Moderate to light moisture.

Plant established plants in spring or fall. Avoid fertilizing. Mulch. After blooming occurs, shear back by about one-third to one-half to promote fresh growth and more bloom. Divide in spring every 3–4 years as needed. It is usually pest and disease free, though cats may roll on it.

Choices: Technically, *Nepeta × faassenii* is catmint and *Nepeta cataria* is catnip, but the two are now used interchangeably to describe nearly any *Nepeta*. *Nepeta × faassenii* is the showiest. *Nepeta* 'Six Hills Giant' is the largest, spreading to 4 feet.

Nicotiana spp.
flowering tobacco

warm-season annual and perennial

Light Needs:

Full sun to part shade

Mature Height: 10"–6'

Mature Width: 8"–3'

Zones: 2–11

Features:

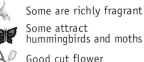 Some are richly fragrant

Some attract hummingbirds and moths

Good cut flower

Blooms summer to frost.

Needs: Usually light shade, but full sun if very humid or in Zones 2–3. Rich, well-drained soil. Moderate moisture.

Plant established plants in spring after all danger of frost has passed. Mulch. Fertilize occasionally. This plant is usually killed by frost, but in Zones 10–11 it may last the winter and act as a perennial.

Choices: *Nicotiana alata* hybrids (also known as *Nicotiana affinis*) are only 1 foot tall and come in several colors. Some types remain open all day but are scentless, including 'Nicki' and 'Domino'. *Nicotiana sylvestris* grows up to 6 feet tall, blooms in white, stays open all day, is richly fragrant at night, and attracts hummingbird moths. *Nicotiana langsdorffii* attracts hummingbirds.

'Nicotiana alata'

Nierembergia
cupflower

cool-season annual or perennial

Light Needs:

Full sun to part shade

Mature Height: 6"–1'

Mature Width: 6"–1'

Zones: 3–11

Features:

 Low-growing

Good flowering groundcover

Blooms summer and fall.

Needs: Full sun in cool summer areas in Zones 3–6; part shade in hot summer areas in Zones 7–11. Rich, well-drained soil. Ample moisture.

Grow as a cool-season annual everywhere except the wetter parts of Zones 8–9, where it can be grown as a perennial. Plant established plants in late winter or in spring a week or two before the last frost date. Group in clusters of 10 or more for best effect. Fertilize occasionally. Mulch. After first bloom cut back by one-third to one-half to prompt further bloom.

Choices: Flowers are purple or white. 'Mont Blanc' and 'Violet Robe' are two favorites.

Annuals and Perennials

Nigella damascena

love-in-a-mist

Light Needs:

Full sun

Mature Height: *1'–3'*

Mature Width: *1'–3'*

Zones: *2–11*

Features:

Good companion for bulbs

Good cut flower

Lovely feathery effect

Blooms late winter or spring.

Needs: Full sun. Sandy or gravelly soil with excellent drainage. Moderate moisture.

In Zones 2–7 sow seeds outdoors in early spring a couple of weeks before last frost date. In Zones 8–11 do so in late autumn. Sow seed directly onto prepared soil and plant in generous clusters of 10 or more plants for best effect. Do not cover. Keep moist. Thin seedlings to 8–12 inches apart. Avoid fertilizing. May need support with a shrubby branch or two inserted into the ground. Trim spent blooms to prolong blooming. However, deadheading may also reduce reseeding, which this plant will do nicely in ideal conditions.

Oenothera spp.

evening primrose, sundrops

Light Needs:

Full sun

Mature Height: *18"–3'*

Mature Width: *1'–3'*

Zones: *3–8*

Features:

Native wildflower

Spreads rapidly

Good for meadow or naturalistic plantings

Blooms late spring or early summer.

Needs: Full sun. Average to poor, well-drained soil. Moderate moisture but will tolerate drought.

Plant established plants in spring. No need to deadhead, mulch, or fertilize. This plant spreads rapidly, especially in rich soil. Each fall and spring, dig up unwanted plants to keep in bounds. It is usually pest and disease free, though spittlebugs can sometimes be a problem.

Choices: Flowers come in pink, white, yellow, and red. Botanical and common names seem to be a jumble with *Oenothera.* Different species go by different common names, depending on the plant reference used. All, however, have approximately the same care.

Paeonia spp.

peony

Light Needs:

Full sun to part shade

Mature Height: *15"–5'*

Mature Width: *2'–3'*

Zones: *2–8*

Features:

Excellent cut flower

Some fragrant varieties

Low maintenance

Blooms early summer.

Needs: Full sun in Zones 2–6; partial shade beneficial in hot areas in Zones 7–8. Rich, well-drained soil; moderate to plentiful moisture.

Plant in spring in Zones 2–6; spring or fall in Zones 7–8. Work in ample compost at planting. Mulch. Fertilize each spring. It may take 3–4 years to bloom after planting. Trim spent flowers after flowering. Provide support to herbaceous types with a tomato cage or other support once plants reach 1 foot high each spring. Do not divide unless more plants are wanted. Ants do not hurt peonies.

Choices: Herbaceous peonies grow about 3 feet tall; tree peonies grow up to 5 feet tall. Fern-leaf peony is an old-time favorite.

Papaver orientale

oriental poppy

Light Needs:

Full sun to part shade

Mature Height: 2'–4'

Mature Width: 6"–1'

Zones: 2–7

Features:

 Large, showy flowers

Striking cut flower

Easy to grow

Blooms early summer.

Needs: Full sun in cool-summer areas and in Zones 2–6; part shade in warm areas in Zones 7–8. Rich to average, deep, well-drained soil. Does best with moderate moisture; somewhat drought-tolerant.

Plant established plants in spring or fall. Mulch. Fertilize occasionally or work in a slow-release fertilizer. Remove faded flowers unless seedpods will be harvested. Foliage dies back after blooming and is unattractive for a few weeks. After bloom time, interplant with African marigolds, cosmos, sunflowers, or other fast-growing annuals to fill the open spots. Or interplant with perennial baby's breath. This plant spreads rapidly in good conditions. Keep in check by digging up new plants each spring.

Papaver spp.

annual poppy

Light Needs:

Full sun to part shade

Mature Height: 1'–3'

Mature Width: 6"–1'

Zones: 2–11

Features:

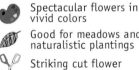 Spectacular flowers in vivid colors

Good for meadows and naturalistic plantings

Striking cut flower

Blooms in early, mid- or late summer.

Needs: Full sun in Zones 2–6; partial shade preferred in Zones 7–11. Average to poor, well-drained soil. Moderate moisture.

Does best started from seed. In Zones 3–7 sow seeds directly onto prepared soil in early spring, 2–3 weeks before last frost date. In Zones 8–10 sow in late autumn. Barely cover seeds. Thin but leave in groups of at least a dozen or so. Mulch. Avoid fertilizing or transplanting.

Choices: In cool-summer, low-humidity areas, Iceland poppy (*Papaver croceum* or *nudicaule*) will grow as a perennial. Annual poppies include *Papaver rhoeas* (corn Shirley and Flanders poppy) and *Papaver somniferum* (opium poppy). See also California poppy on page 181.

'Papaver rhoeas'

Pelargonium spp.

geranium

Light Needs:

Full sun to part shade

Mature Height: 1'–3'

Mature Width: 1'–3'

Zones: 2–11

Features:

Excellent container plant

Easy to grow

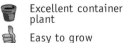 Rabbit-resistant

Blooms spring through frost or all year.

Needs: Full sun in Zones 2–8; light shade in Zones 9–11. Rich, well-drained soil. Moderate water, but ivy geranium (sold as *Pelargonium peltatum*) is drought-tolerant. Grow as annuals in Zones 2–9 and as perennials in Zones 10–11.

Plant established plants in spring after all danger of frost has passed. Mulch. Fertilize frequently. Trim spent blooms to encourage long flowering. Overwinter by digging up and potting. Keep in a sunny area indoors.

Choices: Zonal geraniums (sold as *Pelargonium × hortorum*) are the most common. Scented, Regal, Lady Washington, or Martha Washington geraniums (sold as *Pelargonium × domesticum*) are also available.

Penstemon spp. — *perennial*

penstemon, beard-tongue

Light Needs:

Full sun to part shade

Mature Height: 1'–6'
Mature Width: 10"–2'
Zones: 3–9

Features:

 Drought-tolerant

Attracts hummingbirds

Good vertical accent

Blooms in summer.

Needs: Full sun in most areas; part shade in Zones 8–9. Average to poor, loose, fast-draining soil. Moderate water to drought-tolerant, depending on the type.

Plant established plants in spring. Do not fertilize; do not overwater. Trim spent blooms for second flush. This plant is prone to root rot and black spot. A short-lived perennial, it usually dies out after 3–4 years.

Choices: Flowers are red, pink, yellow, purple, lavender, white, and salmon. Many types are available, especially in the West. 'Husker Red', which has purple foliage, is one of the most commonly available. Heights vary dramatically; check the label.

Pentas lanceolata — *annual*

pentas, egyptian star cluster

Light Needs:

Full sun to part shade

Mature Height: 6"–3'
Mature Width: 6"–3½'
Zones: 3–11

Features:

Excellent container plant

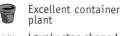 Lovely star-shaped blooms

Blooms summer through frost.

Needs: Full sun, though part shade is appreciated in Zones 7–11. Rich, well-drained soil. Ample moisture.

Plant in spring after all danger of frost has passed. Mulch to conserve moisture. Feed occasionally, every 4–6 weeks, or work in a slow-release fertilizer at planting time. Trim spent blooms to encourage further flowering. In fall, a few weeks before the first frost date, bring inside and place in a sunny spot as a houseplant. It is prone to whitefly.

Choices: Flowers come in pink, lavender, white, and red. Some types grow as high as 3 feet tall, but the dwarf types generally sold for outdoor gardens grow just 6–12 inches tall. 'New Look' is one dwarf cultivar.

Perovskia atriplicifolia — *perennial*

russian sage

Light Needs:

Full sun

Mature Height: 3'–5'
Mature Width: 2'–3'
Zones: 5–7

Features:

Good cut flower

Drought-tolerant

Autumn bloomer

Blooms late summer through fall.

Needs: Full sun. Average to sandy, loose, well-drained soil. Moderate moisture to drought-tolerant.

Plant established plants in spring. Fertilize lightly, if at all. Stake if needed. Doesn't need division. This plant is usually pest free.

Choices: Blue is the only color available.

Annuals and Perennials

Petunia spp.

petunia

Light Needs:

Full sun

Mature Height: *8"–18"*

Mature Width: *8"–4'*

Zones: *2–11*

Features:

Excellent in containers and baskets

Easy to grow

Some are fragrant.

Blooms spring through frost.

Needs: Full sun. Rich to poor, well-drained soil; tolerates alkaline soil. Moderate water.

In Zones 2–7 plant established plants in spring after all danger of frost has passed. In hot-summer regions of Zone 8, plant in early fall. In Zones 9–11 plant in late fall for winter color. Pinch tips by ½–1 inch to encourage much-needed bushiness. Mulch to conserve moisture and to keep sticky leaves clean. Fertilize every 2–4 weeks, or work a slow-release fertilizer into the soil at planting time and supplement with monthly fertilizing after that. Deadhead as time permits. In late summer when plants get leggy, cut back by one-third to one-half to tidy and rejuvenate.

Phlox divaricata

woodland phlox, wild blue phlox

Light Needs:

Part shade

Mature Height: *12"–16"*

Mature Width: *1'–2'*

Zones: *3–9*

Features:

Native plant

Thrives in light shade

Good for wildflower plantings

Blooms mid- to late spring.

Needs: Light shade, dappled if possible. Rich, well-drained soil that doesn't dry out. Ample moisture.

Plant established plants in spring. Work in ample compost at planting time. Mulch to conserve moisture. Each following spring, top soil with 1 inch of compost. Shear back by about half after flowers fade to tidy and to promote fresh foliage growth.

This plant spreads slowly from the roots. For more plants, divide immediately after blooming or in fall.

Mildew and slugs may be bothersome.

Choices: Flowers come in blue, lavender, and white.

Phlox drummondii

annual phlox, drummond phlox

Light Needs:

Full sun

Mature Height: *6"–18"*

Mature Width: *10"–2'*

Zones: *2–11*

Features:

Texas native

Good for sunny wildflower plantings

Good cut flower

Blooms in spring.

Needs: Full sun. Average to rich, well-drained soil. Moderate moisture.

In Zones 2–6 sow directly from seed in prepared soil outdoors in very early spring a few weeks before last frost date. In Zones 7–11 sow in late autumn for late winter or early spring bloom, 2–4 weeks before first frost date. Thin to distance recommended on seed packet. Cluster in groups of a dozen or more for best effect. Trim spent blooms. Heat stops bloom, but plant will revive in fall.

Choices: Blooms come in whites, pinks, reds, blues, purples, salmon, and yellow. 'Dwarf Beauty' is just 6 inches tall, while 'Brilliant' is 2 feet tall.

Annuals and Perennials

Phlox spp.

perennial

garden phlox, summer phlox, and others

Light Needs:

Full sun to part shade

Mature Height: *2'–5'*

Mature Width: *1'–3'*

Zones: *5–7*

Features:

🌬 Lightly fragrant

👁 Lovely masses of domed flowers

Blooms early, mid-, or late summer.

Needs: Full sun in Zones 3–6; light shade in hot summer climates in Zones 7–9. Rich, well-drained soil; ample moisture.

Plant established plants in spring or fall. Place far enough apart to prevent mildew diseases. Mulch. Work a long-term, slow-release fertilizer into the soil each spring. Cut back by about one-third after blooming to encourage rebloom. If mildew becomes severe, cut plant back to just a few inches.

Choices: *Phlox maculata* (wild sweet William or spotted phlox, Zones 5–8), is slightly more resistant to mildew than *Phlox paniculata* (garden phlox, Zones 4–8). Especially resistant are 'Miss Lingard', 'Mt. Fuji', 'David', and 'Eva Cullum'.

Phlox stolonifera

perennial

creeping phlox

Light Needs:

Part to full shade

Mature Height: *6"–8"*

Mature Width: *1'–2'*

Zones: *2–8*

Features:

🌬 Fragrant

🌳 Good woodland or wild flower

❋ Thrives in shade

Blooms early to midspring.

Needs: Light shade in Zones 2–6; full shade in Zones 7–8, preferably dappled. Needs rich, well-drained soil and ample moisture.

Plant established plants in spring. Work in ample compost at planting time. Mulch to conserve moisture, but do so lightly—just 1 inch or so—to prevent smothering the evergreen leaves. Each following spring, top soil with 1 inch of compost. It will probably reseed if you let the flowers ripen on the plant; also spreads by underground runners. Mildew and slugs are occasional problems.

Choices: Flowers come in pinks, blues, purples, and white. The most fragrant is 'Sherwood Purple'.

Phlox subulata

perennial

moss phlox, moss pink

Light Needs:

Full sun to part shade

Mature Height: *4"–6"*

Mature Width: *1'–2'*

Zones: *2–9*

Features:

🍃 Excellent rock garden plant

🍃 Good companion for spring bulbs

Blooms early spring.

Needs: Full sun or very light shade, especially in hot-summer areas. Average to sandy, well-drained, neutral to alkaline soil. Moderate moisture.

Plant established plants in spring or fall. Mulch. Fertilize occasionally, every 6 weeks, or work in a slow-release fertilizer each spring. This plant rarely needs division, but you can divide right after flowering for new plants. It is sometimes prone to spider mites if grown in hot, dry conditions and is prone to root rot in wet winter conditions.

Choices: Flowers come in blues, purples, pinks, and white. Most moss phloxes don't like heat or drought, but *Phlox mesoleuca* (*phlox nana*) does well in the arid Southwest.

Physoslegia virginiana — *perennial*

obedient plant, false dragonhead

Light Needs:

Full sun to part shade

Mature Height: *3'–4'*

Mature Width: *2'–3'*

Zones: *2–9*

Features:

- Blooms in late summer, early fall
- Easy to grow
- Native to the eastern U.S.

Blooms late summer through early fall.

Needs: Full sun or part shade. Average, well-drained soil, preferably acidic. Moderate to abundant moisture.

Plant established plants in spring or fall. Mulch to conserve moisture. Avoid fertilizing, which encourages the plant to become invasive. Cut back after blooming to encourage a second flush.

Dig up spreading plants in spring and fall to keep in check. This plant is usually pest and disease free.

Choices: Flowers are pinks or white. 'Vivid' is one of the most popular. 'Summer Snow' is earlier blooming and considerably less invasive.

Platycodon grandiflorus — *perennial*

balloon flower

Light Needs:

Full sun to part shade

Mature Height: *2'–3'*

Mature Width: *1'–2'*

Zones: *3–8*

Features:

- Interesting balloonlike flower bud
- Long-blooming

Blooms midsummer.

Needs: Full sun in Zones 3–6; light shade in Zones 7–8. Rich, deep, well-drained soil. Ample moisture.

Plant established plants in spring. Mulch. Fertilize occasionally or work in a slow-release fertilizer each spring. Tall types may need staking. Trim individual flowers to promote longest bloom. After the first flush of bloom in spring, cut back by one-third to one-half for more blooms. In fall mark plant with stake. Plants emerge late in spring and may be accidentally dug up during weeding. This plant needs no division but can be divided in spring for more plants. It is usually pest free.

Choices: Flowers come in purples and whites.

Portulaca — *warm-season annual*

moss rose

Light Needs:

Full sun

Mature Height: *4"–8"*

Mature Width: *1'–2'*

Zones: *2–11*

Features:

- Good flowering groundcover
- Drought-tolerant
- Good for containers that dry out easily

Blooms spring to frost.

Needs: Full sun. Average, well-drained soil, preferably sandy. Drought-tolerant.

Plant established plants in spring after all danger of frost has passed. Water sparingly, allowing soil to dry well between waterings.

Aphids, thrips, and white rust may cause problems.

Choices: Flowers come in reds, oranges, yellows, purples, whites, and pinks.

New types that remain open all day (older ones closed at dusk and on cloudy days), include 'Sundial' and 'Sundance'.

Primula spp.

primrose

Light Needs:

Full sun to part shade

Mature Height: *6"–3'*
Mature Width: *4"–2'*
Zones: *3–10*

Features:

Beautiful vibrant colors

Good container plant

Blooms late winter or early spring.

Needs: Full sun in Zones 3–6; light shade in Zones 7–10. Rich, moisture-retentive, but well-drained soil. Ample moisture.

Grow as an annual or a perennial, depending on the type of primrose and the climate. It will not last year after year in Zones 5 and colder, or in very hot, dry conditions, such as the arid Southwest.

To grow as an annual, in Zones 3–7, plant in early spring, 2–3 weeks before last frost date. In Zones 8–10 plant in late autumn for winter and early spring color. Discard when hot weather hits.

To grow as a perennial, plant in early spring. Water well during dry spells. In late fall cover with pine boughs or other lightweight mulch for winter protection.

Pulmonaria spp.

lungwort

Light Needs:

Full sun to part shade

Mature Height: *9"–2'*
Mature Width: *10"–2'*
Zones: *2–8*

Features:

Excellent woodland flower

Good shade flower

Interesting spotted leaves

Blooms early spring.

Needs: Full sun to medium shade. Rich, well-drained soil. Abundant moisture.

Plant established plants in spring, working in ample compost. Fertilize by working in additional compost around the plant each year. Mulch. Trim spent blooms to promote further flowering. Divide in early spring as desired. Powdery mildew may be a problem.

Choices: Bethlehem sage (*Pulmonaria saccharata*) is one of the best, with distinct silver spots on the leaves, Zones 3–8. Jerusalem sage (*Pulmonaria officinalis*) is less showy but an early bloomer, Zones 3–8. Blue lungwort (*Pulmonaria angustifolia*) has no spotting and can be invasive, Zones 2–8.

Pulsatilla vulgaris

pasque flower

Light Needs:

Full sun to part shade

Mature Height: *6"–1'*
Mature Width: *4"–1'*
Zones: *4–8*

Features:

Native plant

Good for woodland or prairie plantings

Blooms very early

Blooms early spring.

Needs: Full sun in Zones 4–6; light shade in hot-summer regions in Zones 7–8. Average, well-drained soil. Moderate water, but more drought-tolerant in cool, shady sites.

Plant in spring. Mulch to conserve moisture. Foliage dies back in summer. Avoid fertilizing. No need to divide or deadhead. May reseed modestly.

It is prone to root rot in wet winter soil.

Choices: Flowers come in deep blues, purples, or red. Most are single, but 'Azure' is a semidouble violet and 'Polka' is semidouble white.

Annuals and Perennials

Rudbeckia spp.

black-eyed susan, gloriosa daisy

Light Needs:

Full sun

Mature Height: *8"–4'*

Mature Width: *8"–3'*

Zones: *3–10*

Features:

Heat- and drought-tolerant

Excellent cut flower

Easy to grow

Blooms mid- to late summer.

Needs: Full sun. Rich to average soil; tolerates clay. Abundant moisture best but will tolerate drought once established.

  Plant perennial types in spring or fall. Plant annual types in spring after all danger of frost has passed. Mulch to conserve moisture. Fertilize rarely. Tall types may need staking. Trim spent blooms to promote longer flowering. Powdery mildew may be a problem.

Choices: Perennial black-eyed Susan or orange coneflower *(Rudbeckia fulgida)* is a popular flower, Zones 3–9. Gloriosa daisy *(Rudbeckia hirta)* is an annual, Zones 3–10. Shining coneflower *(Rudbeckia nitida)* is a perennial in Zones 4–10 and does well in the South.

Salvia farinacea

mealycup sage, annual blue salvia

Light Needs:

Full sun to part shade

Mature Height: *1'–3'*

Mature Width: *4"–8"*

Zones: *2–11*

Features:

Good container plant

Dries easily

Excellent for cutting

Blooms all summer.

Needs: Full sun in Zones 2–6; light shade in hot summer areas in Zones 7–11. Average, well-drained soil. Moderate moisture. Likes warm weather and moderate to high humidity. Grow as an annual in Zones 2–7; as a perennial in Zones 8–11.

  Plant established plants in spring after all danger of frost has passed. Pinch off any flowers and top ½–1 inch of foliage to promote much-needed branching. Mulch to conserve moisture. Fertilize occasionally, every 4–6 weeks, or work in a slow-release fertilizer in spring. It is prone to rust, aphids, and leafhoppers.

Choices: Flowers come in deep rich blues and silvery whites. 'Victoria Blue' is one of the best. 'Strata' has bicolored flowers.

Salvia splendens and Salvia coccinea

annual red salvia, Texas sage

Light Needs:

Full sun to part shade

Mature Height: *6"–3'*

Mature Width: *4"–2'*

Zones: *2–11*

Features:

Attracts hummingbirds

Knockout color

Easy to grow

Blooms summer to frost.

Needs: Average, well-drained soil. Moisture varies depending on type. Plant in spring after any danger of frost has passed. Pinch off any flowers and top ½ inch of foliage section to promote branching. Mulch. Fertilize regularly, every 4 weeks, or work in a slow-release fertilizer. Trim spent flowers to promote longer bloom. It is prone to leaf spot, rust, aphids, and leafhoppers.

Choices: Usually red but also cream, purple, or salmon. Red sage *(Salvia splendens)* does well in full sun or light shade and needs ample water. 'Hotline' is especially heat- and drought-tolerant, Zones 2–9. Texas sage *(Salvia coccinea)* has a long bloom time and is heat- and drought-tolerant, Zones 3–11.

Annuals and Perennials

perennial blue salvia

Light Needs:

Full sun to part shade

Mature Height: *1'–3'*
Mature Width: *1'–2'*
Zones: *4–8*

Features:

Long-blooming

Drought-tolerant

Good cut flower

Blooms early to midsummer.

Needs: Full sun to light shade, especially in Zones 7–8. Average to rich, well-drained soil. Needs moderate moisture until established, then drought-tolerant.

Plant established plants in spring or fall. Mulch. Fertilize every 6 weeks or so, or work in a slow-release fertilizer each spring. Keep spent flowers trimmed for several weeks of bloom. After first flush of bloom, cut plants back by one-third to one-half to promote yet further bloom. Tall types may need staking. It is usually pest and disease free. It seldom needs division but can be divided in spring for more plants.

Choices: Color is usually deep blue or purple. 'May Night' is especially long-blooming. 'Blue Hill' has true blue flowers.

santolina, lavender cotton

Light Needs:

Full sun

Mature Height: *1'–2'*
Mature Width: *2'–6'*
Zones: *6–9*

Features:

Very drought-tolerant

Blooms all summer.

Needs: Full sun. Average to poor, sandy or gritty, well-drained soil. Very drought-tolerant.

Plant established plants in spring. Avoid fertilizing. Periodically shear off spent flowers with hedge clippers.

Each year, in early spring, cut back to just a few inches tall. After a few years, replace if plant becomes too woody.

It is prone to root rot if site is too wet in winter.

Choices: It has only yellow flowers. 'Compacta' is a useful dwarf form that needs less shearing to stay neat. 'Lemon Queen' has pale yellow flowers.

scabiosa, pincushion flower

Light Needs:

Full sun to part shade

Mature Height: *1'–2'*
Mature Width: *6"–1'*
Zones: *3–7*

Features:

Very long-blooming

Attracts butterflies

Excellent cut flower

Blooms midsummer through fall.

Needs: Full sun in Zones 3–5; light shade in Zones 6–7. Rich, moist but well-drained soil. Abundant moisture.

Plant established plants in spring. Mulch to conserve moisture. Fertilize occasionally, every 4–6 weeks, or work in a slow-release fertilizer at planting time. Trim spent flowers to promote several weeks of bloom. Slugs are sometimes a problem.

Choices: Flowers are lovely blues and lavenders; pinks and whites are also available. 'Butterfly Blue' is a 6–12 inch dwarf and one of the most heat-tolerant.

Annuals and Perennials

Scaevola aemula

fan flower

Light Needs:

Full sun to part shade

Mature Height: *6"–8"*

Mature Width: *1'–3'*

Zones: *2–11*

Features:

Excellent for containers and baskets

Pretty blue flowers

Blooms spring to frost.

Needs: Full sun in Zones 2–6; full sun to light shade in Zones 7–11. Usually grown as an annual but can be grown as a perennial in Zones 9–11.

Plant in rich to average, moist but well-drained soil. It needs moderate moisture and excellent drainage. This plant works best in containers or rock gardens. Fertilize regularly, every 4–6 weeks, or work in a slow-release fertilizer in spring. It is usually pest and disease free.

Choices: Flowers are a lovely blue, though pink is also available.

'Blue Wonder' is the most readily available, but other selections, such as 'New Wonder' and 'Purple Fanfare', are also good.

Sedum spp.

sedum, stonecrop

Light Needs:

Full sun to part shade

Mature Height: *2"–2'*

Mature Width: *4"–18"*

Zones: *3–11*

Features:

Low maintenance

May attract butterflies and bees

Drought-tolerant

Blooms midsummer to late fall.

Needs: There are hundreds of different sedums, each with its own needs. Generally they do well in full sun, appreciating light shade in hot summer climates, Zones 8–11. They do especially well in rock gardens, needing average to poor, sandy, well-drained soil, doing best with moderate moisture but tolerating drought well.

Plant established plants in spring or fall. Avoid fertilizing. Trim spent flowers. Usually pest and disease free.

Choices: Flowers come in primarily reds, yellows, and pinks. One of the best-known is *Sedum* 'Autumn Joy', which grows 2 feet tall with wonderful brick red flowers in late summer through fall. Good cut flower, Zones 3–10.

Solidago hybrids

goldenrod

Light Needs:

Full sun

Mature Height: *2'–4'*

Mature Width: *1'–3'*

Zones: *3–9*

Features:

Excellent cut flower

Welcome late-season color

Native plant; good for wildflower plantings

Blooms summer or fall.

Needs: Full sun. Average to poor, well-drained soil. Does best with moderate moisture but is drought-tolerant.

Plant established plants in spring. Mulch to conserve moisture. Avoid fertilizing; tall types may need staking if soil is too rich. Trim spent blooms or cut frequently for bouquets. This plant is usually pest and disease free.

Choices: Wild goldenrod that seeds itself in your garden should be removed—it's invasive. Choose a hybrid that will not spread much and is more compact and disease resistant. Contrary to popular belief, goldenrod does not aggravate allergies.

Annuals and Perennials

Stachys byzantina

lamb's-ears

Light Needs:

Full sun

Mature Height: *8"–2'*

Mature Width: *1'–2'*

Zones: *4–8*

Features:

- Distinctive fuzzy silver-gray foliage
- Beautiful against white, blue, or pink flowers

Blooms in summer.

Needs: Full sun. Rich to poor, very well-drained soil. Moderate moisture but also drought-tolerant.

Plant established plants in spring or fall. Avoid fertilizing. Avoid getting leaves wet when watering. If desired, cut off flowers to keep focus on foliage.

Each spring, gently rake or pull out tattered leaves to make way for new growth.

This plant is prone to crown and root rot in moist or humid conditions.

Choices: Flowers are pink, but plant is grown mainly for its silver-gray foliage.

'Silver Carpet' doesn't bloom at all and is a good choice for edging.

Sutera cordata

bacopa, water hyssop

Light Needs:

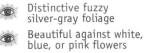

Full sun to part shade

Mature Height: *6"–8"*

Mature Width: *10"–14"*

Zones: *2–11*

Features:

- Excellent for hanging baskets and containers
- Hundreds of delicate flowers

Blooms summer to frost.

Needs: Full sun or light shade, especially Zones 7–11. Rich, well-drained, moist soil. Ample moisture; never allow to dry out. Dislikes heat, so keep out of very hot situations, such as near a driveway or on a sunny patio.

Plant established plants outdoors in spring after all danger of frost has passed. Because this is a thirsty plant that dies quickly if dried out, work water-retaining crystals into the soil under the plant. Mulch to conserve moisture. Fertilize occasionally, every 4–5 weeks, or work in a slow-release fertilizer at planting time.

Bacopa will grow as a perennial in Zones 9–11, but it is best grown as an annual.

Tagetes spp.

marigold

Light Needs:

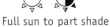

Full sun to part shade

Mature Height: *6"–3'*

Mature Width: *4"–18"*

Zones: *2–11*

Features:

- Exceptionally easy to grow
- Ideal for containers
- Tall types good for cutting

Blooms summer to frost.

Needs: Full sun in Zones 2–6; light shade appreciated in Zones 7–11. Rich to average, well-drained, preferably sandy soil. Moderate water.

Plant established plants in spring after all danger of frost has passed or start from seed indoors.

At planting time pinch off flowers and tips of seedlings to promote branching. Mulch to conserve moisture. Fertilize occasionally. Pluck, pinch, or trim off spent blooms to assure the longest bloom time. Tends to slow blooming when temperatures top 90°F (32°C). Prone to botrytis, root rot, fusarium wilt, slugs, rust, leaf spot, and Japanese beetles.

Choices: Flowers are yellow, gold, orange, russet, deep red, or cream.

Annuals and Perennials

Thymophylla tenuiloba

dahlberg daisy, golden fleece

Light Needs:

Full sun

Mature Height: *8"–12"*

Mature Width: *10"–14"*

Zones: *2–11*

Features:

Drought-tolerant

Often self-sows

Good container plant

Blooms late spring through frost.

Needs: Poor, well-drained soil. Drought-tolerant.

Plant established seedlings in spring as soon as danger of frost has passed. Avoid fertilizing. Discard after frost. This plant may overwinter in warm climates but usually looks too shabby to keep growing.

Pests and diseases are usually not a problem.

Choices: Flowers are yellow.

Tithonia rotundifolia

mexican sunflower

Light Needs:

Full sun

Mature Height: *2'–5'*

Mature Width: *1'–2'*

Zones: *2–11*

Features:

Attracts butterflies

Tall types for back of the border

Deer-resistant

Blooms midsummer to frost.

Needs: Full sun. Average to poor, well-drained soil. Moderate to light moisture; thrives in heat and humidity.

Plant established plants in spring after all danger of frost has passed. Mulch to conserve moisture. Avoid fertilizing. Stake taller types.

Snails and slugs may be problems.

Choices: Flowers are deep orange or yellow.

'Fiesta Del Sol' is a dwarf, growing just 30 inches tall but producing many flowers. Yellow 'Aztec Sun' is especially attractive to butterflies.

Torenia fournieri

wishbone flower

Light Needs:

Full sun to part shade

Mature Height: *8"–12"*

Mature Width: *8"–12"*

Zones: *4–11*

Features:

Good annual for shade

Good in containers

Blooms spring to frost.

Needs: Light to medium shade in most regions but full sun in cool-summer areas where temperatures are not above 75°F (24°C). Humus-rich, well-drained soil. Abundant moisture.

Plant established plants in spring after all danger of frost has passed. Work ample compost into soil. Plant in groups of a dozen or more for best effect. Mulch to conserve moisture. Fertilize occasionally, every 4–6 weeks, or work in a slow-release fertilizer at planting time.

Root rot is a problem in wet, poorly drained soil.

Choices: Flowers have markings in blues, purples, pinks, and white.

'Clown' series is one of the most popular cultivars.

Annuals and Perennials

Tropaeolum majus

nasturtium

Light Needs:

Full sun to part shade

Mature Height: *6"–6'*

Mature Width: *18"–3'*

Zones: *2–11*

Features:

👍 Easy to grow

⬆️ Some types good climbers

🎨 Rich colors

Blooms as long as temperatures don't regularly top 85°F (29°C).

Needs: Full sun in Zones 2–6; part shade in hot-summer areas in Zones 7–11. Average to poor, well-drained, preferably sandy soil. Drought-tolerant.

Plant seed directly in the garden. In Zones 2–7 plant in spring 1 week after last frost date. In Zones 8–11 sow in late autumn for winter or spring bloom. Avoid fertilizing, or leaves will grow higher than flowers.

Choices: Flowers come in oranges, reds, yellows, creams, peaches, and russets.

Choose climbing types to cover trellises. Dwarfs or trailing types are good for beds, borders, and containers. 'Alaska' sports variegated foliage.

Verbena spp.

verbena, clump verbena

Light Needs:

Full sun

Mature Height: *8"–4'*

Mature Width: *16"–3'*

Zones: *2–11*

Features:

💧 Drought-tolerant

🦋 Butterflies attracted to some types

🪴 Excellent in containers

Blooms summer to frost

Needs: Full sun in Zones 2–6; light shade in Zones 7–11. Rich to average, well-drained soil. Moderate water to drought-tolerant.

Plant in spring. If growing as an annual, wait until all danger of frost has passed. Pinch off tips to promote branching. Mulch. Fertilize occasionally. Trim spent blooms. It sometimes self-sows. If growing as a perennial, each spring cut plant back hard by half to two-thirds to keep plants neat.

Choices: Garden verbena *(Verbena × hybrida)* is a warm-season annual, Zones 2–11; a perennial, Zones 9–11. Rose vervain or clump verbena *(Verbena canadensis)* is a creeping perennial, Zones 6–10. *Verbena bonariensis* is annual, Zones 2–6, and perennial, Zones 7–10.

Verbena × hybrida

Veronica spp.

veronica, speedwell

Light Needs:

Full sun to part shade

Mature Height: *6"–3'*

Mature Width: *6"–3'*

Zones: *3–8*

Features:

🌸 Long bloomer

🎨 Lovely blue spires

👍 Easy to grow

Blooms late spring or early summer.

Needs: Full sun best but tolerates light shade, especially in Zones 7–8. Rich to average, moist but well-drained soil. Moderate to abundant moisture.

Plant established plants in spring or fall. Mulch to conserve moisture. Fertilize occasionally, every 4–6 weeks, or work in a slow-release fertilizer in spring. Keep spent blooms trim to keep plant tidy and encourage flowering, which can last several weeks. Mildew and leaf spot are sometimes a problem.

Choices: Flowers come in blues, purples, pinks, and white. 'Sunny Border Blue' is one of the most popular, growing 18 inches tall and blooming summer through fall. Groundcover types are also available.

Viola spp.

pansy, viola, violet

Light Needs:

Full sun to part shade

Mature Height: *2"–18"*

Mature Width: *2"–10"*

Zones: *2–11*

Features:

 Lovely spring color

 Thrives in cold weather

Some types fragrant

Blooms early spring.

Needs: Full sun in Zones 2–7; full sun or preferably light shade in hot-summer areas in Zones 8–9. Humus-rich, well-drained but moist soil. Abundant moisture. Blooms only during cool weather.

To grow pansies and violas, both of which are annuals, plant outdoors in spring in Zones 2–7 a few weeks before last frost date. In Zones 8–11 plant in late autumn for spring bloom. Work ample compost into the soil. Mulch to cool soil and conserve moisture. To grow perennial types of violets (Zones 6–9) plant established plants outdoors in spring. Keep spent blooms trimmed. Each spring, work more compost into the soil around the plants.

Yucca spp.

yucca

Light Needs:

Full sun

Mature Height: *2'–30'*

Mature Width: *2'–10'*

Zones: *4–11*

Features:

 Highly drought-tolerant

Spiky leaves make architectural statement

Blooms in summer.

Needs: Full sun. Average to sandy, well-drained soil. Drought-tolerant.

Plant established plants in spring or fall, spacing as label directs. Use gloves to handle large plants because leaves can be sharp. Avoid fertilizing. Trim off spent flower stalks after blooming. To get more plants, in spring separate small plants that crop up around the base and transplant. It is prone to root rot in wet sites.

Choices: Flowers are white. There are many different species of yucca, some growing as modest-sized perennials and some soaring to the size of trees. The most commonly grown for the flower garden is Adam's Needle *Yucca filimentosa* (Zones 4–11). It has foliage 2–3 feet tall and flower stalks 5–7 feet tall.

Zinnia spp.

zinnia

Light Needs:

Full sun to part shade

Mature Height: *6"–3'*

Mature Width: *4"–2'*

Zones: *2–11*

Features:

 Easy to grow

Attracts butterflies

Excellent cut flower

Blooms in summer to frost.

Needs: Full sun in Zones 2–8; light shade in hot-summer climates in Zones 9–11. Fertile, well-drained, neutral to acidic soil. Moderate moisture to drought-tolerant, depending on type.

Plant established plants in spring after all danger of frost, pinching ends to encourage fuller plants. Or plant seeds directly in prepared soil outdoors after all danger of frost. Thin according to package directions. Mulch to prevent disease. Fertilize occasionally, every 4–6 weeks. Trim spent blooms to promote further flowering.

This plant is very mildew-prone; avoid wetting leaves when watering, and select mildew-resistant cultivars, especially in the humid Midwest and South.

Annuals and Perennials

Bulbs

I n this section you'll find selection and growing information on the most common bulbs, along with tips for using them in the garden. Most bulbs, for example, make outstanding cut flowers. Plant a few, snip a few, and enjoy the beauty of bulbs.

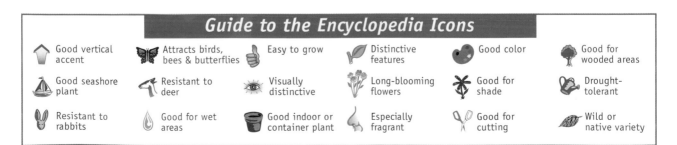

Guide to the Encyclopedia Icons

Good vertical accent	Attracts birds, bees & butterflies	Easy to grow	Distinctive features	Good color	Good for wooded areas
Good seashore plant	Resistant to deer	Visually distinctive	Long-blooming flowers	Good for shade	Drought-tolerant
Resistant to rabbits	Good for wet areas	Good indoor or container plant	Especially fragrant	Good for cutting	Wild or native variety

agapanthus, african lily

Light Needs:

Full sun to full shade

Mature Height: *1'–5'*

Mature Width: *6"–18"*

Zones: *2–11*

Features:

 Excellent cut flower

Attractive architectural flower shape

Needs: Full sun to light shade in Zones 2–6; light to full shade in Zones 7–11. Rich to average, well-drained soil. Moderate water but drought-tolerant when not blooming.

Plant the rhizomes (roots) 1 inch deep outdoors after all danger of frost. Most effective in mass plantings of 2 dozen or more. Work in a slow-release fertilizer at planting time and each following spring. In Zones 2–6, in fall after the first frost, discard or lift and store for winter. (See page 136.) In Zones 2–6 it does best in containers, but in Zones 7–11 it can be planted in-ground.

Choices: Flowers come in blues and white. *Agapanthus orientalis* (5 feet tall) and *Agapanthus africanus* (3 feet tall). Can be used as groundcovers.

allium, ornamental onion

Light Needs:

Full sun to part shade

Mature Height: *6"–5'*

Mature Width: *4"–3'*

Zones: *4–10*

Features:

 Dries well

 Striking round flower heads

Needs: Full sun or light shade, especially in Zones 7–10. Sandy, well-drained soil. Ample water.

Plant bulbs in fall. Depth will vary with type; check label. Plant in masses of a dozen or more for best effect. Fertilize rarely. Keep up on weeding with those that have hard-to-weed, dense, grasslike foliage. Trim spent blooms. Divide every few years when crowded and blooming diminishes. Rodents may eat this plant.

Choices: Flowers come in blues, purples, and whites unless noted. There are many species, all with long grassy or straplike leaves and spherical clusters of small flowers forming a ball atop tall stems.

windflower

Light Needs:

Full sun to part shade

Mature Height: *6"–1'*

Mature Width: *3"–6"*

Zones: *4–9*

Features:

 Good companion with tulips, daffodils

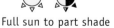 Lovely, delicate flowers

 Good cut flower

Needs: Full sun to light shade, preferably dappled with no midday sun in Zones 6–9. Rich, extremely well-drained soil. Ample moisture during spring; drier summer through fall.

In Zones 4–5 plant tubers 3–4 inches deep in spring a few weeks before the last frost date. In Zones 6–9 plant in October or November. Soak tubers in water overnight first.

In fall, in Zone 4, provide winter mulch for *Anemone blanda.*

Choices: Flowers come in blues, whites, pinks, and reds.

Grecian windflower (*Anemone blanda*) is hardy in Zones 4–8. Poppy anemone (*Anemone coronaria*) is hardy in Zones 6–9 and includes the popular 'De Caen' hybrids.

Bulbs

Begonia tuberhybrida

tuberous begonia

Light Needs:

Part shade

Mature Height: *12"–18"*

Mature Width: *8"–18"*

Zones: *2–11*

Features:

Excellent for containers

Thrives in light shade

Needs: Annual in Zones 2–9; perennial in Zones 10–11.

Very light shade to almost full sun in Zones 2–5; light shade in Zones 6–11. Rich, moist, but extremely well-drained soil (most successful in containers). Water well during bloom.

Plant tubers indoors in spring in pots just deep enough to cover, 2–4 weeks before the last frost date. Transplant outdoors after all danger of frost has passed. Or plant in permanent place outdoors when nights are above 50°F (10°C).

Work a slow-release fertilizer or compost into planting spot. Fertilize every 4–6 weeks. Keep evenly moist. Trim spent blooms. Lift and store tubers in fall (page 136).

Caladium bicolor (Caladium x hortulanum)

caladium

Light Needs:

Full to part shade

Mature Height: *1'–3'*

Mature Width: *1'–3'*

Zones: *2–11*

Features:

Fabulous foliage

Thrives in shade

Good for containers

Needs: Annual in Zones 2–9; perennial in Zones 10–11. Light shade in Zones 2–6; deeper shade in Zones 7–11. Rich, well-drained but moist soil, neutral to acidic. Ample moisture.

Plant tubers 2 inches deep in spring when nights are above 60°F (16°C). Work in a few spadefuls of compost and a slow-release fertilizer. After plant emerges, mulch to conserve moisture. In fall, after first frost, lift and store tubers if desired (see page 136). Store at 40°F (4°C). Bring small pots indoors as winter houseplants or allow to go dormant in the pots. Snails and slugs are a problem.

Choices: Leaves are marked in reds, greens, pinks, and whites. Dozens if not hundreds of cultivars are available in many sizes, markings, and color combinations.

Canna hybrids

canna

Light Needs:

Full sun

Mature Height: *18"–6'*

Mature Width: *10"–24"*

Zones: *2–11*

Features:

Fabulous foliage

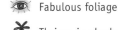

Exotic flowers attract hummingbirds

Good vertical accent

Needs: Annual in Zones 2–7; perennial in Zones 8–11. Full sun. Tolerates a variety of soils, but does best in rich, well-drained soil. Abundant moisture.

Plant in spring after soil has warmed, a week or two after last frost date. Work in ample compost or a slow-release fertilizer at planting time.

In fall, in Zones 2–7, after first frost, lift and store tubers (see page 136). Store at 40–50°F (4–10°C). Snails and slugs are a problem.

Choices: Flowers come in pinks, reds, oranges, yellows, and whites. Foliage has markings of greens, yellows, whites, and purples. 'Pretoria' has lime green and lemon yellow tiger-like stripes. 'Wyoming' has deep purple foliage. 'Pfitzer's' dwarf hybrids grow just 30 inches tall.

Bubls

Colchicum autumnale

autumn crocus

Light Needs:

Full sun to part shade

Mature Height: *6"–8"*

Mature Width: *3"–4"*

Zones: *5–9*

Features:

Unusual fall flower

Needs: Full sun to light shade. Average, well-drained soil. Ample water while blooming; otherwise moderate.

Plant corms in mid- to late summer, 3–4 inches deep. Plant in groups of a dozen or more for best effect. This plant is usually pest free.

Choices: Flowers come in pink, lavender, or white.

Crocosmia x crocosmiiflora

crocosmia, montbretia

Light Needs:

Full sun to part shade

Mature Height: *18"–3'*

Mature Width: *1'–2'*

Zones: *5–10*

Features:

Easy to grow

Drought-tolerant

Excellent for cutting

Needs: Full sun or light shade. Average to rich, well-drained soil. Drought-tolerant but best with moderate water.

Plant corms in spring 3–5 inches deep after all danger of frost has passed. Work in a slow-release fertilizer at planting time and every spring or every other spring thereafter.

In fall in Zones 5 and 6, provide a thick layer of winter-protecting mulch.

Choices: Flowers are red, orange, gold or yellow.

'Lucifer' is one of the few crocosmias hardy to Zone 5.

Crocus spp.

crocus

Light Needs:

Full sun to part shade

Mature Height: *2"–4"*

Mature Width: *2"–3"*

Zones: *5–7*

Features:

One of the earliest bulbs to bloom

Spreads readily

Good for naturalizing in lawns or wooded areas

Needs: Full sun or light shade, especially found under deciduous trees. Rich, well-drained soil. Moderate water.

Plant in October in Zones 3–6 or in November in Zones 7–8, positioning 2–5 inches deep. Plant in groups of 2–3 dozen or more for best effect. An inch or two of mulch is good winter protection in Zones 3–6. Rodents may eat corms.

Choices: Flowers come in yellow, white, purple, and pink.

Snow or bunch crocus (*Crocus chrysanthus*) grows just 2–3 inches tall and blooms especially early, forming little clumps.

Dutch or giant crocus (*Crocus vernus vernus*) grows 3–4 inches tall and blooms as soon as the snow crocuses finish.

Bulbs

Cyclamen hederifolium

hardy cyclamen

Light Needs:

Part shade

Mature Height: *3"–5"*

Mature Width: *4"–8"*

Zones: *7–9*

Features:

Lovely woodland flower

Low-maintenance once established

Naturalizes with time

Needs: Light shade, preferably shade under tall deciduous trees or shrubs. Rich, well-drained but moist soil. Ample moisture during growth; otherwise moderate. Best in climates where summers are relatively dry with cool nights.

Plant established plants or tubers in spring or fall, working in ample compost. Group in masses of a dozen or more for impact. Position tubers just below the soil surface. Mark clearly to avoid disturbing. This plant is unlikely to bloom much for the first year or two but, once established, will take off and even self-sow if not disturbed. Each fall, mulch with 2–3 inches of chopped autumn leaves for winter protection as well as nutrients. In spring, spread 1–2 inches of compost on the planting.

Dahlia

dahlia

Light Needs:

Full sun to part shade

Mature Height: *1'–7'*

Mature Width: *8"–3'*

Zones: *2–11*

Features:

Superb cut flower

Outstanding fall color

Needs: Perennial in Zones 8–11; annual in colder regions. Full sun; light shade mid-day is appreciated in Zones 8–11. Rich, well-drained soil. Ample moisture.

In spring after all danger of frost has passed, plant 6 inches deep. After the first three sets of leaves have developed, pinch the tip of the shoots. A few weeks later, pinch the shoots a second time. Stake as needed. Fertilize with a low-nitrogen formula every 6 weeks. Trim spent blooms. In Zones 2–7, in fall, after the first frost, lift and store tubers in a dry spot that stays about 40°F (4°C) (see page 136). In spring, divide clumps and then replant, including part of the old stem in the division.

Freesia spp.

freesia

Light Needs:

Full sun to part shade

Mature Height: *12"–18"*

Mature Width: *4"–6"*

Zones: *2–11*

Features:

Fabulously fragrant

Excellent cut flower

Needs: Perennial in Zones 9–11 where summers are dry and winters are cool and moist; grow as an annual elsewhere.

Full sun or very light shade, especially in Zones 8–11. Average, well-drained, preferably sandy soil. Ample moisture during growth; less during summer dormancy. In Zones 2–8 plant corms in spring after all danger of frost has passed. In Zones 9–11 plant corms in fall. Plant 2 inches deep. Cluster in groups of a dozen or more for support; stake as needed. Temperatures of 60–70°F (16–21°C) in the day and 50–60°F (10–16°C) at night are best; it will go dormant in summer in hot regions. In wet-summer regions, corms should be dug and stored or treated as annuals. In Zones 2–8 dig corms in fall.

Fritillaria spp.

fritillary, crown imperial, checkered lily

Light Needs:

Full sun to part shade

Mature Height: *1'-4'*

Mature Width: *6"-2'*

Zones: *3-7*

Features:

 Unusual flowers

Deer- and rodent-resistant

Needs: Full sun or part shade. Rich, well-drained soil. Moderate water, though less once dormant in summer.

Plant bulbs as soon as available in fall, usually September, so they don't dry out. Plant 4–6 inches deep. Crown imperial is spaced 8–12 inches; checkered lily 3–4 inches. Place in ground at a 45-degree angle to prevent tops from collecting water. Best in groups of two to three. After blooming, do not cut off browning foliage. It's needed to rejuvenate the plant. Remove brown foliage when it pulls off without resistance.

Choices: Crown imperial (*Fritillaria imperialis*, Zones 5–8) is lovely in beds and borders. Mulch for winter protection. Checkered lily (*Fritillaria meleagris*, Zones 3–8) does not do well in hot, dry climates.

'Fritillaria imperialis'

Galanthus nivalis

snowdrop

Light Needs:

Full sun to part shade

Mature Height: *4"-8"*

Mature Width: *3"-6"*

Zones: *3-7*

Features:

Among the earliest of bulbs to bloom

Good for naturalizing in lawns

Good woodland flower

Needs: Full sun or light shade. Rich, well-drained but moist soil. Abundant to moderate water.

Plant in October, 2–3 inches deep. For best effect, plant in groups of three or four dozen. This plant does best in Zones 3–7 but also in the Pacific Northwest. Where it is well situated, spreading may occur.

It is usually pest free.

Choices: Flowers are white.

Gladiolus hybrids

gladiolus

Light Needs:

Full sun

Mature Height: *3'-6'*

Mature Width: *8"-18"*

Zones: *2-11*

Features:

Showy cut flowers

Good vertical accent

Needs: Perennial in Zones 8–11 but best if grown as an annual. Full sun. Average to rich, well-drained soil. Ample water while growing and blooming, then moderate water.

Plant corms as soon as danger of frost has passed. In hot-summer areas (Zones 8–11) plant in late winter. Plant 4–6 inches deep and work in compost or slow-release, low-nitrogen fertilizer. For a succession of blooms, plant more every 2 or 3 weeks (they bloom 60 to 100 days after planting). Support by staking, especially in windy sites, or mound soil 6 inches around stems. Remove faded flower stalks immediately. When cutting flowers, leave at least 3 to 4 leaves so corms will mature next year. In late fall, lift and store corms to replant next year.

Bulbs

Gladiolus callinathus

peacock orchid, abyssinian gladiolus

Light Needs:

Full sun

Mature Height: *30"–4'*

Mature Width: *4"–6"*

Zones: *3–11*

Features:

Exotic, elegant flowers

Fragrant

Excellent for cutting

Needs: Grown as an annual in Zones 3–6; as a perennial in Zones 7–11.

Full sun. Rich, well-drained soil in a site protected from wind. Ample water.

In Zones 3–6 start indoors in peat pots 4 weeks before last frost date, then transplant after all danger of frost. In Zones 7–11, plant in spring after all danger of frost. Plant 4–6 inches deep. After plant emerges mulch to conserve moisture. Work in compost or a slow-release fertilizer each spring. Stake as needed. Trim spent blooms to prolong flowering for up to two months. In fall in Zones 3–6, if desired, lift and store the bulbs for the winter (see page 136).

This plant is prone to thrips and mosaic virus.

Hyacinthus orientalis

hyacinth

Light Needs:

Full sun to part shade

Mature Height: *12"–18"*

Mature Width: *8"–10"*

Zones: *3–11*

Features:

Intensely fragrant

Good for forcing indoors

Deer-resistant

Needs: Perennial in Zones 3–7; annual in Zones 7–11.

Full sun, though light shade from deciduous trees later in season is ideal. Rich, very well-drained soil, acidic to neutral. Ample water during growth and bloom; moderate water after.

Plant in October on Zones 3–7, working compost and bulb fertilizer into the soil. In Zones 8–11, purchase bulbs and chill in refrigerator for 6–8 weeks (or purchase prechilled) and then plant outdoors. Plant 8 inches deep.

Mulch for winter protection in Zones 3–4. After blooming, allow foliage to brown and "ripen." Do not remove until foliage pulls away easily This plant may come back for several years. Hyacinth are good for forcing (see page 136).

Lilium spp.

lily

Light Needs:

Full sun to part shade

Mature Height: *8"–8'*

Mature Width: *4"–18"*

Zones: *3–9*

Features:

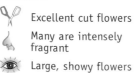

Excellent cut flowers

Many are intensely fragrant

Large, showy flowers

Needs: Full sun in Zones 3–5; full sun to light shade Zones 6–9. Rich, well-drained soil. Regular water during growth; then less.

Plant bulbs in fall 8 inches deep, no later than a week or so after first frost date. Or plant established container plants in spring. Work in compost and bulb fertilizer at planting time. In spring, stake those growing more than a few feet tall. Trim spent blooms. Allow foliage to brown on plant to rejuvenate for next year. When leaves die completely in late summer, cut off a few inches above soil level to mark spot.

Choices: Asiatic lilies grow 2–5 feet tall. Oriental lilies grow 2–8 feet and are often fragrant. Easter lilies (*Lilium longiflorum*) are hardy in Zones 6–11.

Lycoris squamigera

magic lily, suprise lily, naked ladies

Light Needs:

Full sun

Mature Height: 18"–2'

Mature Width: 8"–10"

Zones: 5–8

Features:

🌿 Flowers bloom without leaves

🎨 Pretty pink blooms

Needs: Full sun. Rich, well-drained soil. Abundant moisture while growing; moderate while dormant.

Plant bulbs in mid- to late summer, 5–6 inches deep. This plant dislikes too much water in summer. Plant in clusters and crowd to promote better blooming.

It is prone to root and bulb rot if overwatered.

Choices: Flowers are pink.

Muscari spp.

grape hyacinth

Light Needs:

Full sun to part shade

Mature Height: 6"–1'

Mature Width: 4"–6"

Zones: 3–8

Features:

Good woodland flower

Good for naturalizing in lawns.

Pretty little cut flower

Needs: Full sun or light shade. Average to poor, well-drained, and preferably sandy soil. Abundant to moderate water.

Plant in October 2–3 inches deep. Do not fertilize. For best effect plant in groups of 3–4 dozen. Where well situated, this plant may spread.

Foliage after bloom will gradually fade and "ripen." Do not cut. This is needed to feed the plant for next year. Remove foliage when it pulls away with no resistance. This plant is usually pest free.

Choices: Flowers are usually purple but sometimes also white. The most commonly grown (*Muscari botryoides* and *Muscari armeniacum*) have little round flowers. 'Blue Spike' has double flowers. Tassel grape hyacinth (*Muscari comosum*) has unusual feathery flowers.

Narcissus spp.

daffodils, narcissus, jonquils

Light Needs:

Full sun to part shade

Mature Height: 4"–18"

Mature Width: 4"–10"

Zones: 3–11

Features:

Some sweetly fragrant varieties

Excellent for cutting

Good for forcing indoors

Needs: Full sun, though light shade from deciduous trees later in season is ideal. Rich, well-drained soil, neutral to slightly acidic. Ample water during growth and bloom; moderate water after.

Plant 5–8 inches deep in October in Zones 3–7; and November to early December in Zones 8–11. Work in compost and bulb fertilizer.

Choices: There are thousands of cultivars in a variety of sizes, flower forms, and colorings. Trumpet and large-cup hybrids, the most commonly available, are hardy in Zones 3–9 but not where summers are wet. Jonquils (*Narcissus jonquilla*), pheasant's-eye (*Narcissus poeticus*), and angel's tears (*Narcissus triandrus*) are hardy in Zones 4–9 in the East; in Zones 4–11 in the West.

Bulbs

ranunculus, persian buttercup

Light Needs:

Full sun to part shade

Mature Height: *12"–18"*
Mature Width: *4"–6"*
Zones: *8–10*

Features:

👁 Brilliant blooms

🪴 Good in containers

Needs: Full sun to light shade. Rich to average, very well-drained, preferably sandy soil. Ample moisture.

Where winter temperatures don't drop below 0°F (18°C)—roughly Zones 8–10—grow as a perennial. Plant in late fall to very early winter, 4 inches deep, and select a spot that won't get much summer water. If roots are dried and shriveled, soak for a few hours or place in moist sand for a few days. In the South, where summers are wet, most gardeners lift and store after blooming and foliage yellows (see page 136). In colder zones it can be grown as an annual planted in spring, especially in containers.

Choices: Flowers come in yellows, oranges, reds, pinks, and whites.

squill

Light Needs:

Full sun to part shade

Mature Height: *4"–18"*
Mature Width: *4"–10"*
Zones: *2–8*

Features:

🌿 Among the earliest of bulbs

🌿 Good for naturalizing in lawns

🌳 Good woodland flower

Needs: Full sun or light shade. Rich, well-drained soil. Ample water while blooming; moderate water when it goes dormant in late spring.

Plant in October in Zones 2–6 and November in Zones 7–8. Position 2–3 inches deep. For best effect plant in groups of 3–4 dozen. Avoid watering in summer. No fertilizer needed. Where well situated, it usually spreads. It is pest free.

Choices: Flowers are blue, white, or pink. Siberian squill *(Scilla sibirica)* is the most commonly grown and hardy in Zones 2–7. Two-leaved squill *(Scilla bifolia)* grows 6 inches and has been grown in gardens since the 16th century. Cuban lily *(Scilla peruviana)* is hardy in Zones 4–8 and grows 10–12 inches, blooming in late spring. It's good for warm climates.

trillium, wake-robin

Light Needs:

Part shade

Mature Height: *1'–2'*
Mature Width: *1'–2'*
Zones: *4–8*

Features:

🌳 Native woodland flower

🌿 Spreads readily in good conditions

✳ Thrives in shade

Needs: Light to medium shade. Rich, moist, neutral to acidic soil. Does well under deciduous trees and large shrubs. Abundant moisture.

Plant rhizomes in spring 4 inches deep or plant container-grown plants. Work in ample compost. Mulch to conserve moisture. It will gradually spread to 1- to 2-foot clumps. When plant is dormant, divide clumps if new plants are desired. It is pest and disease free.

Choices: Flowers are usually white but also come in pinks, burgundy, and mahogany. *Trillium grandiflora* has the showiest flowers, growing 2–3 inches across. Others are *Trillium erectum*, *Trillium sessile*, and *Trillium chloropetalum*, which is large at 2 feet tall.

'Trillium grandiflora'

Bubls

Tulbaghia

society garlic

Light Needs:

Full sun to part shade

Mature Height: *18"–2'*
Mature Width: *6"–10"*
Zones: *8–11*

Features:

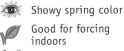 Long-blooming

Low maintenance

Needs: Full sun to light shade. Average, moist, but well-drained soil. Best with moderate moisture but will tolerate some drought.

Plant container-grown plants in spring or fall. Plant bulbs in spring 1–2 inches deep. Trim spent blooms, but otherwise this plant is low maintenance. It is bothered by few pests or diseases.

In Zone 8, mulch for winter protection.

Choices: Flowers are lavender. 'Silver Lace' has white-striped leaves.

Tulipa spp.

tulip

Light Needs:

Full sun to part shade

Mature Height: *4"–30"*
Mature Width: *4"–10"*

Zones: *3–11*

Features:

Showy spring color

Good for forcing indoors

Excellent for cutting

Needs: Perennial in Zones 3–7; annual in Zones 7–11.

Full sun, though light shade from deciduous trees later in season is ideal. Rich, very well-drained soil. Ample water during growth and bloom; moderate water after. Plant in October in Zones 3–7, working compost and bulb fertilizer into the soil. In Zones 8–11 purchase bulbs and chill in the refrigerator for 6–10 weeks (or purchase prechilled) and then plant outdoors.

Mulch for winter protection in Zones 3–4. In spring, after blooming, allow foliage to brown and "ripen." Where well situated, plants will come back for several years but often die out after just 2 or 3 years. Tulips are also good for forcing indoors (page 151).

Zantedeschia aethiopica

calla lily

Light Needs:

Full sun to part shade

Mature Height: *18"–4'*
Mature Width: *10"–24"*

Zones: *3–11*

Features:

Elegant flower shape

Good for wet sites

Excellent cut flower

Needs: Grow as an annual in Zones 2–7; as a perennial in Zones 8–11.

Full sun to light shade, especially in hot-summer areas of Zones 8–11. Average to rich, always moist soil. Ample moisture.

In Zones 2–7 plant in containers in spring after all danger of frost has passed. in Zones 8–11 plant outdoors in containers or in the ground. Plant 4 inches deep. Mulch to conserve moisture. Fertilize once or twice during bloom. This plant will often naturalize.

It is prone to leaf spots, slugs, and snails.

In fall in Zones 2–7, store, pot and all, in garage or cold basement over the winter.

Choices: Flowers are usually white, but yellow is also available.

Bulbs

Shrubs

Flowering shrubs give abundant flowers and require very little work and very little money. For less than you would spend on a best-selling book, one shrub will flower year after year, filling your garden always with beautiful color and often with lovely fragrances.

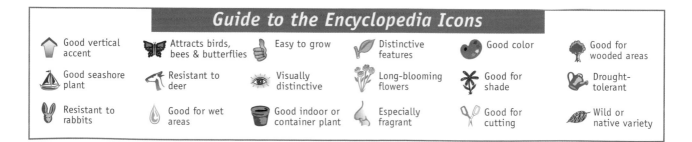

Guide to the Encyclopedia Icons

Good vertical accent	Attracts birds, bees & butterflies	Easy to grow
Good seashore plant	Resistant to deer	Visually distinctive
Resistant to rabbits	Good for wet areas	Good indoor or container plant

Distinctive features	Good color	Good for wooded areas
Long-blooming flowers	Good for shade	Drought-tolerant
Especially fragrant	Good for cutting	Wild or native variety

Abelia x grandiflora

glossy abelia

Light Needs:

Full sun to part shade

Mature Height: 4'–8'

Mature Width: 4'–5'

Zones: 6–9

Features:

- Four-season interest
- Good for flowering hedges
- Ideal foundation plant

Needs: Full sun to light or medium shade. Rich, well-drained, acidic soil. Ample moisture.

Plant established plants in spring or fall. Work compost into the planting hole, but no need to fertilize in most conditions. Blooms appear on new growth each year, so prune in late winter or early spring. Although abelia makes a good hedge, it's prettiest when not sheared. Instead, to preserve this shrub's graceful form, cut out selected branches at the plant's base. It is prone to leaf spot, though usually pest and disease free.

Choices: Flowers are white surrounded by rust-colored sepals. 'Sherwoodii' has fine-textured foliage, 3 feet tall by 5 feet wide. 'Francis Mason', 3–4 feet tall and wide, has variegated leaves.

Buddleia spp.

butterfly bush

Light Needs:

Full sun to part shade

Mature Height: 5'–18'

Mature Width: 5'–8'

Zones: 5–10

Features:

- Attracts butterflies
- Casual, arching habit
- Rabbit-resistant

Needs: Full sun in Zones 5–6; full sun to light shade in Zones 7–10. Average to sandy, fertile to poor, well-drained soil. Ample moisture best; will tolerate drought.

Plant established plants in spring or fall. Mulch. Do not fertilize. This plant dies back to the ground each winter in northern climates.

Buddleia davidii, the most commonly available *buddleia,* blooms on new wood produced each spring. In Zones 5–6, in late winter or early spring, cut back to the ground. In Zones 7–11 cut back less severely, to perhaps a foot or two.

Some buddleia bloom only on the old wood they grew the previous year. In these cases prune the shrubs back by one-fifth to one-third immediately after they flower in summer.

Callicarpa spp.

purple beautyberry

Light Needs:

Full sun to part shade

Mature Height: 3'–4'

Mature Width: 3'–4'

Zones: 5–8

Features:

- Gorgeous berries in fall
- Excellent for cutting

Needs: Full sun for best-formed berries; light shade helps berries last longer. Nearly any type soil; moderate to ample moisture. Tolerates smog and seaside conditions.

Plant established plants in spring or fall. No need to fertilize. Mulch to conserve moisture. This plant produces small flowers in late summer that turn into berries in fall. Birds may eat berries. Throw a net over the shrub to protect and save it for cutting.

In late winter or early spring, when it shows signs of new growth, trim back 6–12 inches from ground. Hard pruning is necessary to ensure new blooming. Rabbits like this plant's new growth.

Choices: Berries are purple or white.

Shrubs

Camellia spp.
evergreen spring-, summer-, or fall-blooming shrub

camellia

Light Needs:

Full sun to part shade

Mature Height: 1'–15'

Mature Width: 1'–15'

Zones: 6–11

Features:

🌿 Alabama state flower

✂ Excellent for cutting

🪴 Excellent in large containers

Needs: Best in part shade, but will tolerate full shade and full sun. Does best in rich, moist, acidic soil. Ample moisture.

Plant established plants in spring or fall. Mulch 2 inches deep. Keep moist first three years; after that most in-ground plants survive on natural rainfall. Fertilize plants under 8 feet every 6–8 weeks or so with an acid plant food. Read label carefully; do not overfertilize. Prune immediately after flowering. Cut out any dead or weak wood, shape shrub, and thin growth as desired. This plant is prone to disease if soil is poorly drained or if there are excessive salts in the soil. It is also prone to camellia petal blight. Pick up fallen leaves and petals immediately to control this problem.

Chaenomeles speciosa
deciduous spring-blooming shrub

flowering quince

Light Needs:

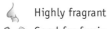

Full sun

Mature Height: 5'–10'

Mature Width: 5'–8'

Zones: 4–9

Features:

👃 Highly fragrant

✂ Good for forcing cut branches

Needs: Average to heavy clay soil. Moderate water best, but drought-tolerant.

Plant established plants in spring or fall. Mulch to conserve moisture. No need to fertilize in most conditions. No need to trim spent blooms.

This plant blooms on old wood. Best to leave unpruned except for removal of dead or damaged wood.

Apple scab, fire blight, and aphids may be problems.

Just as buds begin to swell in early spring, cut branches and bring indoors to bloom in a vase.

Choices: Flowers in white, red, or pink.

Clethra alnifolia
deciduous late summer-blooming shrub

summersweet, sweet pepperbush

Light Needs:

Full sun to part shade

Mature Height: 4'–10'

Mature Width: 4'–6'

Zones: 4–9

Features:

🌿 Native shrub

👃 Fragrant

🌸 Long bloom season

Needs: Full sun to medium shade, especially in hot summer areas in Zones 7–9. Rich, moist to wet, acidic soil. Ample moisture.

Plant established plants in spring or fall. Mulch 3–4 inches to conserve moisture and keep soil cool. No need to fertilize in most conditions. Slow to establish, but once it does, may need to dig up suckers to control spread.

Blooms on new growth, so prune annually in mid- to late winter (before new growth begins or the plant will bleed sap). Cut out very old or very weak growth to base of plant.

It is usually pest and disease free, but spider mites are a problem in dry conditions.

Choices: Flowers are white or pink.

Shrubs

Cotinus coggygria

smokebush, smoke tree

Light Needs:

Full sun

Mature Height: *12'–15'*

Mature Width: *12'–15'*

Zones: *5–8*

Features:

Beautiful purple foliage

Fascinating feathery foliage

Needs: Average to poor, rocky, extremely well-drained soil. Moderate moisture.

Plant established plants in spring or fall. Mulch to conserve moisture. No need to fertilize in most conditions.

Prune as desired to control size in early spring, just as growth is beginning, but do not shear. Selectively cut out branches at ground level or "head off" branches just above a leaf bud. Cut the whole shrub down to just a few inches above the ground if desired. Few pests or diseases bother this shrub.

Choices: This shrub is grown for its often-purple foliage and pink-turning-to-gray inflorescences. Male plants produce a better show than females. Some cultivars have green leaves, but purple are most popular.

Cytisus spp.

broom, genista

Light Needs:

Full sun

Mature Height: *10"–6'*

Mature Width: *3'–7'*

Zones: *6–10*

Features:

Very drought-tolerant

Bold, brilliant color in spring

Needs: Average to poor, sandy, rocky soil. Moderate moisture at first; then highly drought-tolerant. Does well in windy and seashore conditions; good for erosion control.

Plant established plants in spring. Do not fertilize. Pruning not essential, especially in naturalistic settings, but cut stems back by one-third immediately after blooming. Shrub can be invasive. It is bothered by few diseases or pests.

Choices: Flowers are usually yellow but also white, red, or maroon. Warminster broom *(Cytisus × praecox)* is widely grown and is hardy in Zones 6–9.

Do not grow Canary Island broom *(Cytisus canariensis)* or Scotch broom *(Cytisus scoparius)* in the West, where they've taken over in some areas.

Daphne spp.

daphne

Light Needs:

Full sun to part shade

Mature Height: *1'–4'*

Mature Width: *3'–10'*

Zones: *4–9*

Features:

Memorable fragrance

Pretty variegated leaves on some varieties

Needs: Full sun to light shade, depending on the species. Rich to average, very well-drained but moist soil. Moderate to ample water during bloom; otherwise moderate to dry.

Plant in spring or fall. Mulch well. Do not prune. It dies out easily if soil is too soggy.

Choices: Flowers are white or pink. Burkwood daphne *(Daphne × burkwoodii)* is semievergreen and has a number of lovely variegated cultivars. Grows 3–4 feet high and wide. It blooms late spring and late summer, and is hardy in Zones 5–7. Garland and rose daphne *(Daphne cneorum)* grows 1 foot high by 3 feet wide. Good for rock gardens, Zones 5–7. Winter daphne *(Daphne odora)* is very fragrant. Grows 4 feet by 8–10 feet, Zones 7–9.

Shrubs

Shrubs   229

Forsythia intermedia

forsythia

Light Needs:

Full sun to part shade

Mature Height: *4'–5'*

Mature Width: *10'*

Zones: *4–8*

Features:

- Early, brilliant gold flowers
- Good for forcing

Needs: Full sun for best flowering; will tolerate light shade. Average to rich, well-drained soil. Ample to moderate moisture.

Plant established plants in spring or fall. No need to fertilize or trim spent blooms. Mulch to conserve moisture. Flowers bloom on old wood grown the previous year. Little pruning is needed, but do any necessary pruning immediately after flowering. Do not shear, which destroys the plant's natural shape. If pruning is desired, selectively cut out the oldest and weakest stems to just above the ground. Every few years, cut the entire shrub back to about a foot to renew and control size.

This shrub is prone to few serious pests or diseases.

Fothergilla spp.

witch alder

Light Needs:

Full sun to part shade

Mature Height: *3'–10'*

Mature Width: *3'–6'*

Zones: *5–8*

Features:

- Good fall color for leaves
- Interesting, fragrant, bottlebrush-like flowers

Needs: Full sun for the most flowers and best fall color. Rich, acid, moist, well-drained soil. Moderate moisture.

Plant in spring or fall, working ample compost into the planting hole. Do not prune or remove lower stems, which help fill out the plant. This shrub produces suckers; trim these regularly. It is bothered by few diseases or pests.

Choices: *Fothergilla major* (sometimes sold as *Fothergilla monticola*) gets large, up to 10 feet tall. *Fothergilla gardenii* is a more manageable 3 feet tall.

Gardenia augusta (Gardenia jasminoides)

gardenia, cape jasmine

Light Needs:

Full sun to part shade

Mature Height: *2'–6'*

Mature Width: *3'–6'*

Zones: *8–11*

Features:

- Outstanding fragrance
- Gorgeous flowers
- Good cut flower to float in bowl

Needs: Full sun to light shade. Extremely well-drained, humus-rich, moist and acidic soil. Where soil is poor-draining, grow in large pots. Ample moisture.

Very specific climate needed. Survives to 0°F (-18°C), but dies back to ground. Hardy to about 10°F (-12°C) without damage. When forming flower buds, it needs nighttime temperatures of 50–55°F (10–13°C) and sufficient summer heat to bloom.

Plant in spring, amending soil liberally with compost or sphagnum peat moss. Mulch with 2–3 inches mulch to prevent cultivating around shallow roots. Feed monthly with an acidic fertilizer.

Prune only to remove straggly branches or trim spent blooms.

Hamamelis spp.

witch hazel

Light Needs:

Full sun to part shade

Mature Height: 8'–30'

Mature Width: 8'–30'

Zones: 5–9

Features:

- Early, brilliant gold flowers
- Some types are fragrant
- Native shrub

Needs: Full sun for best flowering; tolerates light shade. Rich, well-drained, acidic soil best. Ample moisture.

Plant established plants in spring or fall. No need to fertilize or trim spent blooms. Mulch. Little pruning needed. Do not shear, which destroys the plant's natural shape. If pruning is desired, instead selectively cut out the oldest and weakest stems to just above the ground. Also remove suckers.

Choices: Hamamelis × intermedia grows to 20 feet, Zones 5–9. *Hamamelis virginiana* and Chinese witch hazel *(Hamamelis mollis)* are fragrant, Zones 5–9. Vernal witch hazel *(Hamamelis vernalis)* is a native shrub that likes wet sites and is also fragrant, Zones 5–7.

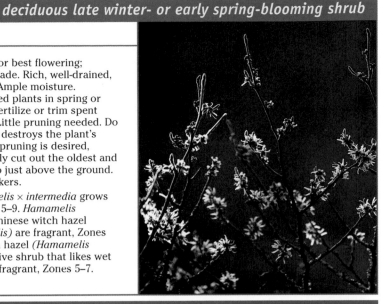

Hibiscus spp.

hibiscus, rose of sharon, shrub althea

Light Needs:

Full sun to part shade

Mature Height: 6'–12'

Mature Width: 4'–15'

Zones: 5–11

Features:

- Big, showy flowers
- Tolerates heat well

Needs: Rose of Sharon or shrub althea *(Hibiscus syriacus)* is a deciduous shrub in Zones 5–9. It tolerates a variety of soils and is drought-tolerant once established.

Plant in spring after all danger of frost has passed. Mulch. Fertilize each spring by working compost into the soil or by adding slow-release fertilizer. Blooms on new wood grown that year, so prune back hard by about half in late winter or early spring just as it starts to show signs of growth.

Chinese hibiscus *(Hibiscus rosa-sinensis)* is hardy only to about 30°F (-1°C) and reaches 15 feet where hardy. Plant in spring in a very well-drained site. Feed occasionally. Water often. In early spring, prune out one-third of the mature wood to keep both types of plants vigorous.

'Hibiscus rosa-sinensis'

Hydrangea spp.

hydrangea

Light Needs:

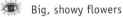

Part shade

Mature Height: 12'–15'

Mature Width: 3'–8'

Zones: 4–9

Features:

- Lovely flower heads are great for drying
- Thrives in shade
- Some are native plants

Needs: Rich, well-drained soil, preferably acidic, with ample moisture.

Bigleaf hydrangea *(Hydrangea macrophylla)*; 2–6 feet, Zones 6–9. Will flower without pruning, but better flowering if in fall shoots that flowered are cut back to a strong, fat flower bud and weak and old stems are cut to the ground. To get blue flowers, choose a cultivar that will bloom blue, such as 'Nikko Blue'. Acidic soil is also needed for blue flowers; fertilize with an acidic fertilizer. Other cultivars bloom in pink and white.

Smooth hydrangea *(Hydrangea arborescens* 'Grandiflora'), Zones 4–9, has white snowball-like flowers. 3–5 feet. Blooms on current year's growth, so prune hard to the ground each spring.

'Hydrangea macrophylla'

Ilex verticillata

winterberry

Light Needs:

Full sun to part shade

Mature Height: *6'–10'*

Mature Width: *6'–10'*

Zones: *4–9*

Features:

Needs wet conditions

Beautiful red berries in winter

Needs: Full sun for the most berries. Rich to heavy, wet to swampy, acid soil.

Both a male and female plant are necessary for berry production. Plant in spring or fall. If soil isn't already acidic, add garden sulfur to the planting hole. Mulch well.

Prune only as necessary, removing dead or damaged wood. Do not shear, which would interfere with berry production.

Use acidifying fertilizer each spring. Birds love the berries, which turn black once temperatures dip to 10°F (-12°C).

Choices: Dwarf male plants, needed for pollination, are available. 'Nana', also known as 'Red Sprite', is just 5 feet tall. 'Winter Red' grows up to 10 feet tall.

Kerria japonica

japanese rose

Light Needs:

Full sun to part shade

Mature Height: *4'–5'*

Mature Width: *5'–6'*

Zones: *5–9*

Features:

 Masses of beautiful golden flowers

Needs: Moderate sun or flowers will fade. Well-drained, humus-rich, moist soil. Ample water.

Plant in spring, summer, or fall. Mulch. This shrub blooms on previous year's growth. Immediately after flowering, cut out flowering shoots to ground or cut back severely. If plant becomes overgrown, renew by cutting entire shrub down to just a few inches. Add an application of compost around the base of the plant each spring. This plant is usually pest free.

Choices: This bush covers itself with golden flowers in midspring. 'Pleniflora' has double, pomponlike flowers. Variegated forms are also available.

Nerium oleander

oleander

Light Needs:

Full sun

Mature Height: *3'–12'*

Mature Width: *2'–12'*

Zones: *5–7*

Features:

Tough, carefree plant

Some fragrant types

Drought-tolerant

Needs: Nearly any type of soil. Little or no additional watering once established.

Plant in spring or fall from established plants. No need to fertilize, though those growing just 4–5 feet may need slow-release fertilizer or compost worked into the soil in spring.

Prune in winter. This bush flowers on new growth, so cut some stems of smaller types back to the ground and remove selected branches of larger types. It is prone to scale.

Choices: Flowers bloom in white, yellow, pink, and red. Mature size varies radically, from 3 to 20 feet tall. Read label carefully. A few, such as 'Double Sister Agnes', are fragrant. Also check hardiness; some are more sensitive to frost than others.

Shrubs

Philadelphus spp.

mockorange

Light Needs:

Full sun to part shade

Mature Height: 3'–12'

Mature Width: 3'–12'

Zones: 4–8

Features:

Lovely fragrance that smells like citrus flowers

Needs: Rich to poor, moist soil. Ample moisture best, but tolerates drought.

Plant established plants in spring or fall. Mulch to conserve moisture. Do not fertilize mature plants or trim spent blooms. Prune regularly to avoid legginess. Immediately after flowering, remove branches at base. Also cut back individual branches to shape. This shrub is usually pest and disease free.

Choices: Flowers are white or yellow. Sweet mockorange (*Philadelphus coronarius*) is the most commonly grown and reaches 10–12 feet tall, Zones 4–7. Lemoine mockorange (*Philadelphus × lemoinei*) is hardy in Zones 4–8. 'Avalanche' grows just 3 feet tall. *Philadelphus × virginalis* is hardy in Zones 5–8.

Potentilla fruticosa

potentilla, shrubby cinquefoil

Light Needs:

Full sun

Mature Height: 3'–4'

Mature Width: 3'–4'

Zones: 2–7

Features:

Durable, low-maintenance plant

Drought-tolerant

Rabbit-resistant

Needs: Average to poor, gravelly or sandy, well-drained soil. Tolerates alkaline soil. Moderate moisture; tolerates drought after a year or two.

Plant established plants in spring or fall. Mulch to conserve moisture. Do not fertilize.

If plant begins to look ragged, in late winter, cut back one-third of stems to ground level.

It is prone to spider mites.

Choices: Flowers are white, orange, or yellow.

'Yellow Gem' grows just 2 feet by 3 feet and flowers well; 'Goldfinger' is bright yellow and also grows and flowers well. 'Abbottswood' has white flowers.

Rhododendron spp.

rhododendron, azalea

Light Needs:

Part to full shade

Mature Height: 2'–10'

Mature Width: 2'–8'

Zones: 3–9

Features:

Lovely color for shade

Excellent woodland plant

Needs: Light shade. Some tolerate deep shade or full sun. Check label. Rich, well-drained, acidic soil. Ample moisture.

Plant in spring or fall. Mulch. In spring use acidic fertilizer on shrubs 4 feet or less.

Pruning seldom needed except to remove dead or damaged wood. If pruning is necessary, do so immediately after flowering. Prune selectively rather than shearing, which disfigures shrub.

It is usually pest and disease free, but mildew and mites can be a problem with some types.

Choices: Flowers come in pinks, whites, purples, oranges, and yellows.

Both rhododendrons and azaleas are members of the rhododendron family.

'azalea'

Rosa spp.

For information on various aspects of growing roses, turn to the following pages:

Designing with roses (page 50–51)
The right rose for you (page 86)
Shrub roses (page 88)
Hybrid tea roses (page 92)
Climbing and rambling roses (page 93)
Miniature roses (page 94)
Standard roses (page 95)
Planting roses (page 96)
Pruning roses (page 108)
Rose diseases and pests (page 110)
Fertilizing roses (page 112)
Winterizing roses (page 113)

Salix spp.   *deciduous late winter- or early spring-interest shrub*

pussy willow

Light Needs:

Full sun

Mature Height: 10'–18'

Mature Width: 6'–8'

Zones: 3–9

Features:

Novel early-season buds

Easy to grow

Needs: Average to rich, moist to wet soil. Moderate to ample moisture.

Plant established plants in spring or fall. Mulch to conserve moisture. Fertilize with slow-release fertilizer each spring if desired.

This bush is prized for indoor display. Cut buds just as they start to swell (they'll do best without water in the vase). After flowering cut back plant hard to encourage new growth and better flowering next year.

It is usually pest and disease free.

Choices: Buds are soft gray.

Spiraea spp.   *deciduous summer-blooming shrub*

spirea, bridalwreath

Light Needs:

Full sun

Mature Height: 2'–7'

Mature Width: 2'–7'

Zones: 3–9

Features:

Pretty minibouquets of flowers

Often has good fall color

Needs: Full sun. Average to rich, moist, well-drained soil preferred, but tolerates a wide range of soils. Moderate to abundant moisture.

Plant established plants in spring. Mulch. Fertilize for the first year or two with a slow-release fertilizer.

Choices: Flowers are yellow, pink, red, or white. Bridalwreath or Vanhoutte spirca (*Spiraea × vanhouttei*) is covered with tiny "bouquets" of white flowers and grows up to 7 feet tall, Zones 3–8. Needs little pruning—do not shear. *Spiraea prunifolia* 'Plena', also called bridalwreath, is the old-fashioned favorite. It's prone to rust, but has nice red fall color, Zones 5–9.

Bumald spirea (*Spiraea japonica* 'Bumalda') grows 3–4 feet tall with pink flowers in summer, Zones 4–8.

Shrubs

Syringa spp.
lilac

Light Needs:

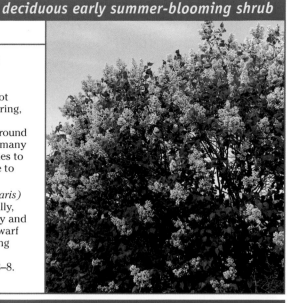

Full sun

Mature Height: 5'–20'

Mature Width: 8'–10'

Zones: 2–8

Features:

Lovely cut flower

Legendary fragrance

Needs: Average to rich, well-drained but moist soil. Moderate moisture; tolerates drought.

Plant in spring or fall. Mulch. Do not prune newer, smaller types. Each spring, after flowering, remove one-third of branches from older, larger types at ground level. Also cut out all suckers. After many years rejuvenate by cutting all branches to about 1 foot high. Old types are prone to mildew in humid regions.

Choices: Common lilac (*Syringa vulgaris*) can top 20 feet and suckers prolifically, French hybrids don't sucker as freely and are somewhat smaller, Zones 3–7. Dwarf Korean lilac (*Syringa patula*) including 'Miss Kim' is good for small spaces, growing just a few feet high, Zones 3–8.

Viburnum spp.
viburnum

Light Needs:

Full sun to part shade

Mature Height: 3'–12'

Mature Width: 3'–12'

Zones: 2–9

Features:

Some are richly fragrant

Berries attract birds

Good fall foliage, berries

Needs: Full sun, especially in Zones 3–5, to light shade, especially in hot-summer regions of Zones 6–9. Rich, well-drained soil. Moderate moisture, but some also tolerate wet conditions or are drought-resistant. Check label.

Plant established plants in spring or fall, working a few spadefuls of compost into the planting hole. Mulch to conserve moisture. No further feeding needed in most conditions.

Needs minimal or no pruning. Pest and disease problems vary by species, but most are fairly problem free.

Choices: Dozens of species and hundreds of cultivars are available. Some are wonderfully fragrant; others produce showy berries; still others have good fall color.

Weigela florida (Weigela rosea)
weigela

Light Needs:

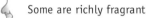

Full sun to part shade

Mature Height: 6'–9'

Mature Width: 9'–12'

Zones: 4–9

Features:

Abundant, arching sprays of flowers

Easy to grow

Needs: Full sun to light shade. Rich, well-drained, neutral to alkaline soil; tolerates poor soil. Moderate moisture, but will tolerate drought.

Plant in spring or fall. Work a few spadefuls of compost into the planting hole; further fertilizing not needed in most conditions. Mulch to conserve moisture. Prune right after flowering each year or every few years. To prune remove branches at ground level that have flowered to keep shrub blooming and maintain shape.

It is usually problem free.

Choices: Flowers are pink, red, or white. Most types grow large, but 'Java Red', 'Variegata Nana', 'Minuet', and 'Tango' grow 4 feet or under.

Shrubs

Vines and Groundcovers

Crawling, sprawling, or leaping flowering vines and groundcovers are great accents in a flower garden. Vines, often climbing 20 feet or more, add vertical interest and color but take up just a foot or two of space at ground level. A single vine can cover a whole wall or conceal a portion of a fence. Groundcovers, too, have their role, clambering over slopes, helping contain runoff, and adding a low blanket of color to a lush garden layout.

Guide to the Encyclopedia Icons

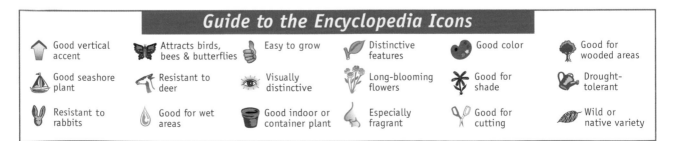

Good vertical accent	Attracts birds, bees & butterflies	Easy to grow	Distinctive features	Good color	Good for wooded areas
Good seashore plant	Resistant to deer	Visually distinctive	Long-blooming flowers	Good for shade	Drought-tolerant
Resistant to rabbits	Good for wet areas	Good indoor or container plant	Especially fragrant	Good for cutting	Wild or native variety

Bougainvillea

bougainvillea

Light Needs:

Full sun

Mature Height: *1'–40'*

Zones: *9–11*

Features:

- Beautifully colored bracts
- Vigorous climber
- Good in containers and hanging baskets

Needs: Full sun, though very light shade tolerable in Zone 11. Rich to poor, loose, fast-draining soil. Moderate water but never soggy; drought-tolerant once established.

This vine does well in Zones 9–11 but can be planted in a protected site in hot summer areas of Zone 8. Low-shrubbery types will also grow in Zone 8 as container plants. Move them to a protected area over the winter.

Plant in spring after all danger of frost has passed. Plant carefully because the roots are very fragile. Tie securely to a support to prevent wind from shredding leaves against plant thorns. Prune heavily in spring. It blooms on new growth and takes hard pruning well. Fertilize in spring and summer. Water in spring only.

Campsis radicans

trumpet vine, trumpet creeper

Light Needs:

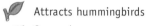

Full sun to part shade

Mature Height: *20'–40'*

Zones: *4–9*

Features:

- Attracts hummingbirds
- Covers large spaces quickly
- Native vine

Needs: Full sun for best flowering but tolerates light shade. Average to poor soil. Ample moisture to drought-tolerant. Tolerates urban shade and pollution well.

Plant established plants in spring or fall. Aerial rootlets cling tightly to walls or supports and need no help attaching. Can reach 20-40 feet, so site carefully, providing heavy, large arbor or pergola. Rootlets and vigorous vines can be destructive to masonry and wood shingles.

Do not fertilize. Mulch to prevent weeds. It blooms on new wood, so prune heavily each spring to achieve best flowering and to control size. Cut out the numerous suckers that emerge.

It is bothered by few pests or diseases.

Celastrus scandens

bittersweet

Light Needs:

Full sun to part shade

Mature Height: *15'–25'*

Zones: *3–8*

Features:

- Attracts birds
- Good for autumn arrangements and wreaths
- Native vine

Needs: Full sun to produce berries, but tolerates light shade. Average to poor soil. Ample moisture to drought-tolerant.

Plant established plants in spring or fall. Both a male and female plant are necessary for berry production. This vine climbs by twining and needs a large, heavy arbor, large tree, sturdy fence, or pergola that will accommodate its full 15–25 foot size.

Do not fertilize. Prune heavily each spring to control size. The colorful berries are poisonous.

Choices: Insignificant flowers are produced; grown primarily for orange and scarlet berries. Do not plant Oriental bittersweet (*Celastrus orbiculatus*), which is spread by birds in Northeast woodlands and is especially invasive. It is often mislabeled as American bittersweet.

Vines and Groundcovers

Clematis spp.
deciduous or evergreen summer- or fall-blooming vine

clematis

Light Needs:

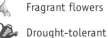

Full sun to part shade

Mature Height: *6'–30'*

Zones: *4–9*

Features:

- Lovely, usually large flowers
- Some richly fragrant types
- Good vertical accent

Needs: Rich, well-drained soil. Ample moisture. Plant in spring, working a few spadefuls of compost into the planting hole. When plant is 2 feet tall, cut back to about 18 inches to further promote branching. Provide sturdy support. Fertilize each spring.

Pruning varies according to bloom time. Clematis that bloom in spring should be pruned, if needed, right after flowering. Clematis that bloom in early summer, or those that bloom nearly all year-round, should be pruned in early spring when new growth is apparent, back to perhaps 6–8 inches and a pair of well-formed leaf buds.

Those that bloom in fall should be pruned in early spring to about 1 foot in height.

Gelsemium sempervirens
evergreen late winter- or early spring-blooming vine

carolina jasmine, yellow jessamine

Light Needs:

Full sun to part shade

Mature Height: *15'–20'*

Zones: *7–9*

Features:

- Fragrant flowers
- Drought-tolerant
- Good vertical accent

Needs: Full sun to light shade. Average to rich soil. Moderate moisture; drought-tolerant after 2–3 years.

Plant established plants in spring or fall. Mulch to conserve moisture. Tie to supports; plant will twine upward.

Fertilize with slow-release fertilizer each spring. Every few years, prune severely right after flowering—by half to two-thirds—to control growth.

This vine is usually pest- and disease free.

Choices: Flowers are yellow. 'Pride of Augusta' is a popular cultivar with double flowers.

Hypericum calycinum
evergreen summer- and fall-blooming groundcover

aaron's beard; st. john'swort

Light Needs:

Full sun to full shade

Mature Height: *12"–18"*
Mature Width: *1'–3'*

Zones: *4–8*

Features:

- Thrives in shade
- Easy to grow; spreads quickly

Needs: Moist, rich, well-drained soil; tolerates drier conditions.

Plant in spring or fall. Mulch to conserve moisture. Technically a shrub, this evergreen plant spreads low enough to serve as a groundcover. It spreads rapidly. Each spring, cut back to ground to encourage good flowering.

Ipomoea spp.

morning glory

Light Needs:

Full sun

Mature Height: *18"–25'*

Zones: *2–11*

Features:

- Attracts hummingbirds
- Beautiful, fast cover and color
- Easy to grow

Needs: Average to poor, well-drained soil. Ample moisture.

Plant seeds in late winter or spring directly in soil after all danger of frost, soaking first in water 24 hours to soften tough coat. Work a few spadefuls of compost into soil or add a slow-release fertilizer. When vine reaches 1 inch high, thin to at least 18 inches apart.

Choices: Most popular is the common morning-glory *(Ipomoea tricolor)*, which blooms morning to afternoon. 'Heavenly Blue' is a favorite, 10–15 feet. Moonflower *(Ipomoea alba)* is white, grows about 6 feet, and opens afternoon through late night, 6–10 feet. Sweet potato vine *(Ipomoea batatas)* is a relatively new arrival that's excellent in containers, 6–8 feet. Start from an established plant.

Jasminum

jasmine

Light Needs:

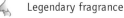

Full sun

Mature Height: *3'–30'*

Zones: *6–9*

Features:

- Legendary fragrance
- Good vertical accent

Needs: Full sun to light shade. Average, evenly moist soil. Moderate moisture.

Plant established plants in spring or fall. Plant against a warm wall for best flowering. As needed, tie to support to get vine started. Do not fertilize; if soil is too rich, blooms are diminished.

Choices: Flowers come in white, yellow, or pink. Most often grown is common or poet's jasmine *(Jasminum officinale)*. Prune as desired in fall after flowering stops. Easy to control, Zones 7–9. Winter jasmine *(Jasminum nudiflorum)* blooms yellow in late winter on old wood, so prune immediately after flowering; it grows to 3–15 feet. It is somewhat drought-tolerant once established, Zones 6–9. Also see star jasmine *(Trachelospermum)* on page 241.

Lonicera spp.

honeysuckle

Light Needs:

Full sun

Mature Height: *8'–30'*

Zones: *3–9*

Features:

- Attracts birds and hummingbirds
- Some types sweetly fragrant
- Native vine

Needs: Full sun to light shade. Rich to average, well-drained soil. Ample moisture. Poor, dry soil restricts growth.

Plant plants in spring. Provide heavy, large support that will accommodate its full size. This vine climbs by twining; all but goldflame types need little assistance. Do not fertilize.

Choices: Goldflame honeysuckle *(Lonicera × heckrottii)* grows a modest 10 feet, Zones 4–9. Japanese honeysuckle *(Lonicera japonica)* is invasive and banned in the East, Zones 5–9.

Native honeysuckle, also called trumpet honeysuckle *(Lonicera sempervirens)*, grows to 25 feet, Zones 4–9. Brown's or scarlet trumpet honeysuckle *(Lonicera × brownii)* grows just 8 feet, Zones 3–9.

'Lonicera x heckrottii'

Vines and Groundcovers

mandevilla

Light Needs:

Full sun to part shade

Mature Height: *3'–30'*

Zones: *2–11*

Features:

🪴 Good in containers

🌸 Some types fragrant

Needs: Grow as an annual in Zones 2–7; as a perennial in Zones 8–10. Rich to average, well-drained soil. Moderate moisture.

Plant established plant in spring, working some compost into the soil as well as some slow-release fertilizer. Pinch stems to encourage bushiness. Provide light support if growing as an annual; sturdy support where grown as a perennial. Fertilize container plants every 2–3 weeks with a liquid fertilizer. In Zones 2–6, container plantings can be overwintered in a sunny spot indoors. In Zones 7 can be overwintered in a garage or other protected spot. Blooms on new wood, so where perennial, cut back by about one-third in late winter or early spring.

Prone to spider mites.

---

black-eyed susan vine

Light Needs:

Full sun to part shade

Mature Height: *6'–10'*

Zones: *2–11*

Features:

🎨 Beautiful, fast cover and color

👍 Easy to grow

Needs: Rich, well-drained soil. Ample moisture. Grow as an annual in Zones 2–9; a perennial in Zones 10–11.

Plant established seedlings or sow seeds directly in soil in late winter or spring, after all danger of frost. Work a few spadefuls of compost into soil or add a slow-release fertilizer.

Once about 1 inch high, thin to at least 12 inches. Support can include trellises, string trellises, latticework, chain link fencing or mailboxes. In Zones 2–9 tear or cut down after frost or when it gets ragged in early winter. In Zones 10–11, frost will kill to the ground but plants will reemerge.

Choices: Flowers are yellow, orange, or cream with dark centers.

'Susie' series is by far the most popular.

---

creeping thyme

Light Needs:

Full sun to part shade

Mature Height: *4"–18"*
Mature Width: *8"–20"*

Zones: *5–9*

Features:

🪣 Drought-tolerant

🌸 Fragrant when crushed

Needs: Full sun, but part shade is good in hot climates. Light, loose, well-drained, alkaline soil. Moderate moisture ideal, but very drought-tolerant. Attracts bees, which are helpful pollinators in the garden.

Plant in spring or fall. Does well between pavers or in rock gardens. Mulch (gravel is good). Do not fertilize. Cut back plants to an inch or two if they become woody or messy.

Choices: Many types available, including many with silver or gold variegated leaves. Some grow taller and bushier, but creeping thymes grow just a few inches high. All thymes are good to use in cooking.

Vines and Groundcovers

Trachelospermum spp.

star jasmine

Light Needs:

Full sun to part shade

Mature Height: *6'–8'*

Zones: *8–9*

Features:

🌿 Legendary fragrance

✱ Thrives in shade

Needs: Average, evenly moist soil. Moderate to ample moisture.

Plant established plants in spring or fall. As needed, tie to support to get vine started. Do not fertilize; if soil is too rich, blooms are diminished.

Seldom needs pruning; but if desired, do so in late winter or early spring.

This vine is sometimes bothered by whiteflies, scale, and mites.

Choices: Flowers are white. Star jasmine (*Trachelospermum jasminoides*) grows just 6–8 feet with white flowers.

Yellow star jasmine (*Trachelospermum asiaticum*) can reach 15 feet with pale yellow flowers.

See also common and other jasmines (*Jasminum* spp.) on page 239.

Vinca minor

periwinkle, myrtle

Light Needs:

Full sun to full shade

Mature Height: *4"–6"*

Mature Width: *12"–18"*

Zones: *4–7*

Features:

🌱 Good flowering groundcover

🌱 Good companion for bulbs

🌳 Excellent in open woodland gardens

Needs: Full sun to medium shade in Zones 4–6; light shade to full shade in hot-summer areas of Zones 7. Average to rich, well-drained soil. Moderate to ample moisture.

Plant established plants in spring or fall. Work in 1 inch of compost as well as a slow-release fertilizer. Mulch to prevent competing weeds and conserve moisture. Keep evenly moist first year; low-maintenance thereafter.

It is prone to few pests or diseases.

Choices: Flowers are blue, white, or pink. Some variegated types are available.

'Bowles' is an especially dense grower and heavy bloomer. 'Aurea' has all-gold leaves. 'Albo-variegata' has green and gold leaves.

Wisteria spp.

wisteria

Light Needs:

Full sun

Mature Height: *30'–100'*

Zones: *5–9*

Features:

👁 Gorgeous hanging flowers

👃 Fragrant

Needs: Full sun; tolerates light shade in South and Southwest. Average to poor, very well-drained soil. Drought-tolerant once established.

Plant in spring, being sure to cover the graft union so its own roots are formed. Site carefully. This vine needs a very heavy, large arbor, large tree, or pergola that will accommodate its full size, usually 30–100 feet with a vine that turns into a heavy trunk. Tie to support for first few years, then it will twine on its own. Do not fertilize. Flowers may not appear for the first 7 to 10 years.

Aggressive, diligent pruning, especially in warm climates, is critical or vine becomes a problem. Prune in late winter and then again in summer after flowering to both shape and control size.

Vines and Groundcovers

Index

General Index

Numbers in *italics* indicate photographs.

A

Accents, *35*
Accessories, garden, 57
Air circulation, 17, 50, 128, 131
American Rose Society, 50
Animals, keeping out, 132–133
Annuals
    for attracting butterflies, 147
    for attracting hummingbirds, 147
    for attracting songbirds, 147
    for California, 23
    choosing, 44
    for coastal gardens, 19
    cool-season, 45
    deadheading, 118, 119, *119*
    designing with, 44–45
    drought-tolerant, 103
    encyclopedia of choices, 158–215
    fertilizing, 107
    for Florida and Gulf Coast gardens, 25
    fragrant, 54
    for Mountain West gardens, 26
    must-have, 44
    no-fail, 33
    for Pacific Northwest gardens, 29
    planting, 76
    from seed, 79
    for shade, 142–143
    for Southern gardens, 17
    for Texas gardens, 21
    warm-season, 45
Aphids, 110, 129, *129*
Arbors, 36
Architects, landscape, 7
Arid climate, 20, 22
Arranging flowers, *154,* 154–155, *155*

B

Bacterial wilt, 130, *130*
Bark mulch, 105
Bed, digging flower, 66–67
Berms, 64, 69
Biennials, 46
Bindweed, 123, *123*
Birdbath, *82,* 146, *146*

Birds, attracting, 146, 147
Black spot, 110–111, 130, *130*
Blight, 130, *130*
Blood meal, 63
Bonemeal, 63
Botrytis blight, 131, *131*
Bubblers, 101, *101*
Bulbs
    for attracting butterflies, 147
    for attracting hummingbirds, 147
    choosing, 48
    companions to, 49
    in containers, 83
    deadheading, 118
    designing with, 48–49
    encyclopedia of choices, 216–225
    fertilizing, 107
    flowering time selection guide, 49
    forcing, 151
    fragrant, 54
    indoor, 151
    planting, 78, *78*
    for shade, 143
    storing, 136–137
    summer-blooming, 23, 48, 136–137
Bunch grasses, 20
Butterflies, attracting, 146, 147

C

California, flower gardening in, 22–23
Chickweed, 123, *123*
Circulation, air, 17, 50, 128, 131
Clay soil, *62,* 65
Climate
    arid regions, 20, 22
    California, 22–23
    coastal, 18–19
    cold, 14–15
    Florida and Gulf Coast, 24–25
    frost date maps, 13
    hardiness zones, 12
    microclimate, 11, 19, 21
    Mountain West, 26–27
    Pacific Northwest, 28–29
    Southwest, 20
    Texas, 21
    warm, 16–17
Cloches, 14
Clover, 123, *123*
Coastal gardens, 18–19
Cocoa hulls, as mulch, 105

Cold-climate gardening, 14–15
Cold frame, 15
Color
    for attracting butterflies and birds, 146
    designing with, 38
    in entry and front gardens, 58
    for moonlight gardens, 150, *150*
    selection guide, 42–43
    year-long, 40–41
Compost, 62, 63, 68, 105, 120–121, 126
    building a compost heap, 121
    materials for, 121
    tips for, 120–121
Conservation of water, 20, 102–103
Container gardens
    annuals in, 72, *73*
    care, 84–85
    in coastal climate, 19
    combining plants in, 82, *83*
    for entry and front gardens, 58
    for Florida and Gulf Coast gardens, 25
    plant selection, 82–83
    planting, 84–85
    positions for, *80,* 81
    shrubs, 114
    size and shape of containers, 81
    types of containers, 81
Contractors, landscape, 7
Cut flowers, 152
Cutting back, 119. *See also*
        Deadheading; Pruning

D

Dandelion, 123, *123*
Deadheading, 40, 41, 47, 108, 118–119
Decks, 36
Deer, 132, 133
Design, 30–59
    accessories, garden, 57
    with annuals, 44–45
    with bulbs, 48–49
    color, 38, 40–43
    combining plants, 38–39
    entry/front gardens, 58–59
    foliage, 38
    for fragrance, 54–55
    garden structure, 36–37
    height, 39
    for outdoor living, 56

Index

Index

Flowers by Common and Botanical Names

Numbers in **boldface** indicate Flower Encyclopedia entries. Numbers in *italics* indicate photographs.

Index

Index

Index

Acknowledgements

Hetherington Studios
3520 S.W. 9th Street
Des Moines, IA 50315
515-243-6329
dhetherington@earthlink.net

Doug Hetherington
Mara Hetherington
Sophia Hetherington
Johanna Hetherington
John Hetherington

Thank You
Michael Bergersen
Maggie Dimson
Marc Fidalgo
Edwin Hubbell
Clair Martin
Andy Zavalla

Home Depot Associates
Joel Adams
Mario Corona
Joe "Papa" Fine
Eric Hagstrom
Mikey Hedrick
Jay Jones
Mike Mitchell
Lorn Patterson
Mo Powers

Bellevue Botanical Garden
12001 Main Street
Bellevue, WA 98005-3522
425-452-2750
www.bellevuebotanical.org

Better Homes & Gardens Test Garden
1716 Locust Street
Des Moines, IA 50309-3023
515-284-3994
www.bhg.com

The Butchart Gardens
800 Benvenuto Avenue
Brentwood Bay, BC V8M1J8
Canada
250-652-4422
www.butchartgardens.com

Des Moines Botanical Center
909 East River Drive
Des Moines, IA 50316
515-323-8900

Fullerton Arboretum
1900 Associated Road
Fullerton, CA 92831
714-278-3579
www.arboretum.fullerton.edu

Heard Gardens Ltd.
8000 Raccoon River Drive
West Des Moines, IA 50266
515-987-0800
www.heardgardens.com

The Huntington Library, Art Collections,
and Botanical Gardens
1151 Oxford Road
San Marino, CA 91108
626-405-2100
www.huntington.org

Iowa Arboretum, Inc.
1875 Peach Avenue
Madrid, IA 50156
515-795-3216
www.iowaarboretum.com

Jackson & Perkins Wholesale, Inc.
1 Rose Lane
Medford, OR 97501
800-854-1766
www.jproses.com
www.surfinia.com
www.jacksonandperkins.com

Minnesota Landscape Arboretum
Andersen Horticultural Library
3675 Arboretum Drive
P.O. Box 39
Chanhassen, MN 55317-0039
952-443-1400
www.arboretum.umn.edu

Missouri Botanical Garden
4344 Shaw Boulevard
St. Louis, MO 63110
314-577-5100
www.mobot.org

Reiman Gardens
1407 Elwood Drive
Ames, IA 50011
515-294-2710
www.reimangardens.iastate.edu

The State Botanical Garden of Georgia
2450 S. Milledge Avenue
Athens, GA 30605-1624
706-542-1244
www.uga.edu/botgarden

Tiny Petals Miniature Rose Nursery
489 Minot Avenue
Chula Vista, CA 91910
619-498-4755
www.tinypetalsnursery.com

Windmill Gardens
5823 162nd Avenue East
Sumner, WA 98390
1-800-628-6516
www.windmillgarden.com

Photo Credits

T=Top C=Center B=Bottom L=Left
R=Right

Front Cover

Doug Hetherington
    Cover C, Cover R

J&P™ roses presented by Jackson &
Perkins Wholesale, Inc.
    Cover L
Peter Krumhardt
    Cover Background

Back Cover

Susan Gilmore
    Back Cover C
Doug Hetherington
    Back Cover R
Peter Krumhardt
    Cover Background

Inside Pages

Cathy Wilkinson Barash
    110 BC, 111 CL, 129 CL
Ernest Braun
    88 BL
Ralph Byther
    129 TR, 130 TL, 130 TR, 130 BR,
    131 TL, 131 CL, 131 BL, 131 CR
David Cavagnaro
    169 C
George De Gennaro
    90 BR
Michael Dirr
    162 T, 206 C, 227 C
Susan Gilmore
    152 TR
Jay Graham
    2 TL, 27 B
J&P™ roses presented by Jackson &
Perkins Wholesale, Inc.
    86 BL, 86 BR, 87 CL, 87 BR, 88 TR,
    88 BR, 90 TL, 90 TR, 91 BL, 93 BL,
    94 BL
Jack Jennings
    172 C, 213 B
Mike Jensen
    158 BR, 200 T
Gene Johnston
    16 BL
Jennifer Jordan
    59 BR
Peter Krumhardt
    8, 9 BR
Michael McKinley
    89 BL, 90 BL, 93 BR
Mike Mitchell
    36 BL, 111 BL, 111 CR, 129 TL, 129 BR,
    197 T
Ron Oetting
    129 BL, 130 BL
Marilyn Ott
    14 BL, 19 BL
Jerry Pavia
    89 TL, 158 TL, 158 TR, 161 B, 163 C,
    168 T, 173 T, 173 B, 174 C, 187 C,
    195 C, 196 B, 197 C, 199 T, 199 C,
    203 C, 228 C, 231 T, 234 C, 237 B
Bill Stites
    89 TR
Judith Watts
    159 B
Mary Howell Williams
    171 B, 183 C, 186 B
Greg Wilson
    24 BL

Take our quick survey and enter to win a $1,000 gift card from The Home Depot®

Thank you for choosing this book! To serve you better, we'd like to know a little more about your interests. Please take a minute to fill out this survey and drop it in the mail. As an extra-special "thank-you" for your help, we'll enter your name into a drawing to win a $1,000 Home Depot Gift Card!

WIN THIS CARD!

OFFICIAL SWEEPSTAKES RULES AND ENTRY DETAILS ON BACK.
No purchase necessary to enter or win.

PLEASE MARK ONE CIRCLE PER LINE IN EACH OF THE NUMBERED COLUMNS BELOW WITH DARK PEN OR PENCIL:

1 My interest in the areas below is:

Cooking	High Interest	Average Interest	No Interest
Gourmet & Fine Foods	○	○	○
Quick & Easy	○	○	○
Healthy/Natural	○	○	○

Decorating			
Country	○	○	○
Traditional	○	○	○
Contemporary	○	○	○

Do-It-Yourself			
Home Repair	○	○	○
Remodeling	○	○	○
Home Decor (painting, wallpapering, window treatments, etc.)	○	○	○

Gardening			
Flowers	○	○	○
Vegetables	○	○	○
Landscaping	○	○	○

2 My plans to do a project in the following areas within the next 6 months are:

	High Interest	Average Interest	No Interest
Bathroom Remodel	○	○	○
Kitchen Remodel	○	○	○
Storage Project	○	○	○
Plumbing	○	○	○
Wiring	○	○	○
Interior Painting	○	○	○
Wallpapering	○	○	○
Window Treatments	○	○	○
Plant/Plan a Flower Garden	○	○	○
Plant/Plan a Vegetable Garden	○	○	○
Deck Building	○	○	○
Patio Building	○	○	○
Landscape Improvements	○	○	○

3 You *must* fill out all of the requested information below to enter to win a $1,000 Home Depot Gift Card.

Also, E-mail me with information of interest to me.

Name: _____

Address: _____ Apt. or Suite # _____

Daytime telephone number: (_____) _____

City: _____

State/Province: _____ Country: _____ Zip: _____

E-mail address: _____

Thank you for completing our survey! Please mail today to have your name entered to win a $1,000 Home Depot Gift Card. But hurry—one winner will be selected soon. See rules on back for entry deadline. To find more home improvement tips, visit www.homedepot.com or www.meredithbooks.com.

Canadian customers:
See mailing details on back!

←

BUSINESS REPLY MAIL
FIRST-CLASS MAIL   PERMIT NO. 8359   DES MOINES, IA

POSTAGE WILL BE PAID BY ADDRESSEE

MEREDITH CORPORATION
HOME DEPOT 1-2-3 BOOKS (LN-104)
1716 LOCUST STREET
DES MOINES IA   50309-9708

▲ FOLD CAREFULLY ALONG ORANGE DASHED LINES ABOVE ▲

Take our quick survey and enter to win a $1,000 gift card from The Home Depot®

No postage necessary if mailed *inside* the United States. If mailed *outside* of the United States, letterfold survey form, place in an envelope, stamp, and mail to:

Meredith Corporation
Home Depot 1-2-3 Books (LN-104)
1716 Locust Street
Des Moines, Iowa 50309-3023

Nathan D. Ehrlich
Atlanta, GA

Tony DiBello
Nashua, NH

Lisa Heredia
Tampa, FL

Sue Mennen
Brentwood, TN

Stephen D. Thomas
Tukwila, WA

Daniel D. Sargent
Torrance, CA

Many thanks to
the employees
of The Home Depot®
whose "wisdom of
the aisles" has made
Flower Gardening 1-2-3™
the most useful
book of its kind.

Robert W. Jacobson
Atlanta, GA

Danny Acevedo
Torrance, CA

Linda La Chance
Salem, MA

Mary E. DiBello
Manchester, NH

Anna M. Mandell
Tigard, OR

Dave Schrader
Natick, MA

Wendy Mersch
Brentwood, TN

Ricky Garrigus
Madison, TN

Nancy G. Siverson
Tigard, OR